AGE OF WOMAN.

ncy to the brink of the grave.

A HISTORY

April 11, 1931 — THE NEW YORKER — Price 15 cents

EDITED BY PAT THANE

A HISTORY OF
OLD AGE

THE J. PAUL GETTY MUSEUM
LOS ANGELES

© 2005 Thames & Hudson Ltd, London

First published in the United Kingdom in 2005 by
Thames & Hudson Ltd, 181A High Holborn, London WC1V 7QX
www.thamesandhudson.com

Picture research: Georgina Bruckner
Editor: Ian Sutton
Design: Derek Birdsall
Editorial assistant: Alice Park
Production: Susanna Friedman

First published in the United States of America in 2005 by
Getty Publications, 1200 Getty Center Drive, Suite 500
Los Angeles, California 90049-1682
www.getty.edu

Publisher: Christopher Hudson
Editor in Chief: Mark Greenberg

Library of Congress Cataloging-in-Publication Data

A history of old age / edited by Pat Thane.
    p. cm.
  Includes index.
  ISBN-13: 978-0-89236-834-1 (hardcover)
  ISBN-10: 0-89236-834-9 (hardcover)
  1. Old age—History. 2. Older people—History. 3. Old age in
literature. I. Thane, Pat. II. J. Paul Getty Museum.
  HQ1061.H54 2005
  305.26'09182'1—dc22

2005007387

Printed and bound in China by C&C Offset Printing Co., Ltd.

Frontispiece:
Youth and age inhabit different worlds, the old observing the
young with a mixture of envy and disapproval. It is a gulf well
expressed by Peter Arno's *New Yorker* cover of 1931: the shocked
amazement of the older generation at the sight of a short-haired,
half-dressed girl sprinter weaving her way along the city pavement.
Peter Arno / April 11, 1931, *The New Yorker*, Condé Nast
Publications, Inc. Reprinted by permission. All rights reserved.

Old age will only be respected if it fights for itself, maintains its rights, avoids dependence on anyone and asserts control over its own to its last breath.

Cicero

Contents

It was the very young who died in such
appalling numbers in every century but our
own, a fact that has distorted the average
life expectancy figures for the past. No one
in the Middle Ages could forget how close
death was. In a Mainz woodcut of 1495,
Death has taken the child's toy and leads
him gently to the grave.

1

PAT THANE **THE AGE OF OLD AGE**

Time and again today, we hear that people are living longer than ever before and that societies are growing older, with old people outnumbering the young. Everywhere this is presented gloomily. Old people are described as helpless dependants, imposing burdens of healthcare and pensions on a shrinking population of younger workers. Insofar as old age is thought to have a history, it is presented as a story of decline: that in 'the past', a vague, unspecified, distant time, few people lived to be old. Because they were few, and not very costly, they were valued, respected, cherished and supported by their families as, it is said, they are not today.

The real history of old age presented in this volume challenges this picture. Past societies, often much poorer than those of today, supported large numbers of old people. At least 10 per cent of the populations of England, France and Spain were aged over 60 even in the 18th century. It is true that at any time before the 20th century, in most places, average life expectancy at birth was only around 40 to 45. But this does not mean that most people died in middle age. Calculations of life expectancy at birth were influenced by very high infant and child death rates. Those who survived the hazardous early years of life at any time in the pre-industrial past had a good chance of survival to 60 or beyond.[1]

In some communities the proportion of older people could be higher still, when young people moved away in search of work, as they very often did, even in pre-industrial times, leaving the older generation behind. Separation of families because of movement around the country or the world is not, as is often thought, a fact only of modern life. In the distant past people did not always live out their lives in one place; and when they left, in the days before mass communications and mass literacy, links with home and family might be lost for ever.

Very many older people were not cared for by their families because they had no surviving children. Their children might have moved to a far corner of the country or even abroad; for instance, in the 19th and 20th centuries they might have left Italy for Argentina or the United

States, Britain for Australia or South Africa and Poland for Western Europe or America. Or they might no longer be alive when their parents reached old age. Given the higher rates of death at all ages at all times before the later 20th century, older people could not be sure that their children would outlive them. In the 18th century just one-third of Europeans had a surviving child when they reached their 60th birthday.[2]

At the beginning of the 21st century older people have fewer children than in the past, but it is rare for them to die in infancy or even in middle age and for an older person not to have, and not to be in touch with, at least one child. Even when the generations live at a distance from one another, they can and do get together at unprecedented speed by telephone, the internet, motor, rail or air travel. One of the constant tropes of today's pessimistic narrative of old age stresses the increasing loneliness of older people in the modern world, with fewer, more scattered children than in 'the past'. Yet all of the evidence suggests the intense loneliness especially of poor, childless, old people in the past and that this is a less, not more, common experience in the present.

Loneliness among older people is often deduced from statistics of older people living alone. The numbers have grown dramatically. In Britain at the beginning of the 20th century 9 per cent of people over 60 lived alone. By 1985 36 per cent did so, 47 per cent of women, 20 per cent of men.[3] But living alone should not be confused with loneliness. Single living – sometimes contented, sometimes not – became common in all age groups in the later 20th century. It is often assumed that in 'the past' older people lived with, and were cared for by, their adult children. As we have seen, these children may not have survived or might have lived far away. Even if they had children nearby, older people often asserted their preference for living in their own homes for as long as they could cope. In northern Europe this preference was reinforced for centuries by folklore, warning of the dangers to older people if they placed their lives under the control of their children. A popular cautionary tale, already old in medieval Europe, told of a man who, tired of caring for his old father, starts to carve a trough from which the old man is to eat, instead of sitting at the family table, or, in another version, starts to exchange his father's bedding for a piece of sacking. As he does so, his own son passes by and remarks that he will make a similar trough when his father is old, or tears the sacking in half and says that he will save half for his father's own old age. The father is duly chastened. In another, bleaker version, the old man is gradually demoted from a place of honour at the head of the table to a bench behind the door, where he dies in misery.

'Those left behind at Christmas' is one of a series of
paintings by Angelo Morbelli around 1901–03, set in
the Pio Albergo Trivulzio, Milan, a rest home for the
aged homeless and destitute. Together they make up
an extended and movingly realistic exploration by
Morbelli of the loneliness of old age.

In another popular tale the old man wins out by his own wiles. He ensures that his son and daughter-in-law continue to treat him well after he moves in with them by pointing out that he has not, after all, given them his entire fortune. The remainder is locked in a chest, to be opened at his death. When he dies, they rush to open the chest. It contains only a large club inscribed: 'He who gives so that he must beg ought to be clubbed until he lies flat.' Such tales were reworked by Shakespeare to achieve their most sublime form in *King Lear*. They prevailed in the peasant cultures of Scandinavia, Germany, Scotland, France and Italy at least into the 18th century. In the later 18th century on the town gates of some cities of Brandenburg hung large clubs with the inscription: 'He who has made himself dependent on his children for bread and suffers from want, he shall be knocked dead by this club.'[4] None of this suggests that comfortable succour in the household of one's children was the expected lot of older people in pre-industrial northern Europe. It was more common for the generations to live together in parts of southern Europe — due to poverty as much as filial devotion, so these relationships should not be romanticized.[5]

Older people everywhere preferred to maintain their independence for as long as they could; most were not helpless dependants. Running your own household and living your own life was generally thought preferable to sharing the lives of younger generations. Older people have always been givers as well as receivers: bringing up orphaned grandchildren, giving a home to a widowed or deserted daughter and her children, caring for sick or disabled children, spouses, neighbours. Support has always flowed downwards as well as upwards between the generations in all social classes.

Younger people also preferred independence, though financial pressure as much as family devotion long forced families to live together. By the later 20th century the generations were more likely to live apart because more of them could afford to do so. Living apart, at any time, does not mean absence of contact or mutual support between surviving members of the generations. From 16th-century Spain to 19th- and 20th-century America or Britain relatives often lived close by and in close contact.[6] And older people moved into their children's homes when they became too weak to live alone, often for a short time before death. If they had no surviving children, they entered hospitals and institutions for the poor, which, throughout pre-industrial Europe and early America, were filled with older people without surviving relatives.[7] Or they died alone.

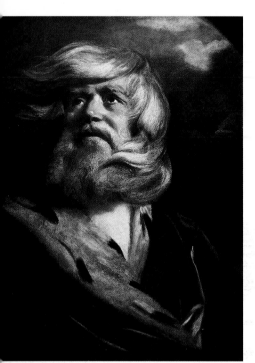

In 'King Lear' Shakespeare drew upon a myth that still keeps its hold upon the imagination — the aged father who is forced to concede authority to his unkind children. Joshua Reynolds painted this image of Lear in the storm in 1773.

'I'll miss my home and I'll miss my stove. It was a wonderful one,' said Mrs Helen Williams who at the age of 78 was bombed out in the London Blitz of 1940–1. With fifty-two grandchildren she was not going to be lonely and — typically of her generation — she could still be comforted by a nice cup of tea. 'I'm taking my lucky horse-shoe with me.'

The tales cautioning older people against placing too much faith in their children implied that they should not assume that they would be automatically respected for the fact of growing old. Indeed, the belief, still common today, that older people are less respected than they 'used to be' is as old as old age itself. In the opening pages of Plato's *Republic*, Socrates meets the elderly Cephalus and asks him what it is like to grow old: 'Is it a difficult time of life or not?' Cephalus replies:

> *I'll certainly tell you how it strikes me, Socrates. For some of us old men often meet together, like the proverbial birds of a feather. And when we do meet, most of them are full of woes; they hanker for the pleasures of their youth, remembering how they used to make love and drink and go to parties and the like, and thinking it a great deprivation that they can't do so any more. Life was good then, they think, whereas now they can hardly be said to live at all. And some of them grumble that their families show no respect for their age, and proceed to harp on the miseries old age brings. But in my opinion, Socrates, they are putting the blame in the wrong place. For if old age were to blame, my experience would be the same as theirs, and so would that of all other old men. But in fact I have met many whose feelings are quite different. ... In all this, and in the lack of respect their families show them, there is only one thing to blame; and that is not their old age, Socrates, but their character. For if men are sensible and good-tempered, old age is easy enough to bear: if not, youth as well as age is a burden.*[8]

Similar complaints, and similarly robust ripostes, resound through history. It is rare in European culture, and indeed in most others, for people to be respected, or not, for their age alone. People of any age earned respect by their actions or because their wealth and power enforced deference. Rich old people might be venerated, outwardly at least. Poor old people might be cared for by the community, or ostracized and neglected. A physician in 17th-century south Germany explained why old women were so often accused of witchcraft: 'They are so unfairly despised and rejected by everyone, enjoy no-one's protection, much less their affection and loyalty... so that it is no wonder that, on account of poverty and need, misery and faint-heartedness, they often... give themselves to the devil and practise witchcraft.' A 70-year-old woman said at her trial: 'The children call all old people witches.'[9] Special knowledge possessed by older people, for example about the cure of sickness, might be valued by the community as the characteristic wisdom of the old, or vilified as further proof of witchcraft.

As Cephalus suggested, in the past as in the present the most striking feature of old age is diversity, and it is this that the essays in this volume explore. They focus on Europe and the European diaspora — the countries colonized by Europe and then long dominated by white

Old women were dangerous – a curious belief founded partly on mistaken medieval ideas, partly on the guilty knowledge that they generally had a just grievance against society. Witches were nearly always women. Goya was close enough to these beliefs to give his satire a touch of the macabre. 'A Fine Teacher' (1797) shows a young woman being initiated into the mysteries of witchcraft by one more experienced.

Europeans, mainly in North America, Australia and New Zealand. This is not, of course, because old age does not have a history in other cultures,[10] but because the diversity of experiences across cultures and over time cannot be compressed into a single volume, and the writers discuss the cultures they know best.

'Old age' is a diverse phase of life partly because of its very length. It is said to extend from the fifth decade of life to past 100. By contrast both 'youth' and 'maturity' cover shorter timespans. 'Old people' include some of the fittest and some of the most decrepit, some of the richest and some of the most powerful and the poorest and most marginalized people in any society. It has become more common to live to a century in the recent past than ever before, but some have always achieved it. As I write (in June 2004), I have just heard a radio interview with a highly articulate man in Australia who has celebrated his 101st birthday by making his first parachute jump. This puts in the shade the former President of the United States, George Bush Snr, who was merely 80 when he chose this same way to celebrate his birthday. Such achievements remain unusual, but less startling than they once were.

More sinister than Goya's witches are his real old people. 'Two Old People Eating Soup', painted when he was about 75, makes them into living corpses.

The Olde Old very Olde Man or Thomas Par, the Sonne of Iohn Parr of Winnington in the Parish of Alberbury In the County of Shropshire who was Borne in 1483 in The Raigne of King Edward the 4th and is now liuing in The Strand, being aged 152 yeares and odd Monethes 1635

Publish'd by I Caulfield 1794.

Thomas Parr became famous for his exceptional age. He claimed to have been born in 1483, though he may, consciously or not, have adopted his father's birth date. He was brought to the court of Charles I in 1635, when this portrait was made. However, the excitement was too much for him and he died the same year, when he would have been 152 or 153. He was buried in the south transept of Westminster Abbey, but the absence of any evidence for his date of birth must cast doubt on his story.

How old is 'old'? These impressive aged parachutists suggest that the boundaries and meaning of old age may be changing. But 17th-century London was enthralled by Thomas Parr, 'Old Parr', who claimed to be 153 at the time of his death and boasted of having done penance for adultery at 105, though it is likely that Parr had, consciously or not, borrowed his father's birth date. He revelled in the celebrity status very old age brought, even then. In fact, over many centuries and places there was remarkable continuity in how old age was defined in both popular and official discourse. In ancient Greece and Rome, throughout medieval and early modern Europe, in 19th-century North America and Australasia, old age was believed to begin somewhere between ages 60 and 70, as it still is.[11] But it was always widely recognized that some people became decrepit at younger ages, in their 50s or even 40s, whereas others remained fit and active into their 80s. Over time, more people were perceived to be active to later ages. In the Crusader kingdom of 13th-century Jerusalem a knight of 60 or over was exempt from military service, as were all men over 60 in 13th-century England. In Castile and León at the same time, 70 was the age at which men were excused from watch duty and war service. The age of exemption from public service in the 13th century was 70 in England, Florence, Venice and Pisa.[12] It was much the same, between 60 and 70, in 19th-century North America and Europe and, indeed, throughout the 20th century, although in reality, as we shall see in the last chapter, this was the century when many more people than ever before lived and remained fit to later ages.

Generally these official definitions would allow the individual who was physically or mentally unfit to be exempted from public obligations at earlier ages, and for the fit and active to carry them on to later ages. Through most of history old age has not been defined by actual number of years so much as by physical fitness. In most times and places people have been judged to be 'old' when they could no longer support or look after themselves, when the faculties essential for survival in adult life were failing. It has always been recognized that this occurs at very diverse ages. The Venetian doge Enrico Dandolo led the Venetians on the Fourth Crusade in 1204, when he was 97. This was exceptional, but he was not the only powerful man of advanced age in medieval Europe.[13] The English religious leader John Wesley was 86 when he wrote in 1789 that he finally felt old because: '1. My sight is decayed... 2. My strength is decayed... 3. My memory of names whether of persons or places, is decayed; till I stop a little to recollect them.'[14] The much larger number of poor and powerless old people, at this and earlier times, were granted poor relief on account of old age finally forcing them into helplessness at ages varying from the 40s to the 80s.

Overleaf:

To defeat old age, turn back the clock and become young again has been mankind's dream for centuries. In the Middle Ages it was embodied in the fantasy of the Fountain of Youth, where decrepit old people entered the water on one side and emerged young and beautiful on the other. This fresco, painted in the first half of the 15th century in the castle of Manta, Piedmont, is attributed to Aimone Dux of Pavia. The dream lives on, but today's generation is more inclined to put its faith in the miracles of chemistry.

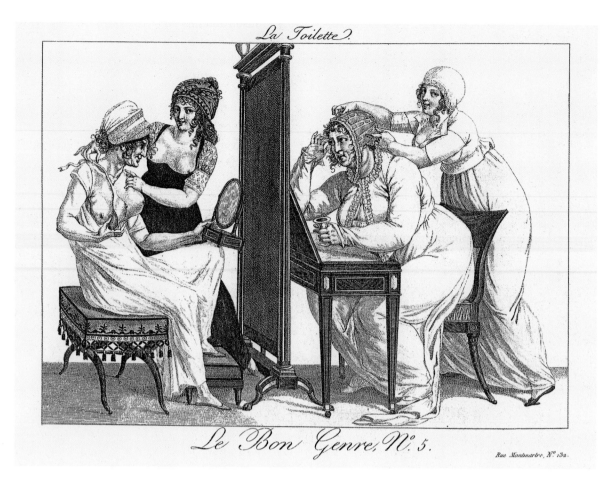

La Toilette.

Le Bon Genre, N.° 5.

Rue Montmartre, N.° 132.

Women were sometimes said to be old after the menopause, when they ceased to be able to carry out their main function in life, childbearing. But this was far from universal. For instance, post-menopausal women were often still mothers of young children since, until the 20th century, it was common for women to bear children for as long as they were physically able. On the other hand, in medieval and early modern Europe and, perhaps, in ancient Greece and Rome, women might gain more independence after menopause, sometimes more public responsibilities, as midwives, chaperones or adjudicators in community conflicts about sexual or other delicate matters.[15] Rich widows had control over their wealth which married women lacked in all societies before the 20th century, and some of them wielded it formidably. For example, in England, Katherine Nevill married John Mowbray, Duke of Norfolk in 1412. He died in 1432, leaving her in control of his substantial estates, which she stewarded well. She lived for a further 51 years, remarrying three times, the last time, when she was in her 60s, to a teenager, Sir John Woodville, to the chagrin of her heirs waiting to inherit the estate – those who survived, that is, since she outlived her son, grandson and great-granddaughter. If Woodville hoped to inherit, which was his right as her husband, he too was unlucky because she outlived him by 14 years. She died in 1483, having deprived a succession of male heirs of the inheritance they expected.[16]

In most times and places women have outlived men, as they still do. In early modern Europe older women were often represented not as sad and decayed but as sexually voracious, once menopause dispelled the fear of pregnancy. Women, like men, were defined as old when they displayed the expected characteristics of old age: physical weakness and dependency. They did so at varied ages and the diversity increased over time. But one thing that did not change over the centuries was the natural lifespan, the maximum time that anyone could expect to live. Since at least medieval times it has been believed that, at some future time, people would live to 150 or 200 or more; indeed, that once, before the Flood, they had already done so, until God punished Man for his sins by shortening his lifespan.[17] But very long life was not always thought desirable. In *Gulliver's Travels* (1726) Jonathan Swift satirized the desire for endless life in describing the Struldbruggs, who were fated to live for ever:

> *They commonly acted like Mortals, till about Thirty Years old, after which by Degrees they grew melancholy and dejected, increasing in both till they came to Fourscore... When they came to Fourscore Years... they had not only all the Follies and Infirmities of other old Men, but many more which arose from the dreadful Prospect of never dying. They were not only opinionative, peevish, covetous, morose, vain, talkative; but uncapable of Friendship, and dead to all natural Affection, which never descended below their Grand-children. Envy and impotent Desires are their prevailing Passions. But those Objects against which their Envy seems principally directed, are the Vices of the younger Sort and the Deaths of the old... At Ninety they lose their Teeth and Hair... The Diseases they were subject to still continue without encreasing or diminishing. In talking they forget the common appellation of Things and the Names of Persons, even of those who are their nearest Friends and Relations... They are despised and hated by all Sorts of People... They were the most mortifying Sight I ever beheld; and the Women more horrible than the Men. Besides the usual Deformities in extreme old Age, they acquired an additional Ghastliness in Proportion to their Number of Years.*[18]

At all times a few people have survived to 100 or a little beyond. At the beginning of the 21st century more people than ever before live to their century, but it still rare to live much beyond that, though there are occasional examples of survival to around 120. The lifespan shows little sign of extending into superlongevity.[19]

In real life the quest for renewed youth and beauty has been a perennial subject for satire. A print from post-Revolutionary France (1800) shows two mature ladies at their toilet. One is acquiring a new bosom, the other retouches the lines around her eyes. The pretty young maids glance directly at us, as if to share their amusement.

Since the beginning of European languages a simple three-part division of the age-span into youth, maturity and old age has been common but not adequate to express the visible diversity of reality. Rather the 'Ages of Man' have been divided, in different times and places, into anything between four and twelve stages, with 'old age' said to begin, even in ancient Greece and Rome, variously between 49 and 70. Most age schema have acknowledged a division within old age between active, younger old age and the last, decrepit stage. The modern expression of this is the sociological distinction between 'young old age' and 'old old age'; or, as the French more elegantly express it, between the 'third age' (which follows the 'first age' of youth and the 'second age' of maturity) and the final, 'fourth age'.

Two attitudes to old age, both from the High Renaissance, reflect two different mentalities, two ways of facing the inevitable, perhaps typical of the north (Germany) and the south (Italy). Giorgione (left) is markedly optimistic; his elderly man, looking straight out at the viewer, is no less confident and healthy (though more thoughtful) than youth and middle age. Hans Baldung (right) in 1510 sees nothing but regret in the contrast between the beautiful young woman, and the old one already arm in arm with death.

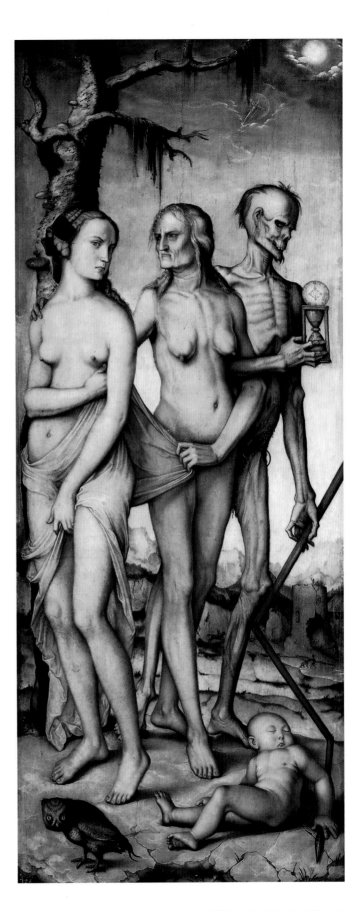

Probably the most famous literary representation of the Ages of Man is that of Jaques in Shakespeare's *As You Like It*. He concludes his description of the Seven Ages:

> *The sixth age shifts*
> *Into the lean and slippered pantaloon*
> *With spectacles on nose and pouch on side,*
> *His youthful hose, well sav'd, a world too wide*
> *For his shrunk shank; and his big manly voice,*
> *Turning again toward childish treble, pipes*
> *And whistles in his sound. Last scene of all,*
> *That ends this strange eventful history,*
> *Is second childishness and mere oblivion;*
> *Sans teeth, sans eyes, sans taste, sans everything.*[20]

This is sometimes interpreted as typical of a negative attitude to old people in Shakespeare's time. Yet Jaques' description of all age groups is negative and he himself is represented as melancholy – conventionally a characteristic of old men in ancient and medieval literature, although he is quite young. There is a satirical edge to the soliloquy which should caution us against taking it at face value. Jaques delivers the speech alone on stage with Duke Senior, who is relatively old yet affects the life of a young man, hunting in the forest. Visually the scene subverts Jaques' verbal message. And, immediately he concludes, his brother Orlando challenges it further by entering with the faithful Adam who has followed him into exile. Earlier in the play Adam, at 'almost fourscore' years, pledges his support to Orlando and claims:

> *Though I look old, yet I am strong and lusty*
> *For in my youth I never did apply*
> *Hot and rebellious liquors in my blood.*
> *Nor did not with unbashful forehead woo*
> *The means of weakness and debility;*
> *Therefore my age is as a lusty winter,*
> *Frosty but kindly. Let me go with you;*
> *I'll do the service of a younger man.*[21]

Adam turns upside down Jaques' description of aged men as dotards. Shakespeare juxtaposes Jaques' representation of the inexorable march of time with Adam's optimistic embodiment of human difference in the process of ageing, one over which individuals have agency if they live temperately.

A variety of images of old age can be found throughout the works of Shakespeare, as they can also earlier in the works of Chaucer.[22]

'Melancholy', one of the four temperaments governed by Saturn, is personified by Hans Baldung as an old man with deep-set eyes and a grim mouth, anticipating doom.

In the Prologue to the Reeve's Tale the Reeve describes himself in miserable terms. Chaucer opens his description of him, conventionally enough, as old, choleric and thin: 'his legs were lean / Like sticks they were, no calf was to be seen.' But he portrays him as a sharp businessman:

> He knew their dodges, knew their every trick
> Feared like the plague he was by those beneath.
> He is wealthy and still active:
> When young he'd learned a useful trade, and still
> He was a carpenter of first-rate skill.

Chaucer portrays other old men as fools, betrayed by young wives. On the other hand the Wife of Bath, clearly past menopause, had, after mixed experiences with four older husbands, found contentment with her fifth, who is 20 years her junior. She presents a strong image of an older woman in control of her life.

Over hundreds of years, writers of philosophy and of literature have expressed this variety, some with more subtlety and self-awareness than others. The French humanist Michel de Montaigne was convinced in 1563, at age 35, that 'I have grown older for a great length of time, but not an inch wiser I am sure'. In later writings he continued to complain that

> I should be grudging and ashamed if the wretchedness and misfortune of my decrepitude were rightly to set itself above my good, healthy, eager, vigorous years, and if men were to judge me not by where I have been but by where I am no longer.[23]

As he aged further, Montaigne became somewhat more reconciled with old age, but never wholly so. He wrote:

> To die of age, is a rare, singular, and extraordinary death, and so much lesse naturall than others: It is the last and extremest kind of dying: The further it is from us, so much the lesse is it to be hoped for: Indeed it is the limit, beyond which we shal not passe, and which the law of nature hath prescribed unto us, as that which should not be outgone by any; but it is a rare privilege peculiar unto her selfe, to make us continue unto it. It is an exemption, which through some particular favour she bestoweth on some one man, in the space of two or three ages, discharging him from the crosses, troubles, and difficulties she hath enterposed between both, in this long cariere and pilgrimage. Therefore my opinion is, to consider, that the age unto which we are come, is an age whereto few arrive: since men come not unto it by any ordinarie course, it is a sign we are verie forward. And since we have past the accustomed bounds, which is the true measure of our life, we must not hope, that we shall goe much further.[24]

However, as the French philosopher Simone de Beauvoir comments (negative though she herself was about old age):

> In Montaigne there is a curious paradox that may have escaped him but that is strikingly obvious to the reader: the Essais become richer and richer, more and more intimate, original and profound as the author of the book advances in age... It was when he felt that his powers were declining that he is at his greatest.[25]

A similar change in attitude to ageing as he himself aged – though a change towards a more relaxed reconciliation with old age than Montaigne attained – is evident in the work of the great German poet Goethe, especially in his successive versions of *Faust*. His *Urfaust* was written in 1773, when he was aged 24; a first fragment of the final work in 1790 when he was 41; the first part of the complete work in 1808, and the second in 1832, shortly before his death at the age of 83. In the work of the young man, old age is dismal, prompting the yearning to return to youth by whatever means, however extreme, even selling one's soul to the devil. In the writings of his later years he has become positive about old age as a time of repose and reflection, though by no means of inactivity, a time when desires are satisfied: 'That which one wishes for in youth, one finds in old age', when illusions have disappeared, but cynicism and melancholy have not replaced optimism or the capacity to love.[26] His best work was written in the last 25 years of his long life. As he expressed it at the end of his life, in the second *Faust*:

> My way has been to scour the whole world through.
> Where was delight, I seized it by the hair;
> If it fell short, I simply left it there,
> If it escaped me I just let it go.
> I stormed through life, through joys in endless train,
> Desire, fulfilment, then desire again;
> Lordly at first I fared, in power and speed,
> But now I walk with wisdom's deeper heed.
> Full well I know the earthly round of men,
> And what's beyond is barred from human ken;
> Fool, fool is he who blinks at clouds on high,
> Inventing his own image in the sky.
> Let him look round, feet planted firm on earth:
> This world will not be mute to him of worth.
> Why haunt eternity with dim surmise?[27]

In 'The Three Ages of Life' Gustav Klimt brought new attitudes and new perspectives to a traditional subject. Vienna in 1905 was at the centre of a whirlpool of revolutionary ideas that produced waves of exciting, often shocking, challenges to received standards in psychology, literature, music and art. Klimt, one of the leaders of the Secession movement, explored this haunting and disturbing world, combining neurosis, eroticism and death.

Another long-lived writer, of the 19th century, Victor Hugo (1802–85), the most important of French Romantic writers, was, like other Romantics, positive about the survival into old age of the spirit and even of physical strength. *Les Misérables* (1862) presents a moving portrait of a strong old man, Jean Valjean. In 1869, aged 67, Hugo wrote: 'My body wanes, my mind waxes: there is an old age coming into flower.' This was no illusion. He continued to publish successfully. He was elected a deputy for Paris in the provisional government of 1870 and a senator in 1876. He continued to be sexually active. In 1877 Flaubert commented of him: 'The old fellow is younger and more delightful than ever.'[28]

These and very many other writers through time and throughout Western culture assume each life to be distinctive, none following quite the same course. They present competing representations of old age with an ease which suggests that these were familiar to and shared by their audiences. A similar diversity, and belief that ageing can be controlled by individuals, is found also in medical, theological and other writings over the centuries.

As some of the examples above show, and the following chapters richly illustrate, throughout history real life was as richly diverse in old age as in literature and the visual arts. Over time, this diversity has increased, especially over the past century, as it has become normal to grow old. Many more people live, and are fit, to later ages and they pursue a greater variety of lifestyles. The story of old age is a much more hopeful one than, all too often, we are led to believe.

The humdrum reality of a woman's life: babyhood (toys), girlhood (ponies), adolescence (boys), maturity (marriage), middle age (pregnancy, childbirth, worry), professional success (schedules), advancing years (keep fit), retirement (family photographs) and old age (loneliness). The date is 1989, the English cartoonist Posy Simmonds.

PICTURES *through the* AGES

2

TIM PARKIN THE ANCIENT GREEK AND ROMAN WORLDS

A Roman jurist, Callistratus, wrote around about AD 200 that 'Old age has always been revered in our state.'[1] But a philosopher whom we know only as Juncus and of whose writings only a few fragments survive wrote slightly earlier in the course of the 2nd century that even to his friends and relatives an old man is 'an oppressive, painful, grievous and decrepit spectacle: in short, an *Iliad* of woes'.[2] That a range of views about old age and elderly people is held in the modern world does not surprise us; neither should we expect anything other than that a wide range of images, attitudes and ideas about ageing and older people survive from classical antiquity, arguably one of human history's richest and more imaginative periods in terms of artistic and philosophical endeavour. The Greeks and Romans observed the realities of ageing and thought creatively about the position of older people within their societies, and the ideas and images they generated have had enormous influence in the Western world, for better or for worse, in the millennia that have followed.

The scholar Isidore of Seville summed up the variety of classical experiences and images thus: 'Old age brings with it many things, some good, some bad. Good, since it frees us from the most violent of masters: it imposes a limit on pleasures, it smashes the force of lust, it increases wisdom, and it grants wiser counsels. Bad, however, because advanced old age is most wretched in terms of both the disabilities it inflicts and the loathing it incurs.'[3] But even the notion that for everyone old age is good until it turns bad is of course heavily generalized. As Seneca the Younger observed in the 1st century AD, 'There is not one type of old age for all people.'[4] Everyone experiences old age differently. The reality for individuals – and not just for philosophers – may also be inferred from inscriptions and documents, and again, variety of experience and of perception is evident. One man who died at the age of 50 years in the middle of the 3rd century AD in the province of Roman Mauretania (modern Algeria) had it recorded on his tombstone that he died 'in the flower of youth'.[5] On the other hand, an orphaned male minor and his guardian in Roman Egypt recorded in a petition against the boy's paternal grandfather's sister that she is already extremely old: apparently she has lived more than 60 years.[6]

A young man's death in Athens in about 340 BC was commemorated by this stele bearing the figures, beside the youth himself, of a boy and an old man, perhaps his son and father, perhaps emblems of the stages of life.

Experiences and attitudes vary; old age was a prospect awaited with mixed emotions. A tombstone inscription from Ravenna, dated palaeographically to the 1st century AD, expresses this well: 'Gaius Iulius Mygdonius, a Parthian by race, born a free man, captured in youth and given over into Roman territory. When I was made a Roman citizen, at fate's command I collected up a nest-egg for the day I should reach 50 years of age. I sought from puberty to achieve my old age; now receive me, rock, willingly; with you I shall be released from care.'[7]

From the classical Mediterranean civilizations of the Greeks and Romans, many depictions of older people have survived, both in iconographic and written forms. While not infrequently old age was glorified or idealized, in some depictions no attempt was made to disguise aspects which might be regarded today as less appealing. In some periods of classical art, particularly in the later Roman republic, the wrinkles and rigours of old age were presented with pride and a marked lack of self-consciousness; in other times the depiction of aged individuals, particularly of women, may strike us as hideously cruel. It is even reported that the painter Parrhasius tortured and killed an aged slave as a model for a painting of Prometheus, whom Zeus as punishment had chained to a rock and had an eagle devour his liver each day.[8]

Life is complex; attitudes to life are varied. Attempts to determine realities and attitudes from literature and art from a distance of two millennia (give or take 500 years) require much care and caution. As diverse as the views may be from Greece and Rome, it must always be remembered that we are heavily reliant on elite male perceptions.

Ideal and reality: Greek art of the classical period idealized the human body and created standardized types according to the nature of the man or woman being portrayed: the philosopher, the soldier, the matron, and so on. In the Hellenistic and Roman periods this yielded to realism, a change particularly marked in the the depiction of old people. Right: Homer, conforming to the stereotype of the venerable inspired poet (Roman copy of a Greek original). Opposite: the closely observed figure of an old shepherdess bears all the marks of age and hardship, yet she walks with dignity.

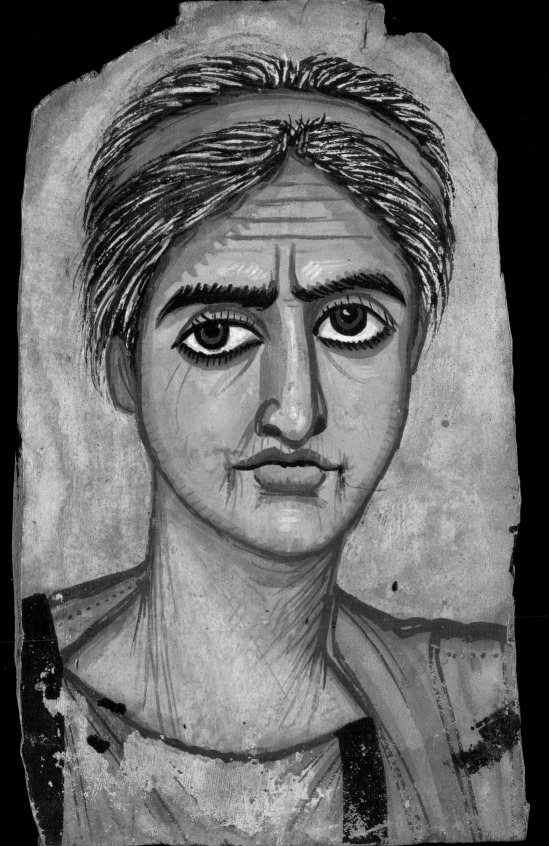

It is also worth noting from the outset that while in this first chapter we are dealing with a vast period of history (in literary terms, well over a millennium from the epics of Homer in Greece's early archaic history to the elegies of Maximianus in the 6th century AD), we cannot map any meaningful chronological development in attitudes towards ageing. It is not true, for example, that the Greeks cherished old age and the Romans detested it, as has sometimes been claimed. There is variety over both time and space (with the classical world we are also dealing with a huge geographical area: the Mediterranean basin and beyond, from Britain to Bactria), and marked differences between one time and place and another are as likely to be the result of the nature of the evidence, or its place of origin, as of any difference in reality.

With these caveats in mind, we can explore prevalent themes that emerge from the art and literature of the Greeks and Romans. But first we must consider how many old people there were in ancient times and, even more fundamentally, exactly what 'old age', or the Greek or Latin equivalents, actually meant.

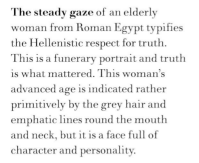

The steady gaze of an elderly woman from Roman Egypt typifies the Hellenistic respect for truth. This is a funerary portrait and truth is what mattered. This woman's advanced age is indicated rather primitively by the grey hair and emphatic lines round the mouth and neck, but it is a face full of character and personality.

Seneca was in his sixties when he died, a renowned philosopher and a strict moralist. In this highly expressionistic bust (1st century AD) the signs of ageing are not disguised, but neither is the independence of spirit that enabled him to die – committing suicide on Nero's orders – with the stoicism that he had always professed.

There is abundant evidence throughout history that some individuals have lived to what was regarded, then as now, as a ripe old age. Indeed, if we were to believe the ancient testimony, people lived a lot longer then than they do today. Whole races of people, mostly far distant if not mythical, were credited with fantastic lifespans. Ages of 300 or 500 years feature in classical literature for pseudo-historical individuals, while lives of several centuries, if not of eternity, were attributed to mythical characters such as Tithonus, Teiresias and the Sibyls. From Homer comes the epitome of old age throughout classical times, the pagan equivalent of Methuselah: Nestor, king of Pylos, who outlived three generations – or, as it came to be commonly understood, three lifetimes or centuries. From the Old Testament we are familiar enough with fabulous ages, up to 1,000 years, being attributed to individuals from the past. St Augustine argued that despite the incredulity of many, the fabulous ages attributed to figures from the Old Testament were to be believed literally; he noted that in the days of Genesis people 'lived such a long time that they did not think a man of one hundred years was old'.[9]

Old age was conventionally associated with wisdom, from at least the time of Homer's Nestor, and Homer himself was said to have lived to a ripe old age. In art elderly men were often depicted as suitably venerable and wise.[10] The Seven Sages of Greece were credited with extended (and usually rounded) lifespans: Myson of Chen was 97 years old when he died, we are told, while Pittacus' age is variously recorded as from 70 to 100 years; Cleobulus of Lindos was 70 years, Periander of Corinth 80 years, the Athenian Solon is usually credited with 80 years, though one source says 100, while Thales is variously recorded as dying at 78, 90 or 100. Likewise the somewhat nebulous figure of Pythagoras in the 6th century BC is usually credited with 80 or 90 years, though one ancient source records that he lived in fine fettle to his 117th year, thanks to a special potion made of vinegar of squill (sea onion). This confusion concerning ages at death is a common one, and it is clear that the longevity of someone long dead, especially someone notable, might be exaggerated as time passed and as circumstances suited.

Conventional images of a limited range of human types – the old man (left), the slave, the matron, etc – were used in the Greek and Roman theatre, even though the characters themselves might be very subtly differentiated.

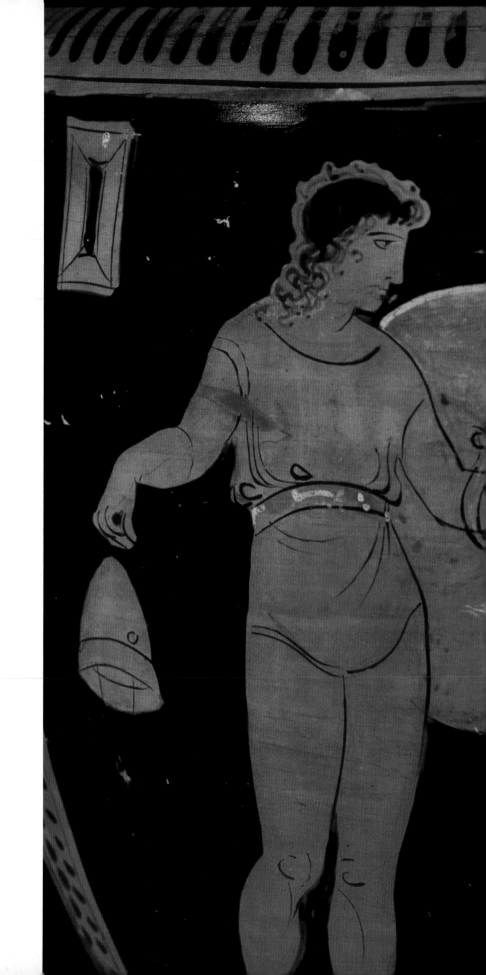

The wisdom of old age was personified for the Greeks in the figure of Nestor, King of Pylos. He was reputed to have lived through three generations, so presumably lived to 90 or 100. Here, on a Greek vase painting of the 4th century BC, he is seen with Telemachus, the son of Odysseus, who visited him after the Trojan War seeking information about his father.

The Athenian people represented themselves symbolically as a wise old man. On this stele, inscribed with a law safeguarding the rights of the people passed in 336 BC, he is being crowned by the figure of Democracy.

Nevertheless, on reaching more historical times, there is ample evidence of people surviving into their 90s and beyond, and often there are few obvious reasons to doubt the figures quoted. It is very important to realize that, despite the 'demographic transition' following the Industrial Revolution and despite the advances in medicine in the last century, people do not live significantly longer today than they did in the historical past. In classical times, dying when one was in one's 60s or beyond was regarded as natural; to die younger was usually seen as a harsh and unnatural fate, as both literary and epigraphic testimony bears witness. Indeed, for a parent to witness the death of an offspring was regarded as an ill-fated but not uncommon consequence of old age. Herodotus has King Croesus memorably remark: 'In peace sons bury their fathers, in war fathers bury their sons,'[11] but that brings in other considerations. The Greek satirist Lucian is much more cynical. In his work *On Grief* a son at his own funeral is imagined as responding to his aged father's grief, pointing out the positive features of dying young: he will not have to grow old, to look like his father (head bald, face wrinkled, back bent, knees trembling); by dying young, he will not be scorned in old age, nor will the sight of him offend the young.[12]

The biblical 'three score years and ten' was held to be a general figure for a good age, not a particularly extended one. At the age of 62 Cicero, in dedicating his philosophical treatise *Cato the Elder, On Old Age* to his friend Atticus (aged 65 at the time), noted that old age was now 'pressing on or at least approaching' them both; by no means did they regard themselves as exceptionally old. Very high levels of infant mortality meant that life expectancy *at birth* was indeed low in the worlds of ancient Greece and Rome. But if you survived your first years, there was a good chance that you would go on to live to be at least 60. It emerges that in antiquity ideas about old age in purely chronological terms were not so different from our own today; while some poets might express horror at the emergence of grey hairs on their head when they were only 40 or so years old, most writers seem to have assumed that you were old once you were in your 60s. No stricter line of demarcation need be expected, especially as there were no general institutionalized schemes of retirement or pensions in ancient times.

While we do not have comprehensive statistical evidence from ancient times, it may be estimated that, for example, around 6–8 per cent of the population of the Roman empire in the 1st century AD was over the age of 60.[13] A very select few would have even survived to be centenarians.

Concern for truth makes the Roman portrait bust virtually unique in the ancient world. Here we come face to face with a living person at the end of the 1st century BC. There are virtually no pretty young girls, but hundreds of interesting mature women, their character and age vividly conveyed with dignity and psychological insight.

Philosophers were almost by definition old men. A Roman mosaic (above), probably derived from a Greek painting, shows Plato's 'Academy' in Athens. He sits in the centre under the tree and seems to be drawing a geometrical figure in the sand. In a box at his feet is a celestial sphere, and there is a sundial on the column behind.

Achilles' tutor, according to Homer, was a wise man called Phoenix, represented (above) in a mosaic of the 2nd century AD in the familiar guise of a bearded elderly man.

Yet another common myth about the classical past is that older individuals enjoyed something of a golden age when they were treated with great respect and held primary authority over political, religious and social spheres. For some, to be sure, old age was not an unhappy or unaccomplished time. We know of many individuals in the ancient world – politicians, writers, priests, prophets and philosophers – admired for their active old age. Instances of 'successful' older individuals, or generalized pictures of wise and active old age, need to be assessed in terms of degrees of idealization or reality, however. Literature provides a host of images, positive and negative. Philosophers attributed old age's perceived negative features to people's dissipated youth and stressed the boons of ageing, not least in the political sphere. Cicero's treatise *On Old Age* is one very powerful statement to that effect, but Cicero's insistence that old men make the best and wisest rulers needs to be read in the context of the time: it was written in a period when Cicero felt his own powerbase eroding, and when the traditional republic itself was on the brink of collapse. He wrote his treatise in 44 BC, the same year as Julius Caesar's assassination; it was also the year following his beloved daughter Tullia's death. Nor is Cicero's work the only ancient treatise on old age; dozens of other works are just as important to the overall picture. Not surprisingly, images of and opinions about older people cover a wide range, from cheerfully positive to bitterly negative.

This makes it all the more evident, in my opinion, that when it comes to political and social realities, old age did not automatically confer the respect and authority that some felt it deserved. Most power, and indeed most wealth, in the ancient world lay with younger generations. From the aristocracy down to the lower-class family and slaves, the realities of life for older people hinged predominantly on one factor: the individual's ability to remain a functioning member of his or her society, be it as a leading politician or as a childminder. In the absence of any form of state welfare or healthcare (as we shall see), responsibility for supporting older individuals rested with their immediate kin.

Classical literature abounds with statements about the respect and care owed by children to their parents, not least in the latter's old age. The picture is not straightforward, since for most aristocratic authors financial security in their later years was almost taken for granted. But ideals emerge. Clearly, from the time of Homer onwards it was seen as a duty for children to care for their parents in their time of need and dependence, basically in the form of repaying the debt of nurture. The duty in many classical societies was traditionally seen as a moral one, at times enforced or reinforced by law. In classical Athens of the 5th and 4th centuries BC, for example, children had a legal as well as a moral obligation to maintain their parents in their old age. The Athenian statute, attributed to Solon, stated that he who did not support

The most famous old man in Greek literature was Priam, King of Troy. When his son Hector was killed by Achilles he came humbly to Achilles' tent to beg for his body, here lying on the ground under the couch.

(*trephein*) his parents was to be *atimos*, deprived of citizen rights – in Athens, it was sometimes felt, a sentence second only to death. Children accused of maltreatment of parents were liable under a charge which any third party could bring without risk of penalty if they withdrew or lost the case. Furthermore, 'Do you treat your parents well?' was one of the questions asked of a candidate for public office. Athenians seem to have taken their duty seriously.

Nor was it simply a case of refraining from maltreating one's parents: positive services were also expected, such as the provision of food and shelter, and the observation of due rites after death. Such a duty, we are told, was laid on all offspring. The only exceptions were those who had not been properly reared by their parents – the reciprocal nature of the arrangement was what mattered. Hence, those who had not been taught a trade by their fathers, those born as bastards and those hired out by their fathers as prostitutes were not regarded as legally bound to support their parents. With an eye to the future, therefore, there was a strong motivation for adults to have children or, failing that possibility, to adopt them. Certainly the child's (moral) duty persisted, as the 2nd century AD Stoic philosopher Hierokles makes clear in his ethical fragments, discussing proper conduct towards parents: 'For our parents, therefore, we should provide food freely, and such as is fitting for the weakness of old age; besides this, a bed, sleep, oil, a bath, and clothing – in short, general physical necessities, so that they should never lack any of these things; thus we imitate the care they took in rearing ourselves when we were infants.' In another passage, he discusses the benefits of marriage, among which is the fact that it produces children 'who help us now while we are strong, and when we are worn out, crushed by old age, they will be fine allies'.[14]

But there were potentially negative aspects to such a system as well as beneficial ones: older people could be seen to be totally dependent on the younger generation and lose their power when they no longer held the purse strings. Such, for example, is the situation described in Aristophanes' *Wasps*, where the son, Bdelykleon, is depicted as the master of the house and his aged father, Philokleon, is shown reduced to childlike dependency. Bdelykleon promises support for his father, but there is a marked lack of any filial respect here: 'I'll support him, providing everything that's suitable for an old man: gruel to lick up, a soft thick cloak, a goatskin mantle, a whore to massage his prick and his loins.' As Philokleon later complains, he is being treated like a child by his own son – a complete reversal of roles: 'At the moment I'm not in control of my own property, because I'm young and I'm closely watched; my little son keeps his eye on me and he's mean-tempered, and a cress-paring cumin-splitter into the bargain.'[15]

It was the duty of a son to care for his father. Aeneas was in this respect a model son. His rescue of Anchises, carrying him on his back from burning Troy, was a favourite subject of classical art: a vase painting of about 510 BC.

This is of course a scene from a stage comedy, not a direct depiction of real life, but its sardonic humour surely draws on an underlying reality, that an aged father could be treated in this way by his own son. Philokleon's complaint of being treated like a child is reminiscent (as an ancient scholiast also realized) of a common proverb, to be found not only in Attic comedy but in classical literature in general, that old age is a second childhood. The life course, in other words, has come full circle. The logic behind such a metaphor, if indeed any underlying logic is to be expected, may be partly explained by the observation of the physical and mental decline experienced by many elderly individuals and the dependence on others brought about by this; it is, of course, a timeless image, still current today. In Athens, in economic terms at any rate, old people may have been seen as children for the very reason that they had lost their independence and, like Philokleon, felt themselves to be prisoners in their own (or rather their children's) homes.

The prevailing attitude in ancient times – and it is one that is becoming ever more familiar again in Western societies – was that it was your own responsibility to ensure that you would be taken care of in your old age. Children were the primary line of defence. Failing that, it might be hoped that your spouse would be capable of providing aid, or at least companionship. Ultimately, you must look to your own resources.

While in Athenian society legislation existed to ensure that children typically looked after their parents, in Rome no such specific legislation is evident; at most, by the 2nd century AD, a judge may require a son or daughter, on the complaint of a parent, to ensure the latter's livelihood if the young person is financially capable. In the Roman context we are usually talking about the oldest living male ascendant, the father or paternal grandfather: the Roman *paterfamilias*, it may be supposed, could look forward to a secure old age, as property owner and ultimate authority in the family. But senile dementia might have altered this image. The physical disabilities of old age tend to be the focus of ancient literature, but an awareness of the mental drawbacks that might come with old age is also there. That the head of the Roman household retained legal control until his death is explicit in the ancient testimony, but this stranglehold on power might be tempered when the abilities of that person to run the family effectively were called into question. A Roman son could in effect circumvent the legal restrictions placed on him, by acting as the *curator* of his own father. It seems plausible that in practice, to avoid such extremes, children were granted an independent role in the running of the house as the father grew older. The tacit agreement would have been that such independence would be repaid when the father and mother were themselves in a state of increasing dependency. Looking at it another way, this legal remedy might also be held to have had the potential effect of placing the parent in a position of childlike dependency.[16]

Modern demographic methods and tools may be utilized in a computer simulation to create an imaginary life-course history, to trace individuals within a defined age range as they age.[17] Modelling a likely population for the Graeco-Roman world, based on high mortality and fertility constraints, it is striking how relatively rarely three generations of a family would have been coexistent (let alone living in the same house). For example, assuming a model in which average life expectancy at birth is 25 years and in which males marry at an average age of 30, females at 20, then it can be calculated that at birth only one in three individuals had their maternal grandfather or paternal grandmother still alive, only one in two had their maternal grandmother still alive and, even more striking, only one in six or seven individuals had at birth a living paternal grandfather. By the age of ten years, the average ancient individual had only a one-in-two chance of having *any* of his grandparents alive. Fewer than one in a hundred Greeks or Romans of the age of 20 would have had a surviving paternal grandfather.

Laertes' reunion with his son Odysseus after twenty years is one of the most powerfully emotional scenes in Homer, confirming the Greeks' reverence for the father-son relationship: a detail of a terracotta relief of about 500 BC.

The difference in terms of paternal and maternal lines is fairly easy to explain, in view of the different average marriage ages of males and females. A woman might become a grandmother by her daughter when the latter was in her late teens, and hence when the grandmother herself was not yet 40 years of age. (Note the scene on the mid-5th century BC Athenian tombstone of Ampharete, with the inscription: 'Here I hold my daughter's child, my darling, whom once I held on my knee when we were both alive and saw the light of the sun; now I am dead and hold her, dead too.') A man would not normally expect to become a paternal grandfather, on the other hand, before the age of around 60.[18] In short, at any particular moment in most people's life courses, living ascendants on the maternal side of the family must have been more common, relatively speaking, than on the paternal side. On the other hand, it must be added, most adult Greeks or Romans would have had only shadowy memories of their grandparents, paternal or maternal. It is a fact that we encounter grandparents in the literary testimony from the ancient world surprisingly rarely, and most references are to the commemoration or listing of deceased ancestors. But even taking into account demographic considerations, grandparents feature more rarely as, for example, dedicators on Latin commemorative tombstone inscriptions than we might otherwise have expected; the nuclear family was the focus of obligations and of affection in the classical world.[19]

Merchants and tradesmen commemorated themselves as freely as emperors and noblemen. The elderly Ampudius, who traded in corn in the 1st century AD, included his own shrewd features on his tomb between those of his wife and daughter.

Cato the Stoic was regarded as the ideal of old age, and is made the spokesman of Cicero's 'De Senectute', the best-known treatment of the subject in antiquity. He was a man of the strictest moral principles, maintaining a dominant presence until his death in 149 BC at the age of 85. The identification of this pair of busts, made as late as the 2nd century AD, is uncertain and may represent his equally famous great-grandson Cato the Younger and his daughter Porcia. An opponent of Julius Caesar, he was defeated in battle and committed suicide in 46 BC. Porcia was married to Brutus, another enemy of Caesar, and is said (though this is disputed) to have also taken her own life after Brutus's death.

The reality was not always quite that straightforward, however, at least in terms of an individual's entire life course. While the traditional image of the extended family as dominant in antiquity (and beyond) has been effectively quashed by recent historians of the family, it must still be realized that it would have been inevitable that, at some points in the lifecycle of a household, some more distant relatives (including grandparents, paternal and maternal, and grandchildren) often remained within the family home, especially among the lower classes and away from the city.[20] Multi-generational households, though rarely mentioned in the written sources, would not have been so very unusual. For example, from the extant sample of around 320 copies of Roman Egyptian census returns, we have nine examples of upwardly-extended families where a husband's or, less frequently, wife's mother or father resides with the younger family. They range in age from 50 to 75 years (in two of these cases the age is lost); on three occasions it is the older person who files the return.[21] The moral duty of caring for one's aged parents may have extended, therefore, to sharing one's roof with them – possibly the elderly relations could perform functions such as childminding, although the presence of slaves in the household may have both provided independent support for older family members and, conversely, made some of the traditional roles of grandparents in pre-industrial societies redundant in the ancient context.[22] As a result of demographic realities, at any rate, any three-generational living arrangements would usually have been of a short-term nature anyway.

Outside of the home, what roles did older people play? In political terms, gerontocracy was neither widespread nor common in the ancient world. The ancient system in the conservative state of Sparta is cited with approval, by Cicero and by others, Greek and Roman, for the way that precedence was given to the aged. Sparta's *gerousia*, whose members were at least 60 years old, is as close as antiquity came to a gerontocracy, but even there the power of the *gerontes* was not absolute, and younger officials, the ephors, over time came to hold greater power. Furthermore, Aristotle for one noted the risks in giving power to men subject to the potential liabilities of old age. In democratic Athens age carried no obvious privilege, and in Rome most authority – emperors (young or old) apart – tended to lie with senators in their 40s and 50s.

If the participation of the aged person in public affairs was at times debated, his or her role in religious practices was not, and this can itself be interpreted as a mark of marginalization: the religious role of elderly women in ancient societies is particularly relevant.[23] Prophets and seers in literature were often depicted as marginal members of society: women and aged men. Plato and Aristotle both remarked that in their ideal states religious duties would be reserved for those in old age.[24] In the Roman state the *paterfamilias*, as the senior male member

An elderly priestess, Roman copy of a Greek 4th-century BC original.

of the household, had the duty to observe the customary religious rites, the worship of Lares and Penates (household gods) and ancestors. Priests at Rome need not be old, though the office normally lasted for life[25] and, in line with traditional ideas of respect for age, seniority would normally be expected to be given to the oldest member of the college, or at least to the individual who had belonged to the college the longest. The impression remains, however, here as elsewhere, that the continued activity of older people depended on their proven capability to perform the duties required. As marginal members of society any rights they held were far from automatic, but had to be won and maintained through continued performance. What may appear at first sight as privileges, such as a greater degree of freedom for women in later life (for example, in Athens, to attend funerals), in many cases should be more closely defined as representing a diminution of status and a lack of concern by other sectors of society.

Caring for the young was, and still is, one of the duties of the elderly. Here, a nurse – or is it a grandmother? – holds an evidently contented baby: a figurine from Tanagra in northern Greece.

While the image of wise old men (and the focus is very much male) is common in classical literature and some ancient art, corresponding negative stereotypes of old age and of elderly people – particularly of women – are widespread and powerful. As a rule classical literature tended to focus on upper-class males (young and old), but a great deal of ink was spent on stereotypical aged females, not uncommonly portrayed in the most virulent and obscene terms as sex-crazed witches or alcoholics. Besides being unpleasant, this points to marginalization in terms of both age and gender. Past reproducing, older women might be dismissed as non-functioning members of society.

The bitterly negative, often extremely personal indictment of old age, especially in satirical and erotic poetry, had a long history which the Roman writers of the early empire adopted willingly and enthusiastically; the tradition in Latin literature extends in painful, clinical and – in my view – rather dreary detail to the six elegies on old age and love written in the 6th century AD by Maximianus.[26]

Portraits of old women in Hellenistic and Roman times could be kindly or brutally cruel. The full-length bronze (left) has dignity and poise. By contrast the drunken woman (right) – a Roman copy of a Greek original – is typical of artists' cruel depiction of people on the edge of society.

Invective against old age, then, has a very long history. It may be traced back almost as far as Homer — and some claim to have found it in Homer too. The early 6th century Greek poet Mimnermus in particular dwells, with heavy and sentimental self-pity, on the flight of time, the loss of youthful pleasures and the hatefulness of old age. In Greek tragedy and comedy alike old people (especially women) regularly — though, of course, not invariably — come in for unflattering, if not harsh, treatment. On the Roman stage, particularly in the plays of Plautus, every conceivable negative quality associated with old age is highlighted, with special emphasis on the old man's sexual, though impotent, proclivities. But other, more 'serious' portrayals may also be adduced.

In the pseudo-Platonic *Axiochos* (traditionally said to date from the 1st century BC), for example, *consolatio* is required for Axiochos as he is on the point of death. As one of his arguments, Socrates states, quite conventionally, that death should not be feared but rather welcomed, since no age in life is exempt from pain and hence death is a blessed release. As part of this argument, he quotes from a discourse given (we are told) by the Sophist Prodikos, in which are described the effects of nature on the aged frame, a force which it is pointless to resist:

The indecency of old age is the subject of the Greek vase-painter Nearchus on this pot of the early 6th century BC. The satyrs' names are as obscene as their actions: Dophios ('wanker'), Terpekelos ('shaft-pleaser') and Psolas ('peeled back').

Little sympathy is evident for a deformed dwarf from Alexandria, 3rd–2nd century BC. The fact that he is also old no doubt made him even funnier.

Then, undetected, there steals over you old age, into which all things pernicious and deadly in nature flow together. And if you do not hasten to give up your life as a debt due, Nature, like a petty usurer, steps in and grabs her pledge – your sight, your hearing, often both. And if you hold out, she paralyses you, mutilates and tears asunder.[27]

Again it is the physical disabilities associated with old age that are stressed, though Socrates does go on to comment on afflictions of the mind as well, saying that old age is a second childhood (a theme we have already seen). In a similar vein but with added complaints, Xenophon has Socrates in his *Apologia* at the age of 70 years declare that his *daimon* or guiding spirit had not offered any sure defence against death for the simple reason that it was not in Socrates' interests to survive any further into old age because of all its negative attributes: loss of hearing and sight, no longer being able to learn but becoming forgetful, general discontent – 'old age, on which all troubles, all privations of comfort, concur to fall... the most burdensome part of life.'[28]

Old age's stereotyped negative repercussions were noted most clinically, perhaps, by Aristotle.[29] The main factor stressed is the old person's wary, pessimistic manner: having lived a long life and made many mistakes, he (and again the focus is on the male) is overly cautious, always using words like 'perhaps' or 'maybe' – unlike the young man who has yet to learn life's knocks and who therefore overdoes everything and lives to excess. This is in direct contrast to the traditional notion that a long life brings with it wisdom, unless one classifies such an attitude as embodying wisdom. Older people are, we are told by Aristotle, overly pessimistic, distrustful, malicious, suspicious and small-minded because they have been humbled by life and so their greatest hopes are raised to nothing more than staying alive. They lack generosity, are cowardly and always anticipating danger ('old age paves the way for cowardice'), and yet they also love life to excess, especially on their last day of life. As a character in a satire by Lucian remarked to an aged beggar half a millennium later, 'men as old as you are such lovers of life, men who ought to be eager for death as a remedy for the evils of old age.'[30]

The signs of old age do not diminish the dignity of this so-called 'old fisherman' (left), a Roman copy of a late 3rd-century BC original. The body is black marble with inlaid eyes, the drapery alabaster. By contrast the little terracotta slave (right) appears pathetically vulnerable.

Aristotle's diatribe continues. Older people are too fond not just of life but also of themselves, a symptom of their petty-mindedness. Always their concern is with what is useful rather than with what is fine or noble. Instead of being shy (as the young are), they are shameless, caring more for profit than for honour, and taking no heed of what people might think of them. Older people, Aristotle states, dwell on and live in the past, dependent on memory rather than hope – their past is long, their future short and uncertain. Thus they continually talk about the past, to the point of garrulity. They are also prone to fits of anger, but even in this they are unsuccessful – such fits are feeble, since all passions have either become enervated or have disappeared altogether. Older people lead their lives more by cold logic (linked to utility) than by moral feeling (linked to *arête*, moral excellence). Pettiness is at the heart of the old man's actions and emotions. Both old and young are capable of feeling pity, but for different reasons: the young out of *philanthropia*, the old out of weakness, since the aged man imagines that anything unfortunate that happens to another could easily happen to himself. Hence again older people's miserable pessimism; they are not witty or given to laughter or general pleasantries – old age has taken away all such qualities.

The picture Aristotle presents here is a depressing one, unrelieved as it is by any mention of positive qualities inherent in older people. It is not that he is unaware of any such positive attributes, only that he is providing a generalized description, for rhetorical purposes, of three stages of life, and it is the negative characteristics that distinguish youth and old age from those at their prime, the ideal middle. If Aristotle was clinical, Juvenal's one hundred lines of satire directed against those who pray for a long life remain most memorable, and focus particularly on the obvious ailments and inadequacies – lack of senses as well as of good sense – advancing age may bring.[31] Pray not for a long life, he insists, but for a healthy mind in a healthy body: *mens sana in corpore sano*. Such positive physical and mental attributes were not routinely associated with old age in ancient thought, medical or general.

While the afflictions old age may bring were well appreciated by the ancient writers, regarding causes the literature is less pragmatic. Medical writers attributed aspects of old age to bad habits in one's youth, but they realized that ageing is inevitable. The most common theory to be found in the extant ancient literature, both medical and philosophical, on the cause of ageing is that in time the body loses its innate heat and fluid, its life force or *pneuma* (like a lamp running out of oil). Hence the infant is warm and moist while the older person – like a corpse – is cold and dry. In other words, ageing is a cooling and drying process, and the desiccation of the heart and liver leads to death. Just as during an illness, in old age the balance of the four humours has been lost: blood and yellow bile are lacking, phlegm and black bile (melancholy) are abundant. As heat dissipates, the body takes longer to recover from illness and injury, but for the same reason symptoms such as fever become less acute in older people, as does activity in general.[32]

Twice in the Hippocratic corpus there appears another theory, namely that the elderly person is cold, but humid or moist (rather than dry). This counter-theory is soundly and insistently refuted by the later medical writer Galen: the mistake is due, he remarks, to the external appearance of moisture about the old person – coughing, a runny nose and the like – but these are merely an abundance of external, phlegmatic secretions or residue of humidity, and are not to be taken as an indication of the innate condition of the elderly individual.

A curious pathos is given to this Hellenistic sculpture (opposite) of the philosopher Chrysippus – curious because he is said to have died, aged around 80, either from excessive wine-drinking or from laughing too much. He was a widely read apologist for Stoicism, but also gained a (possibly undeserved) reputation for eccentricity.

Another philosopher, Diogenes the Cynic (right), lived to be 96. The Cynics owed their name to their supposedly dog-like indifference to human concerns (note the dog by Diogenes' side). Such indifference, however, won him as much admiration as contempt. This figure is a Roman copy of a Greek original.

This idea that old age is cold often recurs in general literature also. As for its dryness, old age is regularly described as having been drained of the moist (and hot) humour of blood (note, for example, the image of the dry and shrunken Sibyl). What blood the ageing body does have is thin and icy-cold, an image Virgil well evokes in the person of Entellus: 'My blood is chilled and dulled by sluggish old age.'[33] Galen noted that the coldness of old age affects not only the body but also the mind: 'So why do many people become demented when they reach extreme old age, a period which has been shown to be dry? This is not a result of dryness, but of coldness. For this clearly damages all the activities of the soul.'[34] Old age, it was concluded, destroys everything.

Furthermore, because ageing was conventionally seen as a process of desiccation, those who were by nature very humid were held to have the greatest chance of a long life. With similar logic it was stated that men, being warmer, age more slowly than women and hence live longer (the latter observation may well often have been accurate in the ancient world, though for other reasons). At any rate, physical exertion dries one out and so hard-working people age more quickly; for the same reason, we are told, excessive indulgence in sexual intercourse is deleterious to the ageing frame.

It was a literary commonplace, adopted by the Pythagoreans in a system of four ages which mirror the four humours, that old age is like winter, at least in its coldness. Part of the theory was that one felt best in the season appropriate or complementary, that is, opposite, to one's age. So it was observed that summer and early autumn were the seasons in which older people might thrive, and winter was the season they should avoid as best they could.

To counter the dryness and coldness of old age, it is necessary to restore the balance of the humours, to give warmth and humidity to the body. Finding a means to warm and moisten the body was the chief aim of what geriatric medicine there was in the ancient world ('the gerocomic art,' as Galen calls it). It was something of a commonplace in antiquity to state that old age was itself a disease; in fact, Seneca the Younger stated that old age was an *incurable* disease.[35] In the 2nd century AD Galen for one disagreed, vigorously: while diseases are contrary to nature, old age is a natural process, just as to die of old age is natural. Therefore, Galen insists, old age, despite what some say, is *not* a disease... but, he goes on to note, it is also not complete health either. Rather old age has a state of health peculiar to itself and this may be maintained through a moderate lifestyle. Hence it was apparently common practice for physicians to recommend a particular regimen or 'diet' which older individuals should follow. Indeed, dietetics was one of the main traditional divisions of ancient medical therapy, the others being pharmacology and surgery.

In the fifth book of his work *On the Preservation of Health*, Galen provides abundant material on the subject, considerably more detailed than anything that precedes it and of considerable influence on treatments of the subject over the following centuries.[36] Galen's concern is with lifestyle, not just diet. His recommendations incorporate massage and gentle exercise – not too much and not too little, depending upon the constitution of the patient; if strong enough, the elderly patient should engage in horse-riding and ball-throwing, or travel on a ship or in a litter; if bedridden, reading aloud is highly beneficial. Galen recommends for the older patient the right amount of sleep (good for moistening and warming the body) and tepid baths (two or three times a month, but never if bedridden). Blood-letting, according to Galen, is good for stronger patients up to the age of 70, though it is not recommended for the *very* elderly, who, Galen adds, need every drop of blood that they have. As to diet, older people, we are told, need little food, which is just as well since most food items were not recommended or permitted. Some foods are beneficial (plums are good as laxatives for the older patient, according to Galen), but many others are dangerous (such as cheese, hard-boiled eggs, snails, lentils, mushrooms and many vegetables). Fish is generally good, as are some types of soft bread. Lean meat, especially young goat's flesh, is useful, but not pork.

The ultimate realism of Roman funerary sculpture is to be found when the face is clearly modelled on a death-mask. The signs are all there: the deeply wrinkled neck, the prominent Adam's apple, the skin tightly stretched on the skull, the lips drawn back around the toothless mouth.

Herakles' encounter with Old Age (Geras) is depicted on a number of vases (below) but is nowhere described in the literature. Here, on a vase from Cerveteri, 480 BC, Geras is shown as a thin, naked old man, and presumably the symbolism is that Herakles, by conquering him, does not grow old.

The old miser was a stock character in the New Comedy. This Greek vase of the mid-4th century BC shows 'Charinus' being dragged off his money-chest by two thieves, all wearing the conventional masks. Later Plautus borrowed the same plot for one of his Latin comedies.

What should the elderly person drink? Water was not recommended, nor was milk. Apparently the latter was believed to rot aged teeth and gums; for older individuals, however, Galen does specifically recommend human breast milk and warm donkey's milk, or milk mixed with honey; he mentions that he himself met one farmer who survived beyond the century mark thanks to goat's milk mixed with honey and wine. Wine, the gift of Dionysus, is particularly commended, and in the name of science Galen devoted much study to the question of which wines were best for medicinal purposes. Wine could have positively rejuvenating effects. Indeed, it was proverbial in antiquity that wine makes an old man dance, even against his will. Wine makes the body warm and, Galen adds, it also serves to counter the sadness and anxieties that long life may bring. Concrete examples of the benefits of wine-drinking may also be found: Augustus' wife Livia attributed her long life (she lived to be 86) to the wine of Pucinum in northern Italy, and Romilius Pollio, an otherwise unknown centenarian from the time of Augustus, credited his aged vigour (as well as, perhaps, his succinct wit) to honeyed wine within and oil without (*intus mulso, foris oleo*).[37] Certainly, for some old age had its pleasures.

What should an old man drink?
Galen recommended wine, and indeed a vase-painting of about 490 BC shows Briseis, the beloved of Achilles, serving wine to his venerable tutor Phoenix. It was one of the substances credited with powers of rejuvenation.

This brings us back to Cicero. We saw at the beginning of this chapter Isidore's summation of the pros and cons of old age; in his *On Old Age* Cicero, via the aged interlocutor Cato the Elder, presented four aspects of old age with which people commonly found fault. Very briefly, they were that (i) old age stops you doing what you did when you were younger (what a blessing!, retorts Cato/Cicero); (ii) old age weakens the body (good – one can devote oneself more to one's mind); (iii) old age lacks pleasures (good – it is easier to be wise and virtuous then); and (iv) old age is not far from death. The sense of Cicero's reply to this last *vituperatio* is, in true Stoic fashion, 'Death, where is thy sting?' As Plato's Socrates had observed hundreds of years earlier, there is nothing to fear in death.

The link between old age and death is an inevitable and ever-present one in ancient art and literature. In Greek and Roman mythology personified Youth was worshipped or at least glorified. Old Age enjoyed no such prestige. In Hesiod's *Theogony*, 'Hateful Old Age' (*Geras*) is the offspring of Night, and has as siblings Doom, Fate, Death, Sleep, Blame, Nemesis and Deceit, among others.[38] The references to *Geras/Senectus* in literature are several, and virtually identical. Old Age is one of a hideous troupe, incorporating all the malevolent features of life: grief, misery, disease, hunger, discord, envy, fear, poverty, greed, war and the like, normally relegated to the Underworld but all too often unleashed on frail mortals. The contrast with desirable youth could not be more evident; old age is feared rather than worshipped. In art, one of Herakles' (Hercules') lesser-known labours was battling against personified old age, typically an emaciated figure with grotesquely swollen but flaccid genitals. Aside from this episode, *Geras* plays little role in classical myths. The exception proves the rule, itself not overly surprising, that old age as a personified concept to the Greeks and Romans merited not worship but awe, if not dread.

Old age, as the final stage of life rather than as a personality in its own right, does feature in the mythological depictions of mortal heroes and villains, but not of gods, who are held to be ageless and immortal, an honour on rare occasions also accorded to privileged mortals. Many grotesque figures from mythology, such as the Furies and the Fates, are old and haggard for the very reason, however, that this will invoke fear in the hearts of mortals; some of the most fearsome and loathsome creatures might in fact be classified as old spinsters (the Graeae, for example), a sign of their complete isolation or marginality from 'normal' society.

Overleaf:
Medea preparing to rejuvenate
Pelias, a vase-painting of about 500 BC.
For the full story see p. 68.

Medea the sorceress determined to avenge the injuries suffered by her lover Jason from King Pelias by offering to restore the aged king to his youth. To prove that she could do this she cut an old ram into pieces, boiled them in a cauldron and then restored it to life as a young lamb. This is the scene depicted on a vase from Vulci of 470 BC. Delighted by the experiment, Pelias's daughters happily did the same to their father, but Medea declined to complete the process and Pelias's bones remained in the cauldron. The possibility of rejuvenation seems to have haunted the Greek subconscious.

On the other hand attempts at rejuvenation and immortality by mortal men are frequently remarked upon, and both have been aspirations of humankind throughout history.[39] Galen mentions the intriguing case of a contemporary Sophist who had, at the age of 40, published a book on how to avoid the effects of old age and remain perpetually young. By the time this fellow turned 80, however, age had indeed taken its toll, making him appear shrivelled and dried out, and earning him general mockery. He then revised his book and brought out a second edition, stressing that only *some* individuals may enjoy eternal youth and that it is necessary to prepare from the earliest years. This Sophist declares that, while he himself unfortunately started the process too late to save himself, he is prepared to undertake such a task for the benefit of the children of his fellow citizens—presumably for a substantial fee.[40]

Even for the wealthy elite, with whom most of our surviving evidence is concerned, old age in antiquity tended to be a time to be endured rather than enjoyed. For the poorer classes old age must have been singularly unenviable: it was a common proverb that old age and poverty are both burdensome — in combination they are impossible to bear. In the case of the vast majority of the individuals we know of from ancient times, however, because of the elite bias of our sources, poverty was not a problem, and wealth, as well as the existence of slaves, must have helped to ease the problems for them. But if a person's failing health led to inability to be self-supporting, then, in the absence of effective medication, dependence may have been short-lived anyway.

The key was not how old, but how active or useful. Cicero's words are timeless, and speak across the millennia: 'Old age will only be respected if it fights for itself, maintains its rights, avoids dependence on anyone, and asserts control over its own to the last breath.'[41]

A kind of rejuvenation seems to be intended in this bronze statue of the emperor Trebonianus Gallus, 251–53 AD. The head is an authentic likeness, but it is attached to a much younger body, endowing him with exaggerated physical power.

Human life, like everything else, was ordered according to God's plan, and the thinkers of the Middle Ages dedicated their minds to explaining that plan, often devising visual equivalents to clarify it. Old age had its place in the sight of God. 'The days of our years are threescore years and ten; and if by reason strength they be fourscore years, yet is their strength labour and sorrow; for it is soon cut off and we fly away.' This diagram from the De Lisle Psalter (English, early 14th century) traces the life of a man from the child in his mother's arms (bottom left) through youth and maturity to old age and the tomb.

3

SHULAMITH SHAHAR

THE MIDDLE AGES
AND RENAISSANCE

Old people in the Middle Ages, as in all other times, were regarded as part of the symbolic order of the world as well as an actual component of society. This is indicated by their various representations in written texts and in art. As has been noted earlier, because of the low life expectancy of the period the dominant view is that people in the Middle Ages and the early modern period were considered old in their 40s, but research done in recent decades has dispelled this notion. Life expectancy was indeed low: the highest life expectancy at birth in the Middle Ages and the Renaissance was 40 years. In periods of plague and famine it was much lower.[1] However, this low average was due mainly to the high infant mortality. People who reached early adulthood had a fair chance of reaching the age of 60 or 70. There were also men and women who lived to be 80 or even 90.

Much like 21st-century gerontologists, medieval scholars were aware of the gradual nature of the ageing process, as well as of individual variations on it. And as in contemporary Western culture, there was also in the Middle Ages a chronological definition of the onset of old age. People were defined as old not at the age of 40 but between the ages of 60 and 70. Thus, wittingly or unwittingly, medieval people followed similar earlier traditions: biblical, Greek and Roman.[2]

In the schemes for the division of life into stages (anything between three and seven) various numbers were presented as the onset of old age: 35, 45, 50, 58, 60 and 70. The schemes were developed in different contexts − scientific, medical, didactic, homiletic and literary − and were related to various configurations of nature and time. They conveyed the symbolic identity of each stage in human life, rather than an evaluation based on biological or social criteria, and their variety makes them impossible to use as a source for the discussion. A more reliable source is the legislative texts. The privileges accorded to the elderly almost without exception took the form of exemption from certain duties and from liability to various services rather than positive benefits.

'The Death of Adam', Piero della Francesca's great fresco at Arezzo, is one of the supreme images of old age. Adam lies naked on the ground, the aged Eve standing at his head. The monumental stillness that is such a hallmark of Piero's style gives the scene an unforgettable inwardness, as if time were standing still.

The three other figures, the bearded man facing us (Seth) and the adolescent boy and girl, bring it into the long iconographic tradition of the Ages of Man.

The way life's stages were represented schematically throughout history is used as a *leitmotif* in this book. It was a convention that remained remarkably constant from the 14th to the 19th century: a man or woman, usually from the leisured classes with no apparent worries except growing old, proceeds from happy childhood to healthy old age, reaching a peak of prosperity in middle age (here, in a mid-14th-century psalter by a Catalan artist, apparently as a scholar). Such pictures are almost blueprints for the good life as it was imagined in each century. When, in the 20th century, the stereotype was undercut by cynically introducing a note of reality (see pp. 29 and 276), the humour largely consisted in confounding expectation. An equally rigid matching sequence was used in the Middle Ages for the Labours of the Months. February was invariably an old man warming his feet at the fire. Below right: detail of a stained-glass window in Lausanne Cathedral, c. 1170.

iminifu ueds. rzpha noui.
n quã dispensatione iste ps
pitieno˚. e̅ n̅ q̅d moises eu̅ con
ferit.
mo q̅d̅e̅ passibit̔ f̔, di uban
s.q̅i.hoc dauib q̅d ꝉ moyses
unt.
s de defetu gn̅s. h̔.q̅ ꝑ xp̅m
eret̔.
rimo eternu̅ ꝑponit refugi-
i temporali.

All the relevant texts specify 60 or 70 as the age of eligibility for exemption. Exemption from the various forms of military service, town watches and trial by battle was generally granted to those who had reached the age of 60. (There are examples of exemption from military service in England, the Latin kingdom of Jerusalem and Paris, and from trial by battle in almost all countries.) In some regions, however, exemption from military service came only at the age of 70 (Castile and León, Modena, Florence). The age of exemption from compulsory public service (e.g., jury service in England) was generally 70; from the payment of taxes 60 or 70, and from compulsory labour 60.[5] The idea that after the age of 60 a man was no longer capable of hard physical tasks and found it difficult to make a living took other expressions. According to the Christian laws which were incorporated into the laws of Iceland in the 12th century, people had to observe the established fasts until they were 70.[4] Scourging oneself was considered a harsher form of mortification, so in Italy the rule of the *Scuola della misericordia* of Venice exempted brothers who were over 60 from this obligation. They were supposed to remain in the chapel and pray, while the younger brothers marched in procession through the city and scourged themselves.[5] According to a 1503 statute of Henry VII of England, male and female beggars and vagabonds over 60 (as well as pregnant women and the sick and disabled of both sexes) were not liable to the same punishment as younger ones.[6]

All medieval sources focus on the male, and there is a general tendency to masculinize the data. The same is true of the various schemes of the division of life's course. Though none of the schemes states explicitly that it does not apply to women, it is quite clear that they relate to men alone.[7] The absence of women from most of these statutes and ordinances is explained by the fact that women were not liable to them at any age: they were not subject to military service; they were entitled at any age to have a proxy represent them in a trial by battle; they filled no public offices. Furthermore, most of the taxes were paid by heads of household, who were generally men (except for a few widows, or independent female merchants and craftswomen). The translation of the differences between the sexes into codes of behaviour and customs was much less marked in the lowest than in the upper strata of society. Women were not free from compulsory labour, and poverty also drove some of them into begging and vagrancy. The Statute of Labourers, which was passed in England in 1349 in the wake of the Black Death, obliged both men and women to accept the work offered to them.[8] And a statute of Henry VII applied to both female and male beggars and vagrants. Exemption from a female-only obligation – to marry by order of the feudal lord – is mentioned in Jean d'Ibelin's compilation of the Laws of the Crusading Kingdom of Jerusalem. A widow who reached the age of 60 could not be compelled to remarry.[9] References to the age of 60 to denote an old woman in various other sources show that it was the common view that this marked the onset of old age in the female as in the male.

Dürer's mother looked older than her 63 years. He gives her grace and dignity but makes no attempt to disguise her sunken cheeks and bony neck, and even truthfully portrays the divergent squint from which she suffered.

Few rewards or advantages could, in the eyes of a Renaissance painter, compensate for the loss of beauty. Hans Baldung in 1544 (opposite) sees nothing but regret in the passing years; so much so that he can hardly bear to show the seventh age at all.

The old and infirm beg Death to take them, but he passes them by in order to feed upon the young and healthy: a detail from Orcagna's fresco 'The Triumph of Death' (1344), once in S. Croce, Florence, of which only fragments survive.

Right: an earlier image of the elderly disabled, who must have been so numerous in the Middle Ages. An old woman is drinking from a fountain, now dismantled, by Arnolfo di Cambio, 13th century.

The percentage of the elderly – people of 60–70 and older – in the population as a whole was much less than in modern Western society, although medieval records containing demographic data are few and incomplete and historical demographers are able to make only a rough estimate. But according to these, the elderly generally constituted not more than 8 per cent of the population, and in some regions and periods it was not above 5.[10] Only in exceptional circumstances, as in the post-plague periods, did their proportion rise. The plagues killed more young people than old ones.[11] Thus in Florence in 1427, 14.6 per cent of the population were over 60, and in Ravenna 15.9 per cent. A similar increase in the ratio of old people took place in other parts of Europe as well. This high percentage gradually declined during the period of recovery and the steady growth of the population from the late 15th century.[12] In modern Western society women live longer than men, a fact attributed to genetic rather than environmental factors. In the Middle Ages, however, it appears that the latter factors were decisive. In the nobility, elderly women indeed outnumbered men because of the frequency of violent death among males.[13] In the general population, however, a number of factors combined to shorten women's life expectancy. Many women died in childbirth or soon after. In the rural areas they were worn out by work. Moreover, it was the women who looked after the sick and were thus more exposed to infection.[14] The reason for the large number of widows, some old and some younger, was not a higher life expectancy among women, but the age gap between husband and wife, especially in the prosperous strata. Women who married early outlived their older husbands. Only at a later stage, after they had stopped bearing children, did the gap between the life expectancy of males and females shrink; sometimes women's life expectancy even exceeded that of men.[15]

The literary genre known as the *sermones ad status*, popular from the 13th century onwards, reflected a new social model. In these sermons society consisted of socio-professional estates and conditions – from emperors, kings and popes, via various workers and professionals, to serfs.[16] But the elderly, like women and children, were represented as a single marginal group irrespective of social stratum, rank, profession or lifestyle. In some texts they were classed with the invalids, foreigners or the very poor, the emphasis being on their physical or mental weakness, or on their social inferiority and their exclusion from political influence.[17] The exemption from services and payments expressed consideration for the elderly and the intention to alleviate their lot, but at the same time it also implied marginalization. (Some of the elderly secular peers in the later Middle Ages asked to be exempt from attending the sessions of the House of Lords.) Women were doubly marginalized, as female and as old.

The only privilege accorded to the elderly as such was exemption from certain obligations. There were no positive benefits and no extra roles or honours were accorded to them merely because they were old. This is clearly expressed, *inter alia*, in the Rule of St Benedict of Nursia. According to article 63 of the Rule, the position of the brothers in the monastery should depend on their length of service there, or on their virtue, or on the abbot's decision. A brother's position never depended on his age.[18] In secular society, although ideally mature middle-aged active males were expected to wield authority, some senior positions were hereditary, so it often happened that young people held office. In the church, on the official level, there was a minimum age for holding various positions, but in practice this was often disregarded.

It appears that discrimination in favour of age operated only in the Venetian republic, where young and even middle-aged citizens were disqualified from holding the highest offices. Between 1400 and 1600, the average age of the doges, when they were elected from the Procurators of San Marco (themselves rather old), was 72. Some of them were in their 60s, and some in their late 70s or even in their 80s when elected. Their age was regarded as ensuring wise and balanced government; and in addition that their term in office would not be too long.[19] Most church prelates were also elderly people, but this was not so much because of a belief in their special suitability, as because usually they reached the level in the ecclesiastical hierarchy that made them eligible to the highest offices only in their 60s. Yet just as the absence of a prescriptive criterion of age for authority and power did not guarantee roles for the elderly, it did not disqualify them from continuing to hold office, or bar them from being elected or nominated to new ones.

Though rarely mentioned in the normative texts, there was one function the elderly performed in their capacity as old men (and sometimes also as old women). They served as witnesses in disputes over land possession, contested demands of service and matrimonial affairs, and were regarded as repositories of local custom and tradition. To cite one example: in a suit for divorce on grounds of consanguinity before the ecclesiastical court of York five men testified. One was in his 60s, two were in their 70s, one was in his 80s, and one who testified from his bed was said to be 100 years old. Records show that there was a tendency to round up a person's age to the nearest decade, but even if the witnesses added some years to their age it is clear they were old. (They succeeded in proving a fourth degree of consanguinity between the couple.)[20] The legislation of Alfonso X of Castile and León stated that sick and aged witnesses could be questioned before a trial for fear they might die before it actually took place.[21] Wisdom and experience, and hence the ability to offer advice, were components in the positive stereotype of the old person, but the aged were called to testify not on the assumption that they possessed special wisdom but rather in the belief they had the necessary information.

The doges of Venice were, by the very nature of the constitution, fairly elderly when they were elected, but often proved surprisingly long-lived. Andrea Gritti, a military commander and diplomat of wide experience (he spent several years in Constantinople), was appointed in 1523 at the age of 68 and remained in office until he was 83. Titian's portrait of him in his late 70s shows a man very much in control. The power of Venice was declining, but Gritti held his own against France and the Empire and did his best to appease the Turks. But he was never a popular doge, partly because of his unsavoury private life. He was reputed to have fathered at least five bastard children, three in Turkey and two in Venice, one of them by a nun.

La nefera de ma bocha oftra
sfera ma goria bien aroffea

fetu nclanfes laborgla
fetr dumear orfus lorrgla

Old people who took advantage of the Fountain of Youth were, according to the revered opinion of Aristotle, not only feeble but also bad-tempered and irritable. In the same castle of Manta in Piedmont (see p. 18) are represented a very disagreeable trio consisting of an old man on a donkey, a woman helping herself to a wine-flask and an angry old man in a wheelbarrow.

Old age, it seemed, could affect both the body and the soul. What was the relationship between these two? There were three main views. According to the first, the person constituted a psychosomatic unity of body and soul. The second emphasized the idea of their possible development in two opposite directions, though its proponents did not imply a dichotomy between them in old age. The third entailed an explicit separation of body and soul, and the texts that represent it are the only ones that disregard the body.

The concept of the person as a psychosomatic unity of two linked entities, body and soul, was developed in scientific and medical texts. Old age, it was argued, entailed a deterioration of both physical and mental capacities, as well as the development of negative traits of character. The changes in the composition of the humours in the body – that is, the increase of external bad humours and a decrease in natural heat and innate radical moisture – were regarded as the immediate cause of all the *accidentia senectutis*, which included both physical and mental elements.[22]

Aristotle believed that physical and intellectual abilities peaked and declined at different ages, the latter occurring later than the former.[23] As a consequence some medieval writers distinguished between old age and extreme old age, usually denoted *senium*, and attributed the mental decline only to the second stage. At that time, because of the physiological changes occurring in his body, primarily the decrease in natural heat, man becomes once more like a child.[24] Mary Carruthers has shown that in medieval literary culture 'memory' was a sign of the moral strength and humanity of the person.[25] Its weakening was thus a sign of their diminution. Melancholy, moreover, had a hint of sin; it signified lack of belief in divine grace. However, the development of these characteristics, as well as of negative traits of character, was described in a neutral manner, with no moral judgment attached. The development of certain negative traits of character was considered part of the inevitable process of ageing, just like the body's deterioration, over which man has no control.[26]

Medical knowledge was limited. The purpose of the detailed instructions for the elderly in the health manuals was not therapeutic but preventive – namely, to delay further deterioration and enhance well-being, not to cure or rehabilitate.

The authors of medical texts, like those who composed the schemes of the 'stages of age', did not state explicitly that they referred only to men, but the texts themselves clearly show that normally they did. Some writers, however, did devote a separate discussion to one particular change in the body of the elderly woman: the cessation of menstrual flow. The theory concerning the consequences of this physiological phenomenon is implicit in the scientific texts and explicit in works of scientific popularization. According to both scientific and popular belief, menstrual blood was impure, harmful and of destructive power.[27] Yet, according to this theory, after menopause the woman was even more dangerous, because she was unable to eliminate the superfluous matter from her organism. As stated in *De Secretis Mulierum* – attributed (wrongly) to Albert the Great – 'The retention of menses engenders many evil humours. The women being old have almost no natural heat left to consume and control this matter, especially poor women who live on nothing but coarse meat, which greatly contributes to this phenomenon. These women are more venomous than the others.'[28] Being venomous by virtue of her very physiology, the poor old hag who concocted love philtres and death brews was engaged in an activity analogous to the physiological transformation in her organism. The conception of the process of ageing of the male was also a deterministic one. The changes in personality attributed to men (including poor ones), however, were not thought of as harbouring social danger and destructive actions.

In religious and didactic writings the old body served as a metaphor for the transience and vanity of all worldly things. Its unidealized stereotype was meant to arouse contempt of self and of the world (*contemptus sui, contemptus mundi*). Pope Innocent III (1160–1216), in a text influenced by Horace and which itself had an impact on various later medieval texts, from sermons to literary works, depicted the vicissitudes, sufferings, sins and vanities of earthly life from conception to death. He devoted a detailed and unsparing description to the old man's body – his heart weakens and his head shakes; his face becomes wrinkled and his back bent; his eyes grow dim and his joints grow shaky; his nose runs and his hair falls out; his hand trembles and he makes awkward movements; his teeth decay and his ears grow deaf. 'Young men! Be not proud in the presence of a decaying man; he was once that which you are; he is now what you in turn will be.'[29] This description of the degradation of old age was not meant to evoke empathy but to caution against pride and arouse contempt of the flesh. The Pope was not exhorting the young to respect the wisdom and morality of the old, but emphasizing the fact that old age is part of the human condition which none who live long enough can escape. The old body does not merely indicate the approaching biological end, as suggested in the medical works, but also symbolizes the terrible judgment in the next world which man in his folly and sin chooses to ignore. In Petrarch's (1309–74) philosophical treatise *De Remediis utriusque Fortune* (On the Remedies to the Two Kinds of Fortune), the metaphoric use of the old body serves the same purpose as in Innocent III's religious text. In a dialogue between Joy and Reason, the function of pessimistic Reason is to curb Joy, bring home to him the folly of his happiness and convince him that all that now causes him happiness will one day become a source of evil and pain. The degradation and increasing unloveliness of the body and the loss of physical pleasures are indicators of the fragility, impermanence and insignificance of this world. The young body is like a flower, but a flower whose fading is inherent in its blossoming. Faithful to the concept of the unity of body and soul, after describing the changes in the old body and the diseases which are its lot, Petrarch depicts the dimming of understanding, the weakening of memory and the disturbance of speech.[30]

'Sorrow', a medieval French miniature illustrating the sorrows of women. This old woman, apparently sitting on a grave, expresses the sadness accompanying bodily decay.

Prejudice against the old is all too clear in a series of illustrations to a French allegorical text of about 1400, 'The Pilgrimage of Human Life'. The Virtues are all shown as beautiful young women (top, Penitence and Charity), but the Vices as old and ugly: Pilgrim (with staff) meets Sloth and Pride, Gluttony and Avarice.

Preachers and authors of moralistic and didactic treatises depicted in detail the unsightliness of the old male body, but avoided the female one. Some of them only mentioned in general terms the transience of female beauty, and accompanied their statements with critical and sarcastic comments on the vain efforts of old women to conceal their decline with lavish clothing, cosmetics and feminine wiles.[31] The texts that present the binary contrasts of young/old, and especially those that use the old female body as the personification of winter, the enemy of love, evil traits, sin, old age itself and death, contain detailed and cruel descriptions of such a body. One example will suffice. In *Le Pèlerinage de la vie humaine*, written in the 14th century by William of Deguileville, the virtues of Mercy, Charity, Reason, Penitence and Diligence, as well as God's Grace, are personified by young women splendidly dressed, while the vices of Sloth, Pride, Flattery, Hypocrisy, Envy, Treachery, Anger, Avarice, Gluttony and Lust, as well as Tribulation, Heresy, Disease and Old Age, are represented by ugly old women. Sloth is an ugly, hairy, dirty and stinking old woman. Pride is a monstrously obese old woman. Because of her obesity and swollen legs she cannot walk alone. She rides on Flattery, holding in one hand a stick (to spur her mount on), and in the other a mirror into which she gazes. The image of Hypocrisy is not sharply delineated – she is covered by a cloak such as is worn by old women to hide their ugliness and infirmities. Envy crawls on her belly like a snake; she is shrivelled and dry without flesh and blood. Disease leans on crutches; and Old Age has legs of lead, while Mercy, leading the pilgrim to the infirmary, is a young woman with an exposed breast to suckle the suffering.[32] The old woman, whose milk has dried up, can never be the image of the Holy Mother nursing her infant – the symbol of goodness and unstinting giving. Caroline Bynum has demonstrated the association of the young woman's body with food in medieval culture, and the use of food as metaphor in describing the female mystical experience.[33] There was no place for that association in the case of the old woman's body.

In medical and scientific texts the development of negative traits of character in the elderly is neutrally described as inevitable. In moralistic and didactic treatises, however, the tone is more critical, implying moral responsibility as well as consciousness of individual differences between people. Aegidius Romanus (*c.*1247–1316) wrote a manual for the education of kings, dedicated to his former pupil the French king Philip the Fair. Here, following Aristotle, Aegidius describes the old as cowardly, suspicious, shameless (because advantage is more important to them than honour), miserly and without hope. On the other hand, he also states that they tend to show pity and avoid passing judgments hurriedly. However, the source of these apparently positive traits is equivocal. Unlike the mercifulness of the young, which derives from their belief that everybody is as good as themselves who have not yet done harm to anyone, writes Aegidius, the mercifulness of the aged derives from their weakness. They want everyone to take pity on the weak. They do not hasten to pass judgment because they are no longer sure about anything, having been humiliated by life. Aegidius also concurs with Aristotle's conclusion, adopted by other medieval thinkers too, that the most suitable age for positions of power is middle age (*in statu*). At this stage, the negative traits of youth have disappeared while the negative traits of old age have not yet developed. However, in Aegidius's day monarchy was hereditary: thus a young man might inherit the throne and, at least in theory, so might an old man. Aegidius's diplomatic solution was that both young and old could transcend their natures: 'Young and old alike can act against the tendency [of their age].'[34]

Bernardino of Siena, like Cicero in his *On Old Age*, distinguished between 'good' and 'bad' old people. Enumerating the spiritual calamities of old age – impatience, melancholy, ignorance, gloominess, perversity or vice, stupidity and mental blindness – he added that all these were found mainly in the 'bad elderly' (*et maxime in senibus malis*). He rejected determinism and ignored physiology.[35] Vincent of Beauvais, a compiler who recorded various, often incompatible, views, noted the two different conceptions of old age, and in this case, did try to reconcile them. He wrote about the good in old age, with wisdom increasing and passion subsiding, and then went on to list the manifestations of mental decline: absence of energy, forgetfulness, gullibility. Aware of the contradiction, he proposed a solution based on the acknowledgment of individual differences between people, their dissimilar personalities: just as passions and wantonness do not characterize all *adolescentes*, so also senile folly (*stultia que deliratio dicitur senium*) is not evinced by all old people.[36] Unlike Vincent of Beauvais, who wrote an encyclopedia of natural philosophy and was obliged to refer to the theory of humours, the physically determined basis of personality, the authors of moralistic and didactic texts were exempt from this duty. They rejected determinism and emphasized man's will and choice, together with divine grace.

The most influential treatise on old age during the Middle Ages was Cicero's 'De Senectute'. This takes the form of a dialogue between Cato, Scipio and Laelius. Dedicating it to his friend Atticus, Cicero wrote: 'In order to give their reflections the greatest force I have represented them as delivered by the venerable Cato. To this end I have introduced Scipio and Laelius, as expressing to him their admiration of the wonderful ease with which he has supported his old age ... I have only to add that in delivering the sentiments of Cato I desire to be understood as fully declaring my own.' In this 15th-century French version Cato is seated at his desk addressing Atticus, Laelius and Scipio, whose close friendship Cicero had praised in another book, 'De Amicitia'.

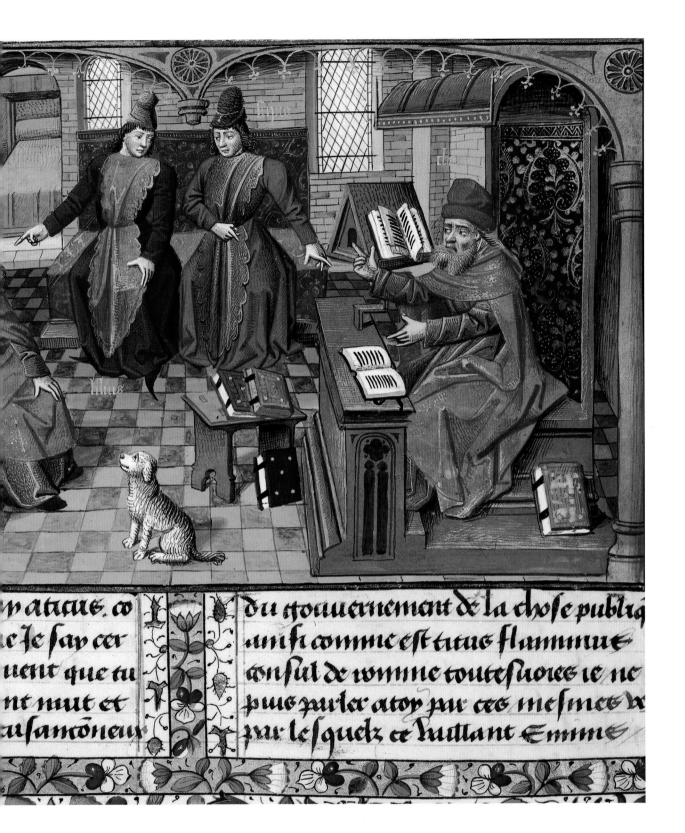

y atiaus. co
e le lap cer
uent que tu
nt nuit et
u lamoneul

du gouuernement de la chose publiq
unli comme est titus flamninie
consul de romme toutesluoies le ne
puis parler atoy pur ces mesmes u
par les quelz ce liultant Emme

This denial of determinism, arising from the conception that body and soul can develop in two opposite directions, could offer consolation and hope. It could open up various expectations from the old person regarding behaviour and state of mind. A clear separation between the developments of body and soul is found in the writings of John Bromyard, a 14th-century compiler of an encyclopedia for preachers. He asserted: 'To the extent that old age decreases the power of youth it increases the devotion of the soul; what is suppressed in the one is elevated in the other.'[37] Some writers placed greater emphasis on the expiation of sin; others, like Dante, emphasized spiritual elevation. In his *Convivio* he compared the last stage of life to a ship gradually lowering its sails before entering harbour. Tranquilly and gently, without bitterness, the ennobled soul proceeds in due order towards its ultimate destination. Like other thinkers and authors of medical manuals, Dante compared the death of the old person to the ripe apple falling from the tree. In medical works, the emphasis was on the naturalness and lack of pain; in Dante, on the end of the road, acceptance and great peace.[38] Old age thus becomes a time not only of expiation of sin but also of possible spiritual elevation.

God Himself is invariably represented as old, 'the Ancient of Days'. Right and opposite: two images from the early 16th century, one by the German limewood sculptor Master H.L. in the parish church of Breisach, the other by the Italian painter Gaudenzio Ferrari in the sacristy of S. Maria dei Miracoli, Saranno, surrounded by a crown of flames, circles of putti and exuberant angel musicians.

Yet the purest consolation was offered by the idea of the ever-youthful soul, which related to both men and women. A full elaboration of this idea is found in one of Meister Eckhart's sermons, on the Epistle to the Romans, 6: 4: 'Therefore we are buried with him by baptism into death; that like as Christ was raised up from the dead by the glory of the father even so we also should walk in newness of life.' God, who created *ex nihilo*, wrote Eckhart, who always is, and who always acts, is new. Life and newness are his domain. All that is new comes from God and there is no other source of renewal. Therefore, 'Come close to God,' said Eckhart; 'draw near, come back, turn round to God.' All who draw near to God will be renewed (*innovantur*) and purified; they will be good and sanctified, as says Psalm 103:5: 'Thy youth is renewed like the eagle.' In a life of grace, man will always be renewed, and renewal is life. On the other hand, those who move away from God will grow old (*veterascunt*) and be lost. 'For the wages of sin is death' (Epistle to the Romans 6:23). The soul formed in the image of God is created young. It may have grown tired and feeble in bodily existence, but it can renew

Combining age and authority, Claus Sluter's Isaiah (left) is both convincingly realistic and deeply symbolic. Begun in 1383, this figure and other prophets and forerunners of Christ were intended to stand at the base of a Calvary in the cloister of the Carthusian monastery of Champmol in Burgundy – the Old Testament supporting the New.

God the Father stares down from a stained-glass window in the church of Clavering, England, dating from the 15th century.

and purify itself. Only the material and visible are destined to age. Eckhart does not refer to the body, nor does he perceive the old body as an opportunity and means of spiritual purification through suffering, release from passions and expiation of sin. It is the renewal of the soul that is a constant factor, and this renewal is not a single act but is repeated. If a man delves into his inner resources, detaches himself from the world and concentrates on divine grace, he will be renewed. Only the soul of him who draws way from God will grow old, and the further away he moves, the more will his soul age (*antiquatur*).[39]

As already mentioned, the rejection of determinism not only offered consolation, it could also entail expectations from the old person. And the expectations were quite high. There are in the various discourses expressions of empathy for the plight of the elderly: their physical sufferings, their poverty and the fact that they are considered a burden and a nuisance. Bartholomaeus the English, author of a popular encyclopedia, described the old man who coughs and spits, who is a burden to everyone and is judged and despised by all.[40] However, little tolerance was shown for the deviations of the elderly from their expected state of mind and behaviour. The old person was exhorted to exhibit resignation, free himself of worldly ambitions and passions, refrain from complaining, accept his age and his approaching death and prepare for it, gaze into his own soul and act for his salvation. Old age is presented as a gift the old person is privileged to receive. The gift is longevity itself, which the old enjoy while so many others die prematurely, in childhood or in youth. Castigating the elderly for their murmurings and complaints, Bernardino of Siena says (or rather shouts): 'You strove to reach it, you desired to achieve it, you were afraid you would not reach it, and now, arriving, you lament. Every one wishes to reach old age, but nobody wishes to be old.' On a higher plane, the gift consists in the opportunity given to the old person to repent, make penance and draw closer to God by means of his weak and ailing body. It is up to him to use the opportunity afforded to him, or not to use it. The very ageing of the body prevents the person from committing some of the most heinous sins. Having lost his teeth, the preacher said, the old man will laugh less, gnaw less at the good name of others and talk less. His weakening eyesight will relieve him from gluttony, avarice and lust. If his hearing fails, he will be less able to listen to nonsense, and instead will read religious books and gaze in silence at the works of God — at heaven and earth and all they contain. The abating of the libido will free him of the sins of the flesh.[41] A lustful old man or woman looking for sexual adventures was flouting the laws of nature and behaving like a madman or madwoman. Moral, social, aesthetic and medical arguments combined with views on the 'natural' and 'unnatural' to condemn the amorous old man (*senex amans*) who does not act as befits his advanced years.[42]

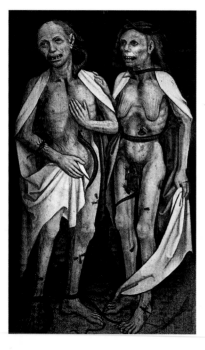

Dead lovers: a grim reminder of the transience of earthly happiness by Matthias Grünewald, c. 1470.

The few elderly men who wrote about their old age in the first person (no such writings by women have come down to us) depict it as a time to be endured rather than enjoyed. They lay emphasis on their disabilities and the tone is usually one of sadness and bitterness.[43] Margery Kempe (1372–c. 1439) did not write about the plight of her own old age, but (with a marked tendency to self-pity) about the difficulties of caring for her old husband, who was an invalid.[44] A rare exception is the 16th-century Italian Alvise Cornaro, who wrote four *Essays on the Sober Life* (*Discorsi intorno alla vita sobria*): the first when he was 83, the second at 86, the third at 91 and the fourth at 95. (He died peacefully at 98.) The essays advocate a health regimen and describe Cornaro's peaceful and pleasant later life.[45] It is well to keep in mind that Cornaro was a nobleman, free from economic anxiety and thus able to follow the recommended health regimen.

Foolish old men still susceptible to the charms of young women have been the target of satirists throughout history (a vein of humour that is by no means exhausted). Lucas Cranach's painting is called 'The Old Fool'; he is blithely unaware that the girl's hand is in his purse (detail).

Another expectation was that the old should withdraw to the margins and make way for younger people. Philip of Navarre declared that a man who reached the age of 60 was exempt from service. Given the meaning of the word service in Latin, and in the French of Philip of Navarre's time, it is clear that he was not referring to personal services only, but also to serving public office.[46] Vincent of Beauvais too stated that the old man ought to quit his occupations and the management of his estates.[47] In the 13th century, estates entailed administrative functions and sometimes also positions of government and command. In Alberti's *Book of the Family* (*Della famiglia*), old Giannozzo, a model wise and respected old man, is depicted as having withdrawn to the margin. He helps, to the best of his strength and ability, those of his friends who are as old as he: he commends them to the city authorities and aids them financially, while serving the younger members of the family as counsellor and arbitrator. But it seems that he no longer does any business, holds no public office, and is already removed from the centre of affairs.[48]

The theme of the Ten Ages could challenge the inventive faculties of artists. In these woodcuts from Antwerp, 1520, the child (whipping a top), the youth (with falcon) and the soldier (in armour) are clear enough, but the next three (the merchant?) are virtually indistinguishable, and the advance of old age is chiefly indicated by the length of beard.

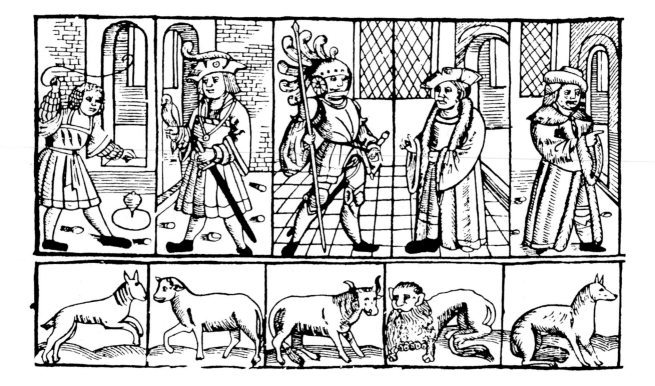

Images influence attitudes which can affect actions, but they need not reflect reality. Turning from the images, attitudes and advocated norms to the social reality of the elderly, it is clear that the degree of participation of old people in society as individuals varied according to gender, social stratum, economic resources and level of wellbeing. There was no mandatory age of retirement, and legal disqualification of the elderly was exceptional. (The only case of a disqualification from office due to chronological age encountered is in the statutes of Lucca, where people aged 55 and over could not be elected to public office.)[49] As a rule it was the minimum age, not a maximum one, for the appointment or election to various offices that was fixed both by canon and secular law. But kings and feudal lords could sometimes force their office holders or servants to retire. In England from the second half of the 14th century to the middle of the 15th, scores of the king's coroners were compelled to retire, although in theory they were appointed for life. The justification for the dismissal of these minor royal functionaries was that they were too old or infirm to perform their work properly.[50] As the individual's capabilities were the primary criterion for continuing to hold office, this justification might be at least partly true. But otherwise, most of the elderly could continue to fulfil their roles. A person's precise age was not always known anyway and, even when it was, it had less impact on their rights and participation than in modern bureaucratized societies. Age was not a basic organizing principle, and the age of 60 or 70 was not necessarily a major landmark in life's course.

Many of the popes and other prelates − archbishops, bishops, abbots and abbesses, as well as heads of religious orders − were elderly. As already mentioned, this was not due to a conscious preference, but resulted from the fact that they had reached the peak of their careers when already in their 60s or even their 70s. Some of them lived to their 80s, and died in office. Those who did retire did not do so before they reached their 60s, and sometimes much later. A few examples will suffice. Lanfranc (*c.* 1005−89) was appointed archbishop of Canterbury by William the Conqueror when he was about 65 years old. He died in office when he was 84. Anselm of Canterbury (*c.* 1033−1109) was elected archbishop when he was 60 years old, and served until his death at the age of 75. Arnulf, bishop of Lisieux, retired to the monastery of St Victor in Paris when he was 81. Hato, bishop of Troyes in the 12th century, retired to Cluny when he was 69, while Gilbert of Sempringham finally retired as head of his order when he was at least 89. Humbert of Romans retired as master-general of the Dominican order when he was 65. Another member of the same order, Stephen of Bourbon (1182−1261), an active preacher and Inquisitor, retired only in his late 70s. Hildegard of Bingen (1098−1179) founded her independent community of nuns at Eibingen when she was 67 years old and remained at its head until her death at the age of 81. Ela, Countess of Salisbury (*c.* 1191−1261), after she was widowed founded a Cistercian nunnery and became its abbess. She retired at the age of 68 (two years before her death). Héloïse remained abbess of her nunnery, the

Paraclete, until her death at the age of 63. (She became abbess at a younger age than the minimum one fixed by canon law, when she was about 30.) The holders of high church offices did not suffer economic hardships when they retired, and generally enjoyed the same privileges in retirement as in office. Parish priests were neither allowed to retire nor forced into retirement (on the grounds that they were feeble, ill, semi-blind, deaf or senile) before they reached their 60s. The church had some pension schemes for retired clergymen, but poor parish priests or chantry priests received only meagre sums which more often than not did not suffice for subsistence.[51] The advanced age of the monks or nuns did not guarantee respect or an honourable standing in the community. It was their individual personality that determined their status. They were, however, taken care of and nursed by the community's younger members, and insured against want as well as against loneliness.

Popes and prelates (left), like doges, normally reached their high positions at an advanced age. Pope Paul III (Alessandro Farnese) was elected aged 76 and lived to be 81. Cardinal Filippo Archinto, Archbishop of Milan, was probably painted when he was in exile in Venice in 1554–56. Both portraits are by Titian, the second incorporating a virtuoso piece of illusionism in the half-drawn transparent curtain.

Among the remarkable women of the Middle Ages – and there was no shortage of them – none was more impressive than Hildegard of Bingen. Mystic, theologian, poet, artist and musician, she founded her community of nuns when she was 67 and ruled it until her death in 1179 at the age of 81. Her scope was wide; she corresponded with popes and emperors and only narrowly failed to be canonized; from a manuscript of about 1250.

'La Vecchia' – the Old Woman (opposite) – like so many of Giorgione's paintings, is an enigma. One tradition says that it is a portrait of his own mother. But is it sympathetic or not? Is it an expression of reverence for old age, as some have thought, or (more likely) a harsh comment on the corrosive effect of time on female beauty? The inscription on the paper, 'Col tempo' ('with time'), is consistent with either view.

A hostile view of old age is suggested in a double portrait by Marinus van Reyerswaele (1493–1567), but it may merely depict variety of attitudes to age.

Unlike popes, kings tended to be young. It was the dynastic principle that was decisive here. When predecessors died relatively young, they inherited the throne at an early age. Of all the kings of Europe from the 11th to the beginning of the 15th century, the longest living king was Alfonso VI, king of Castile and León (1030–1109), who reached the age of 79. Of all his predecessors and successors only two made it into their 60s. Only three of the kings of Aragon reached their 60s, and only four of the German emperors. Three of the kings of England reached their 60s, but only one of the Capetian kings of France – Louis VII (1120–80). All other kings, in all European countries, died younger. In the most dramatic struggles in the Middle Ages between church and state, young kings confronted elderly popes. At Canossa, in 1077, the emperor Henry IV was 22 years old; Gregory VII was 57. Frederick II (*Stupor Mundi*, 1194–1250) was 34 years old when he was excommunicated in 1228 by Pope Gregory IX, who was then 73. When, in 1303, Pope Boniface VIII was attacked by the envoys of Philip IV, king of France, the pope was 68 years old, the king 35.

Among men of the nobility there was a high rate of unnatural death. Noblemen met their ends in wars in Europe as well as in the Crusades, in military training, in tournaments, or by execution in civil wars (towards the late Middle Ages), often long before they reached old age. Of those who survived, some continued to render in person the military service due for the fief as long as they could, and to fight in battles. Robert Guiscard (*c.* 1015–85), founder of the Norman state in southern Italy, who died at the age of 70, commanded his troops until the day of his death. Raymond IV (*c.* 1041–1105), count of Toulouse, became one of the leaders of the First Crusade when he was about 60 years old, and fought in battle until his death at the age of 63. William Marshal was appointed regent of England (since Henry III was a minor when he inherited the throne) at the age of 71, and at the age of 72 was still taking part in battle. John Howard, duke of Norfolk, fell in battle aged about 75. Others preferred to retire (through commutation of the military service by money payment, or by hiring someone to replace them), although they did not lose their fief, which was hereditary, continuing to enjoy its income and control its administration. However, even in the later Middle Ages, when feudal service had long ceased to constitute the main source of military levy, retirement must have entailed diminution of status and distanced the person from the centre of activities. Service, like honour and the right of command, constituted a basic element in the ethos of the aristocracy. In chronicles which described aristocratic kinship groups, a nobleman valued his kinship group according to the power and standing of its middle-aged *seniores*, not its oldest members. However, the honour of the group and the representation of the *seniores* as a source of support and advice to the younger men blur the image of the conflict between the generations. It is in the literary descriptions of old men in epics and romances that the raw intergenerational tension is exposed. The old man is an object of contempt. He tries to do things he no longer can: he wants war when he himself can no longer fight; he is feeble and senile, but tyrannizes over his sons, and his commands are disastrous. Above all, he still holds his fief and can marry for the second or third time, taking to wife a young girl, while the young men in his kinship group have no fief and cannot marry.[52]

There must have been less diminution in the status of the heiresses of fiefs than in that of their male counterparts. Some women who inherited fiefs that entailed political and legal powers, like Matilda of Tuscany (1046–1115) who died aged 69, or Margaret of Flandres (1202–80) who died at the age of 78, ruled their feudal principalities to the ends of their lives. At no stage did they have to render military service in person and, though they were legitimate heiresses, they were debarred from participating in the representative assemblies that arose in the 14th century. When women entered the public domain they were rarely in a situation where their female identity was irrelevant. In old age, however, it became blurred. Possibly when they were no longer young, they became more assertive and freer in their contacts and negotiations with both their subordinates and their superiors.

Marriage was an area where the older man had the advantage over the younger woman. He is assumed to be easily able to marry for a second or third time. Quentin Massys represents him as decidedly unsympathetic. Heaps of money and jewelry lie on the table. The other men are as repulsive as the bridegroom, and the old woman just as unattractive in her disappointment and envy.

Like many office holders who did not wish to retire, there were also in urban society burghers who were disinclined to abandon their economic activities as they grew old. Bankers, merchants and artisans, lawyers, notaries and physicians were independent and could not be forced to retire. (Guillaume de Harcigny, a good and experienced physician, treated Charles VI of France when he had his first attack of madness. He was then 92 years old.)[53] Owners or partners in merchant companies could choose to retire partially and gradually by transferring some of the work to their sons, or younger relatives. The women of the prosperous urban stratum were as secure in their old age as noblewomen. The right of dower, or the marriage settlement, the dowry, and sometimes an inheritance from the husband or the family of origin, ensured a comfortable existence. The problem of retirement from economic activity did not exist for women of this social group.

Artisans rarely retired. The family constituted the production unit, including the artisan's wife, the children who had not yet left home, an apprentice or two, and sometimes also a journeyman. The ageing artisan could thus leave the hardest tasks to others. Moreover, the rate at which a medieval artisan worked was not dictated by machines or by management practices, such as piece-rate work or time bonuses. Such changes as occurred in the methods of production in a man's lifetime were small and gradual. They did not make his skills obsolete or inefficient, and it was not beyond his ability to adapt. Nevertheless, some artisans undoubtedly experienced economic hardship as their working capacity declined. As guild members, they were entitled to some support, which took a variety of forms, from their craft guild and/or from the fraternity in which they were members.[54] Though daughters and wives of artisans worked with their fathers and/or husbands, very few craft guilds admitted women as full members, and all-female guilds were rare.[55] Members' widows generally received assistance, but few of the guilds permitted them to continue working at their late husband's craft, even if they had the capacity to do so.

Artists never retired and many left records of themselves in later life. Left: Michelangelo as Nicodemus from a late Pietà, when he was about 75. Opposite, clockwise from top left: Leonardo da Vinci (1510, aged 58), Titian (1562, in his 80s), Tintoretto (c. 1589, aged about 70) and Lucas Cranach (1550, aged 77).

Manual workers in the Middle Ages continued as long as they could.
This Bohemian miniature from a Bible of 1411 shows a range of
building techniques including the treadmill for lifting stones. Those
at work are distinctly elderly by modern standards, but the dress of the
man in the foreground is evidence that some fashions do not change.

It was the lot of elderly wage-earners, both male and female, that was the hardest. Few were hired for life (examples include primary-school teachers and a summoner).[56] Those who were probably continued to receive their modest wages even when they could no longer carry out their duties. In some cases a prior agreement was made with an artisan that in return for his work he would receive a subsistence for the rest of his life, and a smaller pension would be paid to his widow. (There is an example of such an agreement between a monastery and a gifted painter who also specialized in 'glazed windows', and another between a monastery and its victualler.)[57] But most labourers were neither hired for life nor guaranteed a pension. Journeymen who were not admitted into an occupational guild were taken on for a limited period or a specific task and received daily or weekly wages. Most of them were unable to save enough for their old age during their working years. They could thus not afford to retire and were obliged to continue working as long as they could. They were not able to assure subsistence for their widows either. Female wage-earners, married, widowed or single, probably likewise continued to work as long as they could – except the wet nurses and prostitutes, whose working life was naturally limited. As women generally worked in more poorly paid occupations than men, they were even more exposed to dire want in their old age.

The harshness of Pieter Bruegel's portrait of an old peasant woman (c. 1564) and of the drawing by Hans Baldung is typical of the prevailing male prejudice that was widespread in the past. Baldung's picture is usually called 'The Witch' or 'The Hag'. The exposure of one breast makes it likely that Baldung intended her to be a procuress and perhaps planned to use her in a brothel scene.

There were bishops, kings, feudal lords, burghers and lords of the manor who left in their wills small sums to provide for their faithful soldiers, office holders or long-time servants in their old age. Monasteries also made provisions for some of their servants and employees. But providing a pension of some kind to one's workers was not a duty in law, nor even a generally accepted norm. It was voluntary, and most of the sums left were too small to secure a livelihood.[58]

In southern Europe, where the extended family was dominant, elderly peasants did not retire but kept their status as heads of the household. They cultivated their land together with a married son, or a number of sons, daughters and sons-in-law, depending on the demography and traditions of the region. All sons and daughters who remained on the family farm also remained under the authority of the head of the household. In Languedoc, even the latter's death did not always liberate the younger generation from control: the widowed mother replaced the father and assumed authority over her married sons and daughters-in-law.[59] The custom was quite different in northern and some parts of central Europe, where the nuclear family was dominant. At a certain stage in his life the peasant handed over his farm to one of his offspring by an agreement (often a written one), whereby the latter undertook to keep him and look after him until the end of his days. If he had no offspring in the village, either because he was childless or because his children had died or emigrated (which was common in the 14th century after the Black Death of 1348), the agreement was drawn with a relative or with non-kin. What determined the time of retirement was not only the decline in the person's functional capacity, but also demographic and family circumstances. Some widows handed over their farm before reaching old age, because they felt incapable of working on their holding and rendering to the lord of the manor the services that their tenement was charged with. In periods of demographic pressure peasants sometimes retired while still relatively young in order to enable a son to marry and establish a household. In periods of demographic decline, when more opportunities were available to them outside their birth village (to earn better wages or acquire land), many of the young emigrated. To ensure that a son (or a married daughter) remained in the village to continue cultivating the land and provide support in old age, older peasants sometimes retired and handed over the farm to the son or daughter. A lord of the manor who wanted his lands to be cultivated properly and the manorial services rendered sometimes exerted pressure on a widow or aged peasant to retire.[60] Then the retired couple (or widow or widower) moved from the main room to a back room, or to the attic, or to a spare cottage, and the new head of the household settled in the main room — a painful symbol of the changed status of the elderly. In didactic literature there are many detailed stories about the plight of the

Peasants too never retired –
because they could not afford to.
In a 15th-century English stained-
glass window (opposite), Adam,
like any peasant worker, goes on
working for as long as he can.
In a painting by Pieter Aertsen,
an elderly farmer brings his
produce to market.

elderly who handed their property over to their children in their lifetime, and there were many medieval versions of *King Lear* – a father divides his assets (in some versions it is a kingdom, in others it is a peasant's farm) among his sons or daughters, and they insult him and treat him badly. In reality, as in all periods, there must have been both 'good' and 'bad' sons and daughters. The warnings in the didactic texts, as well as the sayings that were common in Austria – e.g., 'sitting on the children's bench is hard for the old'[61] – express anxiety and fear of ageing, and the dependence and loss of status that it entailed. They also express sadness because of the lack of symmetry in the relations between parents and children, even when the latter were 'good'.

The church set the conjugal family above the birth family, in conformity with the biblical verse 'Therefore shall a man leave his father and mother and shall cleave unto his wife and they shall be one flesh' (Genesis 2:24) and St Paul's dicta (I Corinthians 7:4 and Ephesians 5:2–22). At the same time, the biblical commandment to honour parents (Exodus 20:12; Deuteronomy 5:6; repeated in the Epistle to the Ephesians 6:1–3) was reiterated in the didactic literature and in the various discourses. And though not incorporated in law, the duty of honouring parents and supporting them materially was a binding moral duty everywhere. However, as already mentioned, not all elderly men and women (not only in the peasantry) were taken care of, even when they had children and the children were not too poor to assist them. 'Corrodies' (the right to live in a monastery, nunnery and hospital) were widespread in the higher echelons of society. Some were bought or obtained by patrons for their officials as a way of providing for them in their old age. But most men and women retired to a monastery or a hospital after purchasing the pension for themselves with a single payment, or by promising a bequest.[62] How many of those who had a choice (i.e., had offspring and purchased a pension) did so because they preferred it to living with their children, we cannot know.

Retirement had its disadvantages and doubtless entailed a diminution of status. Yet the absence of obligatory retirement and that of pension schemes were obviously linked. Pensions granted to private individuals, even minute ones, were scarce, and public ones, including government-administered relief in general, almost nonexistent. (The only assistance given by governments to the needy took the form of tax exemptions for the poorest and, in time of famine or war, deferment of taxes and debt payments, prohibition of the export and hoarding of grain, and the supervision of its market price.) Only the church created something which approached a pension scheme for retired clergy. Both in the towns and in the rural areas, those who had never had any assets but the work of their hands were exposed to dire poverty and humiliation when they ceased working. The elderly were not, as were the widows and orphans, among those whom the Scriptures defined as deserving assistance. Nevertheless, there was an awareness of the fact that old age was often accompanied by want, and that the elderly could not always be cared for by their offspring. In practice, it cannot be said that the elderly were discriminated against by the charity institutions administered by the church, the village community or the fraternities. They suffered worse because they were unable to take advantage of changes in the land and labour market as they happened, as could younger people. Charity was never sufficient.

The voice of the old man is rarely heard in medieval sources, and that of the old woman hardly ever. Such a voice might have told us more and in a direct way about the experience of the elderly. The means of production in the Middle Ages were limited. It was a society poor in resources, and because of its hierarchical structure assets were concentrated in the hands of the privileged few. It was violent; it was impotent against disease and epidemics; and poverty was considered an unavoidable feature of human society. It was not a golden age for any stage of life. Attitudes and images were constantly veering between the 'positive' and the 'negative'. A considerable part of the ageing process is biologically determined, and its unpleasant aspects universal and unavoidable. A better understanding of the experience of old people in the past can help us to distinguish between the biological and the socially constructed, the inherent and that which is open to change and amelioration.

A ninety-year-old man is derided by a young child, a Viennese woodcut of 1579. Attitudes of disrespect for old age are as easy to find as those of respect.

4

LYNN A. BOTELHO THE 17TH CENTURY

Rembrandt's insight into old age
is unique among the great masters.
He was not alone in preferring a
rough elderly face marked by
character and experience to a young
smooth one. But his interest went
further, and there is no precedent for
the series of self-portraits in which
he recorded his own advancing years.
Penetrating in some inexplicable way
beneath appearances, he seems to
make manifest the conflict between
spirit and flesh, the one shining
more brightly as the other slowly
deteriorates. Most of these paintings
are inevitably sombre in mood;
here (about 1668, when he was 62)
he looks unusually happy, but there
is a theory that he is assuming a part,
that of the Greek painter Zeuxis
who, according to legend, 'departed
this life laughing immoderately,
choking while painting a funny
wrinkled old woman.'

To be 'old' in 17th-century Europe was not to be a rare commodity, an oddity or somehow divinely set apart. There was no rarity value in advanced age. The century's demographic structure resembled that of England and America in the early 20th century with roughly 10 per cent of the population over the age of 60. Becoming and being old was a common expectation of 17th-century life.

What did it mean to be old in the 1600s? Was it to be alone and isolated from friends and family, having outlived one's companions as well as one's usefulness? Or to be the proud matriarch or patriarch at the core of the community's political and social networks? At what age was someone considered old? Did 17th-century Italians, Germans, or French men and women share the modern demographers' definition of age 60 as the line of demarcation between middle and old age? Did men and women share the same experience of old age?

In the modern West, there is a strong and growing belief that 'one is as old as one looks or acts' and that age 70, while *older*, can still be a time of vitality and productivity. Similar sentiments prevailed in the 17th-century. Seventeenth-century Europe was a visually-centric society, where dress and carriage were daily manifestations of authority and where displays of wealth equated with real-world power. Italian noblemen hosted elaborate carnival masquerades, such as on 27 February 1679, in Venice, when the Duke of Mantua rode on horseback, accompanied by Indians, Africans, Turks and Tartars; the Venetians' French counterparts produced equally complex masques, including Jean-Baptiste Lully's *Le Carnival Mascard*, while the English team of Ben Jonson and Inigo Jones concocted *Pleasure Reconciled to Virtue*, all in an effort to assert the social and political superiority of the nobility. Therefore, it comes as no surprise that entry into old age was organized on similar principles: one was considered old when one looked old. 'Who is an old woman?' asked the 12th-century polymath Maimonides: 'One who is called old and does not protest.'[1]

Not everyone, then or now, ages physically at the same pace or with the same intensity. Diet and occupation, and indeed sex, heavily influence the outward signs of ageing. But although masked by the medical and cosmetic advances of the modern West, the physical characteristics of old age have not changed much. Men tend to lose hair on their heads; women tend to grow it on their faces. Hearing begins to fade. Eyesight dims owing to calcium avidity. Yet, as eyes collect calcium, other parts of the body lose it. Bones become brittle and tend to break. The 'Dowager's Hump' of osteoporosis was the stereotypical hallmark of the elderly woman in the 17th century, as were the broken hips and arms of the aged male. Old people shrink. Other signs of advancing age appeared as well. Skin becomes drier and less elastic, resulting in wrinkles and bags. Noses grow and gums recede. The picture painted here is a grim one – and, indeed, overstated. Only the most unfortunate would have suffered the simultaneous breakdown of all the parts of their body. For most people, as we shall see, the ageing process was much slower and much gentler.

Further complexity is added by the very nature of 17th-century Europe. The continent was not a unified and united mass. Its peoples did not share the same climate, the same access to food, or even the same diet. It was fiercely regional in its social, political and religious make-up and identity. Finally, and most significantly of all, Europe was socially stratified and hierarchical. Consequently, there was no one single point marking the threshold of old age, but rather many, with a few general principles gently shaping its contours.

Women were considered 'old' at a younger age than men. Menopause and its physical manifestations produced telltale signs, due to inadequate diet and poor living standards, which prompted community members to consider poor women to have entered old age around age 50. English records often document the use of honorific titles such as 'Mother' or 'Old' for poorer women, beginning around their 50th year. For poorer men, similar titles of 'Old' or 'Father' were not tightly bunched around a benchmark year or event, but were more widely scattered, though still roughly centred in their sixth decade. Lacking a shared biological turning point, it was the appearance of other physical markers – perhaps those produced by long years of manual labour – that triggered the community's use of 'Old' or 'Father' to connote both age and respect.[2]

'Mother' was an honorific title given to women over 50. 'Mother Louse' (opposite top) was so called because she kept a pub called Louse Hall near Oxford. 'Mother Shipton' was a prophetess, reputed to be a witch. She was born in Yorkshire at the end of the 15th century and was so ugly that she was known as 'the Devil's child'. One of her most sensational prophecies concerned Cardinal Wolsey, hence his appearance in the background of this 17th-century woodcut.

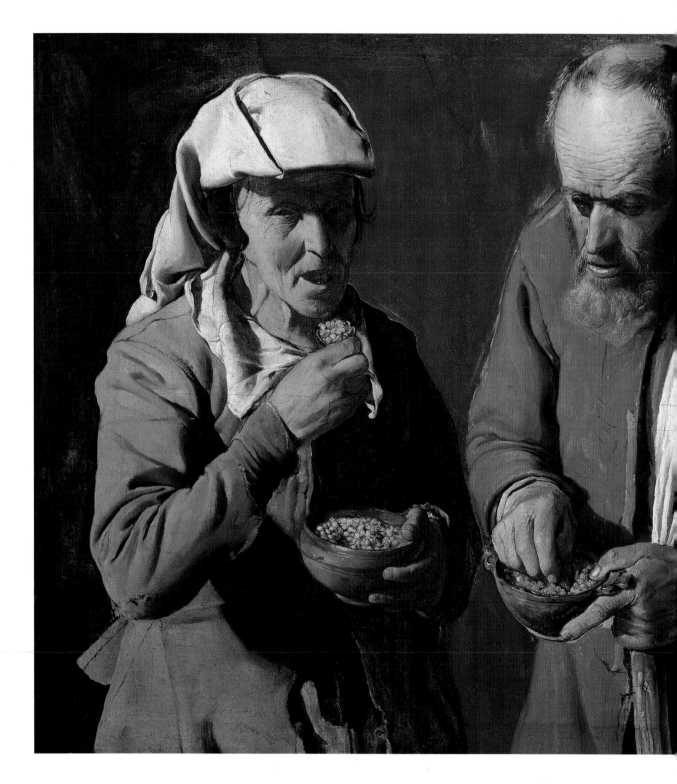

Poverty was integral to the story of old age. While the rich could remain healthy and youthful until their 60s, the poor, subsisting on a limited and unnourishing diet, became 'old' at 40 or 50. Georges de La Tour specialized in intimate devotional works and scenes of peasant life, both of which reveal his compassion for the unhappy and oppressed. His picture 'Couple Eating Peas' was painted about 1618.

Another shaping element of old age was social status. For the elites, entry into old age was held at bay for at least an extra decade. A protein-rich diet, comfortable (and sometimes luxurious) housing and a less physically demanding lifestyle kept the most obvious markings of old age off the faces and figures of both sexes longer. As a result of this higher standard of living, menopause played only a minor role in the social construct of female old age: consequently, the onset of old age was not sharply gendered among the elites. Ironically, the toothlessness that was typically associated with old age came to the faces of the wealthy at a precocious age. Able to afford the luxury sugar, and using it liberally as an overt status-marker, the effect was the rapid decay and loss of most teeth by richer old people. The well-recognized toothless smile was not a signifier of age, but rather of wealth.

Other variables played their parts. Occupation was critical. Weather-beaten seafaring men, such as sailors in the North Atlantic and pale-skinned miners of the German tin mines and elsewhere, grew old earlier and died younger. The physicality of their employment accelerated the ageing process just as it did for female lacemakers in Lyon, who suffered debilitating blindness and stiff fingers. Ageing in such circumstances could begin in one's 40s and become unquestionably present by one's 50s. Conversely, less physically demanding professions, such as the religious life, could contribute to a later and gentler old age. Those with religious vocations, whether male or female, Protestant or Catholic, seem to have aged slowly and lived long. With a steady diet and a roof consistently over their heads, priests, nuns and clergy grew old in ways similar to the wealthy.[3] What one did, what one ate, where one lived, as well as one's sex and status, all converged upon the body in an idiosyncratic manner.

Despite the individualistic pacing of the lifecycle, general guidelines and rough cut-offs are nonetheless useful tools as we contemplate the early modern ageing process. The poor became old earlier than the rich and women sooner than men. Poor women aged the quickest of any group due to a calcium-deficient diet, calcium-draining pregnancies and, all too often, inadequate food and shelter. They entered old age at 50 and represent one end of the ageing spectrum. Wealthy and leisured men mark the other. They did not publicly enter old age until after their 60th birthday.

The onset of old age, however, was not sudden. What must be borne in mind when assessing and assigning thresholds is that one did not cross a chronological barrier and tumble head first into decrepitude. The process was much more subtle. 'Age,' wrote Honorat de Bueil, the Marquis de Racan, 'imperceptibly washes us to doom.'[4] One manner of marking the cultural start of frail old age is to use the age-exemptions offered across Europe that excused the elderly from a range of civic and military obligations, such as serving in Florence's Council of Six, representing Venice as a foreign ambassador or serving in the military in any number of countries. These were used, as we have seen, by Shulamith Shahar in the preceding chapter to mark entry into old age during the Middle Ages. In the 17th century these chronologically triggered exemptions marked a generalized functional decline in ability – advanced old age – somewhere between age 60 and 70, but not the onset of this process. They also reflect the experiences of the elites and not the hard world of the poor. Individuals may have been considered 'old', but still thought active, useful and vitally engaged with the world.

After seventy there was only heaven to look forward to.
A series of etchings by the Swiss-German artist Conrad Mayer made in 1675 chronicles the last thirty years of the Biblical Isaac and his wife. In the first, still hale at 70, they sit by the fire while Jacob and Esau manage the house.
At 80 they listen to a reading of the Bible (the Ten Commandments are displayed on the wall behind).
At 90 they need careful tending by their pious children.
At 100, helpless and bedridden, they await death patiently and prepare to meet God.

We shall see many examples of the 'Ages of Man' schema. His earthly term commonly divided into three, four, seven, ten or 12 such ages, man is seen climbing the stairs of life, whose apex is 'middle age', before he begins an equally measured descent into decrepitude. Popular in Germany in the 16th century and probably familiar still in the 17th was this description of the decades of life:

10 years – a child
20 years – youth
30 years – a man
40 years – standing still
50 years – settled and prosperous
60 years – departing
70 years – protect your soul
80 years – the world's fool
90 years – the scorn of children
100 years – God have mercy.

This highly structured manifestation of the 'Ages of Man' had taken on a special resonance in Northern Europe by the start of the 17th century. Its very ordered and prescriptive nature offered solace and stability, a template of how to proceed and how to behave, in a world whose very fabric of living had been turned upside down during the course of religious upheaval.[5]

Overleaf:
The Ages of Man as a cross-section of life in 17th-century Holland: after the last image – death – the gates of Paradise open to the sound of trumpets.

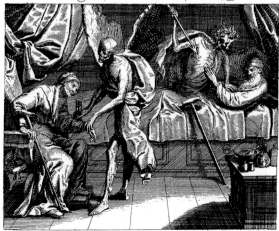

The early part of the 17th century, especially in the northern areas of France, Germany and the Low Countries, witnessed Europe's struggle to regain its feet after a sometimes bloody and always disruptive religious conflict between traditional Roman Catholicism and the growing number of Protestant groups that began with Luther and ended with the Calvinists, but also unhappily harboured the Anabaptists and their offshoots. In many aspects of dogma and doctrine the differences between Roman Catholic and Protestant, indeed even between Protestant and Protestant, were sharp enough and deeply enough felt to result in bloodshed, war and religiously sanctioned murder. Yet, much was shared between these groups, including their understanding of the position of the elderly within the Christian community and church.

Paramount to the Christian view of the aged was the biblical command: 'Thou shalt rise up before the hoary head, and honour the face of the old man, and fear thy God: I am the Lord' (Lev. 19:32). Protestant and Catholic alike were taught when young to follow Moses' words and to respect the elderly for their wisdom and piety, as well as to honour the subjugation by the elderly of the carnal lusts that otherwise clouded the judgment of the young. 'Allwaies have a respect to a gray-haired Experience and samed understanding [i.e. the elderly's understanding of life],' echoed the 17th-century Earl of Carbery. Even the aged widow was to be accorded her fair share of Christian respect and if need be charity. She was seen to be a worthy recipient of God's miracles in the Bible, such as in II Kings 4, where the oil of a widow's lamp is made to last days longer than it should. Ancient widows and honourable old men were both afforded particular respect in Christianity, regardless of creed.

This idea is one of the fundamental precepts of the Ten Commandments: honour thy father and mother. The Commandments also had a particular resonance in Europe's Protestant communities, as painted word replaced painted image on the walls of many churches as part of an iconoclastic drive towards the recreation of the Apostolic church. Pictures of saints, such as St Christopher who universally adorned pre-Reformation churches, were literally whitewashed over and the word of God painted in their place. The tablets of Moses called upon all men and women to honour their parents and by extension *all* elderly people who stood before them as their elders and betters. The author of *Dives and Pauper*, an extended commentary on the Ten Commandments, described this obligation in morally reciprocal terms: your parents raised you while helpless, so now you must care for them.[6]

'This is my beloved son': one of Mattia Preti's frescoes in the Cathedral of St John, Valletta, Malta. ('No painter has ever had a more difficult labour than the vault of St John's,' he wrote to a friend in the 1660s.) This is part of a cycle on the life of St John the Baptist – God spoke those words at the moment of Christ's baptism – and Preti follows convention in representing God as old: 'Thou shalt rise up before the hoary head and honour the force of the old man.'

The God-like image of infinite wisdom is applied traditionally to all sages, law-givers and prophets. Neither Jewish nor Christian moralists really underrated the drawbacks of old age, yet in these contexts both present it in idealized form, from Moses, through whom God communicated the Ten Commandments (above: meeting the messengers from Canaan with their luxuriant grapes, by Gianlorenzo Bernini) to St Jerome (right, by Guido Reni) who translated the Bible into Latin under God's direct inspiration.

The thematic linkage notwithstanding, Protestant women and men were often appalled by the explicit *visual* connection between honour due to one's parents and honour due to God the Father. Traditional Roman Catholic iconography often depicted God as an ancient man. 'I was very much scandalized at a large silver image of the Trinity,' wrote Lady Montague during her extensive travels in Catholic Europe early in the 18th century, 'where the Father is represented under the figure of a decrepit old man, with a beard down to his knees, and a triple crown on his head.'[7] Not all aspects of old age and the elderly straddled the confessional divide.

Despite the teachings of Moses, the well-rehearsed directive of the Ten Commandments and Roman Catholicism's explicit conflation of God the Father and earthly parents, Christianity was aware that old age was not always a time of respect and retirement. The aged poor of any denomination would have been in sympathy with the sentiments expressed in Psalm 71: 'Now also when I am old and grey-headed, O God, forsake me not' (Psalm 71:18). Similarly, the following lines from the same psalm summed up the pan-European fear of growing old: 'Cast me not off in the time of my old age; Forsake me not when my strength faileth' (Psalm 71:9). Regardless of wealth or social standing, the elderly Christian was to be esteemed. For the old and financially impoverished, this might have been cold comfort without Christianity's explicit direction to give alms and charity to the poor and needy.

The failing strength of the elderly, which often drove them to seek and receive Christian charity, was directly linked in the minds of 17th-century Europeans with the failing 'heat' of their bodies. In a century alive with medical innovations and competing medical theories – such as alchemy, chemistry, as well as those of the Paracelsians and the Helmontians – the prevailing understanding of the body remained that of Galen and his theory of the humours.

By the 17th century, the four humours (blood, phlegm, yellow bile or choler, and black bile or melancholy) had become linked to Aristotle's four elements (earth, water, air and fire). Both humours and elements were formed from the four qualities or building blocks (hot, dry, cold and wet) of the world. In turn, these were paired with the four seasons (spring, summer, autumn and winter) and the four ages of man

(childhood, youth, adulthood and old age). Each person was considered a unique mixture of temperaments, humours, constitutions and complexions, and it was the interplay among all of these that produced individual dominant psychological characteristics: phlegmatic, sanguine, choleric or melancholic, the distinctive feature of the aged.

As people aged, the body's vital heat was slowly burned away and consumed. The older one got, the colder and, at least inwardly, the drier: 'But in ensuing time, as all the organs become even dryer, not only are their functions performed less well but their vitality becomes more feeble and restricted. And drying more, the creature becomes not only thinner but also wrinkled, and the limbs weak and unsteady in their movements. This condition is called old age.'[8] This cold dryness was old age's inner or primary nature. Yet, the elderly also had 'external moisture' and a secondary nature. Often viewed as 'bad', these external moistures were produced by the elderly themselves, through their tears, phlegm and mucus, rendering their secondary natures cold and moist. In this manner, the elderly could be drying up and wasting away physically while at the same time manifesting a melancholic and phlegmatic temperament.

The ageing female body was even more problematic in its nature, as we have seen in the previous chapter. As they aged and dried, old women became harder and more 'male' in their physical selves. Consequently they were considered capable of more reason and level-headedness, and thus due more respect. On the other hand, they were thought to grow increasingly evil and dangerous as menopause set in. Good health was predicated on the balance of humours and, with the end of menstruation, women no longer expelled the poisonous blood from their system, leaving their humours dangerously out of balance. The situation was exacerbated by the natural loss of heat that could otherwise consume and control the now-trapped menstrual blood. Instead, this noxious substance turned to deadly venom. Menstrual blood was long reputed to be deadly to the touch. It was said that a menopausal woman could cause grass to dry up, fruit to wither on the vine, and trees to die. Dogs would become rabid and mirrors crack by her mere presence. Such women, without even trying, could cast the evil eye.[9] With malice aforethought, the glance of the post-menopausal woman could kill. At this conjuncture the world of women and witches combines, contributing to the rash of witch hunts and crazes. Seventeenth-century Europe was both patriarchal and hierarchical: not only did women only have poisonous ageing bodies, but it was only poor women who manifested these traits. Wealthy women did not exhibit as marked physical changes at menopause, and seldom were they tried for witchcraft.

The Seasons and the Ages of Man formed a parallel series, with Winter naturally linked to old age. Here he warms his cold hands by the fire, an engraving by Christian van der Passe.

Just as the body's humoral composition changed over the lifecycle, until the very old once again resembled the very young, the physical body showcased a series of changes. The discomforts and diseases of the elderly were myriad, there was a strong tendency towards respiratory problems, such as pneumonia, influenza and bronchitis, in addition to colds, coughs and general bodily aches. Winters were a particularly trying time for the old. General, age-related problems included ringing or buzzing in the ears, stomach complaints, difficulty in urinating, dizziness and annoying skin complaints and itches. More serious problems also plagued the elderly. They suffered from declining eyesight, if not blindness. There was also a high probability of some physical disability stemming from earlier, work-related injuries, or falls resulting in broken and poorly healed bones.

Despite the repetition of Galen's advice to consider all aspects of the patient, including age and lifestyle, most European doctors treated the elderly's aches and pains in very much the same manner they did those of the younger population. They prescribed egg whites for eye ailments and 'for sleepyness, hold[ing] the fresh leaves of pennyroyall under the tong'.[10] However, there were a few significant areas where treatment *was* modified. Drastic interventions with the body's functioning, for example, were thought best avoided. Bleeding was to be done lightly, if at all, because loss of blood also meant loss of vital heat. Strong enemas, a common way to remove an imbalanced humour or to relieve constipation, were not to be used, the problem instead being treated more gently and organically with massage, figs and herbal drinks. By and large, however, the medical response to the 'diseases of old age' remained fundamentally unchanged from the medieval period: it was preventative, not corrective. In other words, medical practitioners did not seek to cure, but rather to comfort their patients.

The goal was to *prevent* premature ageing and to prolong youth. Early modern Europe's fascination with longevity was not distinctive to the continent or to the century, but was part of a long and global preoccupation that led the Spanish to search for the Fountain of Youth and found 17th-century England obsessed with the idea of the supposedly 153-year-old Thomas Parr. The keys to postponing old age were diet and regimen, habits of eating and living that needed to be established firmly in youth as they were considered powerless if instigated only after strength had begun to fade. Here too medical commentators recognized the various stages of old age and shaped their regimen accordingly. Those in the first years of old age should continue with moderate exercise, such as walking, not as a means to build up strength in the manner that prompted youth to do the same, but to maintain the strength they already had.

Ioan. Stradanus invent.   Ioan. Collaert. fe

15.

CONSPICILLA.

'With spectacles on nose' is one of Shakespeare's defining attributes of old age next to the 'last scene of all': 'the lean and slippered pantaloon'. An Italian 17th-century engraving of a market shows a pathetic collection of old people trying on glasses, then a comparatively new invention. They were no doubt a blessing to their owners, even if a modern optician might find the techniques of sight-testing on the primitive side.

Food and drink were the basis upon which successful ageing was built. During these years of vigorous old age individuals should concentrate their calorific intake around food and drink that was warming and wet, consuming that which did not diminish their already declining heat. Red wine, the flesh of young and vibrant animals, and milk were to be consumed regularly. 'Wine,' as the saying went, 'is the old man's milk.' In fact, an old person who ceased to drink wine was viewed by the Italians as approaching death: 'When the old man will not drink, go to see him in the other world.'[11] Further, the old were instructed to eat small amounts but often. Warmth was to be preserved in all ways possible, including taking plenty of sleep in a heated or sunny room. Those in advanced old age were to follow these guidelines strictly, without deviation or modification. At this stage of life, strict warnings were issued to avoid excessive exertions and heat-dissipating foods: old people were instructed to avoid work, bleedings under any circumstances and sexual intercourse, and to eat smaller amounts of food but with increased frequency. The physical and dietary regimes were designed to preserve heat and moisture – to hold old age at bay, not to restore youth.

'When the old man will not drink, go to see him in the other world' ran an Italian proverb. Red wine was recommended to old people to prolong life. So this detail of a ceiling fresco in the Villa Albergati, Theodoli (1665) by Angelo Michele Colonna is surely an allusion to the passing of time.

Just as the humours were held in a delicate balance, each reflecting and affecting the others, so too were the body and the soul. The mental or soulful state was directly reflected in the physical health of the body. Towards that end, the elderly were advised to avoid being anxious, angry or sad, while at the same time they were urged to strive towards happiness and contentment. Medical commentators suggested music, good company, intellectual and religious pursuits and red wine as means simultaneously to drive away melancholy and find joy. A full regimen of health and the potential to prolong youth, therefore, involved food and drink, friends and family and a judicious amount of physical and intellectual activities. The key to physical success was the same as the key to moral success: to start in one's youth. 'That which one learns in youth,' said the French, 'will continue til old age.'[12] Old age itself was much too late to repent either lifestyle or morals.

Medical writing was shot through with sayings, proverbs and adages singing the praises of age and experience and warnings against youth and experience, such as the Portuguese 'Beware the young Physitian, and an old Barber'; or the French attack: 'Old Chyrurgeons, and young Physitians make the church-yards swell.'[13] Europe shared a common view of the ageing body, as well as of the merits of its medical practitioners. It also shared common cultural stereotypes of what old age entailed: the north did not substantially differ from the south, or the east from the west. Many proverbs were universal in meaning, if not identical in construction. The theatres and operas too shared many stock characters, with Pantaloon and the Doctor chief among them, and referenced a shared set of stereotypes, such as lustfulness and avarice. Commentators and critics also drew on a shared ethos that paradoxically encompassed both the biting criticism of Europe's supposed gerontocracy as well as a call to respect the hard-earned wisdom of age.

At the same time, there was the sense that everything has its season. 'Each age has its mood,' wrote Mathurin Regnier (1573–1613), 'its tastes, and its games; As hair grays, likewise do our whims.' Closely tied to this was the strong sense, as we have seen already, that the nature of old age was directly related to how youth was spent, for good or for ill. The French reminded people that 'An idle youth makes a needy old age', which the Italians echoed with: 'When we are young, we lay up for old age; when we are old, we save for Death.' Old age was closely connected with death, whose harbinger it was. Both French prose writers and dramatists found this a rich theme. François Maynard (1582–1646), in *A une belle vieille* (1638), positioned old age as a liminal stage between the quick and the dead: 'My foot is on the brink of the other world, Age robs me of desire, strength, and sleep; And soon will be born from the depth of the sea the first radiance of my last sun.' The great French playwright Pierre Corneille (1606–84) phrased the same idea thus: 'Every moment of life is a step toward death.'[14]

The positive and negative traits of old age were mirror images of each other: knowledge was paired with foolishness and good counsel with craftiness. 'Be advised by the aged, and thy opinion will prevail in Council' was a common Portuguese expression that closely echoed the disquisitions of the early 15th-century Spaniard the Marques of Santillana: 'The deed that's done by good advise, doth always firmly stand, and seldome seene to crave amendes at any second hand. Be ruled by counsaile evermore, whatsoever thou dost intend, and from thy side let never go thy faythfull aged friend.' An alternative view was voiced with equal vigour: 'An old bird is not caught in nets.' Proverbs could express contradictions: the elderly could be challenging competitors, but also old age was a time of foolishness. 'There's no fool like an old fool' was axiomatic in the 17th century and it still resonates in the 21st. Andriano Banchiere's Italian opera *The Madness of Old Age* (1598) revolves around this very conceit, with an old father insisting 'on loathsome, arranged marriages' while simultaneously being made a fool of by his own wife.[15]

Reflecting the patriarchal nature of 17th-century society, with its heavy emphasis on the moral, social and religious unworthiness of women, old women were assigned a smaller and much more negative range of traits than men. Their few redeeming characteristics were not those of personal strength and wisdom, but of perseverance and of a mother's devotion to her family. 'By little and little the old Woman spinnes the bundle of flax' speaks to the old woman's understanding of the steady movement of time and the value of slow, but constant, progress. Unlike the wealth and power coveted by old men, an elderly woman's dreams were much more modest and in keeping with her womanly role: 'A sheep and a bee, A stone which grinds, A jewel in his ear, the old woman wisheth her son.' There are important reminders of what European society valued about old women: patience and care for their family's wellbeing. But such descriptions were rare. Generally old women were feared or held in contempt.

Respect for the elderly is prominent in 17th-century Dutch didactic literature on family life, a respect reflected in the painting of the period. Nicolaes Maes gave dignity to mundane scenes of work in domestic settings. His 'Lacemaker' (left) was painted in 1655. In a similar vein is Rembrandt's drawing of about the same date of an old woman teaching a child to walk.

Most old widows were considered lustful, driven by sex and the desire for a husband. The very concept of elderly women engaging in sexual relations was repugnant to 17th-century society since the only approved aim of sex was reproduction and they were unable to bear children. Furthermore, the means used to achieve these ends were also unsettling to a society preoccupied with good order. 'She took care to paint and to adorn her face,' wrote Jean Racine (1639–99), 'to repair the irreparable outrage of the years.' Plutarch had earlier condemned similar practices: 'Now you're an old woman, do not drench yourself with scent.' Vilified with greater vigour was the behaviour of the merry-making old woman. Horace's words were much quoted in early modern Europe: 'The fleeces shorn near famed Lucera are fit work for you; not yours the dance-band and the red, red rose, nor the cask drained to its last dregs: you're an old woman now.' Make-up and merry-making were for the young and fair, not the old and wrinkled. The young man caught in a widow's machinations tended to be pitied, if slightly mocked: 'He who doth an old wife wedd, must eat a cold apple as he goes to bed.' (James Howell, a 17th-century recorder of European proverbs, explained, 'this relates to the flatulence of the apple which causeth Erection.') A Portuguese saying, however, concluded that 'An old woman with money is better than a young one with beauty.'[16]

'**To repair** the irreparable outrage of the years,' wrote Racine, 'she took care to paint and adorn her face': a cruel judgment but not as cruel as Bernardo Strozzi's graphic depiction of the same subject, 'The Old Flirt'.

Old men fared better in the court of common opinion. Their love of wine was considered benign under most conditions and positively healthy when compared to contemporary medical treatments: 'There be more old drunkards then old Physitians.' Ancient men were held up as an example to youth as a reminder that what they did in their salad days would directly, for good or ill, shape their final years. The English expression 'An old serving-man, a young beggar [i.e. if a young man does not work, he will not have saved up money for his old age and then has to work]' was echoed throughout Europe, as was the Italian peninsula's 'Who is not something at twenty, nor knows not at thirty, nor hath not at forty, He never will be, nor will he ever know, nor will ever have any thing.' These sayings were intended, as we saw earlier, to instil a proper work ethic into the young, lest they suffer a poverty-ridden old age. The Portuguese bestowed similar advice on ageing parents regarding the education of their sons: 'a gathering father, a scattering son' and 'a pinching father, a prodigal son', the common phrases ran. In other words, the elderly needed to be reminded to provide a positive model for their children. This part of the cultural construction of male old age was neutrally charged: it expressed neither disapproval nor admiration.

Other stereotypical attributes were thought of as positive, reflecting the elderly man's wisdom born of long experience that generated sage advice, in contrast to the rash and beardless counsel of the young. 'An old dog barks not in vain' expresses the same thing, while the French played upon the same image with: 'There's no hunting but with old hounds'. Seventeenth-century Europe thought of old men in ways that they did not think of women, as valued counsellors and living moral examples for the young.[17]

While old men were viewed with a degree of benign amusement while in their cups or listened to with purpose at the council table, the overwhelming image of male old age and a common view of old age in general was that of financially greedy, physically lustful, self-important, talkative and meddling individuals; consequently, they were the butt of jokes and targets of mockery. Italian theatre abounded with the 'avaricious old father insisting on loathsome, arranged marriage', which when consummated in real life was lamented publicly: 'This strange alliance between youth and old age, which avarice has suggested to our fathers,' wrote the 17th-century actress Isabella Andrein, 'permits many abuses... Girls do not willingly accept the rewards of such marriages; or when accepted, they hate the austerity demanded by spectacled husbands.' Further, it was popularly thought that when they were not forcing their daughters to marry their friends and business partners for financial gain, aged fathers were themselves in hot pursuit of women of their daughters' age. 'His lust is as young as his limbs are old' was axiomatic in England;

while in Italy, with its very real age inequalities in marriage, old men were thought to be consumed by lust: 'Lust dirtieth young men, and drowns the old.' Outside of Italy, such marriages were frowned upon – 'To marry a young Mayd to an old man, is to cover a new house with old straw' – and collectively protested with Charvaris and Rough Music, devisory cacophany, made by clashing pots and pans. It was assumed without debate that such old men were quickly cuckolded.[18] While old age as a concept was held in respect, the elderly themselves were frequently derided.

Greed and lust were the vices of old men, as vanity was of old women, and 17th-century moralists showed little mercy to either. David Teniers' portrait of 'The Covetous Man' makes him almost obsessively avaricious. The amorous old man (opposite) in an anonymous Dutch painting (detail) is equally in the grip of passion, but here is treated as laughable rather than grim.

The Commedia dell'Arte offered a range of character types revealing the way they were popularly perceived. Pantaloon, the representative old man, is an object of contempt, petulant, pretending to be young, falling in love with unattainable young women and being deceived on all sides. Right: Jacques Callot's etching of Pantaloon in about 1620.

The Italian theatrical genre of Commedia dell'Arte reflected the Europe-wide characterization of old men as objects of mockery and disdain. Originating in Venice, by the 17th century this improvisational style of performance with stock characters (Pantaloon and the Doctor as representatives of old age) and common plots (lustful old men, deceitful youth, and the war between youth and age) had spread across the continent.

Pantaloon is a 'decrepit old man who tries to pass himself off as a youth'; 'a man ripe in years who pretends to be a tower of strength and good counsel for others, whereas in truth he is blinded by amorous passion and continually doing puerile things which might lead an observer to call him a child, for all that he is almost a centenarian'. His behaviour reinforces the Italian proverb 'Anyone who falls in love when he is old should be put in the stocks'.[19] Pantaloon was also miserly, despite his hidden chests of silver and gold. 'His most sumptuous feast,' his fellow characters complained, 'consists of dog or alley-cat soup, that he draws his wine from the fountain at the corner, and partakes of a duck egg as the chief dish of the banquet.' It is little wonder that Pantaloon's daughters worked hard, in plays such as *Magnifico* and *Zingana*, to avoid his parental authority and to dupe him into permitting their marriage to the young men of their choice.[20]

The aged Pantaloon, with his lust and greed typically unfulfilled, was paired both on the stage and in the minds of 17th-century European audiences with the equally elderly Doctor, an academic of the university. The latter, like his friend Pantaloon, acted the young gallant and chased maids, but was primarily associated with book learning and rhetoric. He was famous for constantly talking, rarely making sense and frequently stating the obvious.

Pantaloon and the Doctor: two more Commedia dell'Arte types, the first absurdly vain and pompous, the second pedantic and incomprehensible. These are watercolours by L.O. Burnacini.

In this 17th-century exchange the Physician is the one whom we should identify as a medical doctor:

> *Physician: Yes, sir, I practise medicine out of pure love for it. I nurse, I purge, I sound, I operate, I saw, I cup, I snip, I smash, I split, I break, I extract, I tear, and cut, and dislocate, I dissect, and trim, and slice, and, of course, I show no quarter.*
> *Doctor: You are a veritable avalanche of medicine.*
> *Physician: I am not only an avalanche of medicine, but the bane of all maladies whatsoever. I exterminate all fever and chills, the itch, gravel, measles, the plague, ringworm, gout, apoplexy, erysipelas, rheumatism, pleurisy, catarrh, both wind-colic and ordinary colic, without counting those serious and light illnesses with bear the same name. In short, I wage such cruel and relentless warfare against all forms of illness that when I see a disorder becoming ineradicable in a patient I even go as far as to kill the patient in order to relieve him of his disorder.*
> *Doctor: That is an excellent cure.*
> *Physician: I know no other. (He talks himself out of breath before the Doctor can stop him.) The jaundice, symptoms… Itching, symptoms… Gravel, symptoms… the… the… the… symptoms… …*
> *Doctor: He's making my ears buzz.*
> *Physician: The ear, you say? The skin that covers it adheres to the cartilage by means of a nervous membrane which makes it sensitive.*
> *Doctor: I'd like to bash in his nose.*[21]

In matters more prosaic than medicine the old Doctor is no more useful, frequently pronouncing solemnly and pompously: 'Anyone who is sleeping has not yet awakened.'[22] And often people fell sound asleep to the drone of the Doctor's words.

Pantaloon and the Doctor were the physical embodiments of all that 17th-century Europe held in contempt and associated with old age, male or female. They were the opposite of what a good old person should be like: instead of being wise, they were foolish; instead of having outgrown the cravings of the flesh, they indulged them; instead of offering good counsel, they spoke in platitudes. Consequently, they were ridiculed instead of revered. Clearly, such cultural constructions are not the same as the lived experience. Each negative proverb could be cancelled out by another, more positive one. These example nonetheless give valuable insights into the mind-set of 17th-century Europe. Contemporary commentators, playwrights, opera librettists and recorders of proverbs, sayings and adages spoke to Europe's fears and mirrored its values.

How women saw themselves as they reached old age can (rarely) be understood through written memoirs and (more rarely) through paintings. Sofonisba Anguissola, one of the most accomplished artists of the 17th century, was prevented by her sex from studying anatomy and life-drawing, and therefore concentrated especially on self-portraiture.

In the last of these (1610), she is aged 78, and depicts herself with unsentimental honesty. She lived to be 92.

The question of what the reading, theatre-going and indeed the talking public did with these expressions, of how – if at all – they related such cultural forces to their own lives, has always been a difficult one to answer. Certainly, we know – as did they – that not all old people were frail, talkative, fearful or any other number of attributes commonly associated with that stage of life. Yet, and it can sometimes be a significant caveat, was there not some aspect of those stereotypes that hit uncomfortably close to the mark? Lady Sarah Cowper offers an as yet unrivalled window into how one old and literate woman interacted with the cultural norms of ageing.

Lady Sarah was in no way representative of 17th-century women. Her literary output, over 2,300 pages of diary alone, sets her at some remove from other women, as does her rank. But her life engaged with the same questions of appropriate behaviour for the elderly and, as she aged, she experienced the same sort of physical decline as other women and at the same age, her mid-50s. While Lady Sarah's responses may have been heightened or amplified by rank and inclination, they nonetheless articulated a set of shared concerns.

She saw herself as 'elderly', but other people as really 'old'. 'I see objects abroad which plainly shew mee I am not yet arriv'd to the worst condition of old age by much,' wrote Lady Sarah. 'I mett Mr. W.G. who labors under it I believe with patience; yet sure it must be very tedious if not terrible.' Even as old age had her in its grip, she managed to find a gap between her and others, even though at the time she had difficulty reading or even feeding herself.

> *My Coz: Mas[ters]... being a 100 lack 3... thath reduc'd her income to £40 yearly paid on May: day to her daughter who keeps her handsomely well. However she ceases not to call for the mony into her own custody and refused meat or drink till she might have it. The daughter no doubt had it not in her power then to produce, but to satisfy and make her eat she gott 40 quilt counters and put in her purse which serves as well to count ten times a day and lay under a pillow at night... such kind fraud I think commendable.*

The very act of recording the plight of her kin confirmed for her that she herself was not yet truly old. She viewed old age as something to be held at bay for as long as possible. Ultimately, and not happily, Lady Sarah finally placed herself in that long-resisted category of advanced old age, at age 65. What it meant for her was the eventual loss of her favourite activities, reading, writing and learned contemplation. These projects were diminished and finally stopped during the last three and a half years of her life as her health failed her. Before she died, at age 76, she was, even to herself, truly old.

In the process of distancing herself from old age, and through her eventual acceptance of the same, Lady Sarah articulated a full set of behaviours deemed appropriate for those of advanced years. In short, one was to act one's age. The most egregious violation was for the elderly to act younger than their years and in ways that transgressed the sombre and dignified office of ageing. Remarriage to younger spouses, talking too much, and women's use of make-up were the three most censured traits.

Marrying a significantly younger man, particularly after menopause, was the source of much comment in Lady Sarah's diary.

> *Sir T. L. is newly married to a lady old, decrepid with the palsey and other inWrmities. Covetousness is thought to be his excuse (if it be one) for 'tis said she is rich; but none can imagine her meaning to be otherwise than to serve a beastly end. The end of marriage (say some) is society and mutual comfort; but they are rather an eVect of marriage none of the principle end which is procreation of children and so the continuance of mankind. As for comfort and society they may be betwixt man and man, woman and woman and therfore not proper end of marriage. That conjunction which hath no respect to the right ends for which marriage was ordain'd by God is no lawfull marriage.*

She condemned it in no uncertain terms, and without the strain of humour found in more literary representations of the same event. It was, simply, a sin.

No less sinful, at least socially if not quite as regarded their eternal souls, were those elderly ladies who talked too much in public and those who wore make-up.

> *I mett with Lady W___o, of whom it may be said she hath rent her face with painting. She is at least old as I am and hugely infirm yet affects the follys and aires of youth, displays her breasts and ears adorns both with sparkling gems while her eies look dead, skin rivell'd, cheeks sunk, shaking head, trembling hands, and all things bid shutt up shop and leave to traffick with such vanities or affectation of superfluities which signifys nothing but weakness.*

Lady Sarah's construction of what it meant to be old conformed quite closely to that of popular culture.

There is no melodrama in Rembrandt's portrayal of old women. They accept their age philosophically and still have an assured position in the family and in society. Below: Frau van Wassenhove of 1634 and the artist's own mother.

She also matched society's positive views of old age, although giving them her own distinctive twist. It was her *looks* as an older woman that Lady Sarah felt were the outward signifiers of a mature and wise person, who might now offer opinions concerning religion and political life, topics normally out of bounds for younger women. The proper course of life for the elderly was withdrawal from the social whirl into a contemplative state that focused, as the popular proverbs indicated, on approaching death and the meaning of life. For Lady Sarah, this was achieved with the aid of prolonged reading and extensive writing: 'Books every way assist mee, they comfort me in age, and solace me in solitariness.'[23]

Lady Sarah expressed the same views and held the same expectations of old age as peasants did in their proverbs and dramatists in their dialogues. The old were to be wise and sombre; they were to make peace with their lives and with their souls; and they were to be mocked for clinging too tightly to the ways of youth. As such, the very actions of the elderly themselves reinforced and gave credence to the stereotypes concerning old age.

Atropos, one of the three divinities who presided over human fate, was the goddess who cut the thread of life. Pietro Bellotti makes her stern and inflexible (right) but not without a touch of pity. Another portrait by the same artist (opposite) has the same expression and could even be the same model.

Overleaf:
True understanding of those approaching old age, as distinct from the production of class icons or conventional judgments based on prejudice, especially in the case of women, seems to have become commoner in the 17th century. Hyacinthe Rigaud's double portrait of his mother, Marie Serre, was painted in 1695, possibly as a guide for a sculptor. He lived on until 1743, and one can see in his work a foretaste of that interest in individual psychology that would lead to the rise of the novel in the 18th century.

The population of 17th-century Europe, when taken as a whole, was fairly static. Certain areas experienced staggering losses, such as those caused by war in the German States and the Italian experience of recurrent plague. From the mid-century, however, northern Europe began to experience a steady climb in population numbers, first in the Netherlands and then in England.[24] The reason was improved diet, economic developments leading to improved transportation (of food as well as goods, thus limiting the effects of regional famine) and 16th-century social-welfare programmes that were beginning to mature and bear fruit in terms of increased survival of poor mothers and children. The result was more people living into old age. The demographic data from Austria illustrates the general trend. In 1632, 5.5 per cent of the population was over the age of 60. In 1671, there were 6.9 per cent and, in 1779, the percentage of elderly inhabitants was 8.6.[25] In England and the Low Countries, the numbers of elderly began to increase earlier and reached more robust proportions.

The poor were also being rendered with compassion. Georges de La Tour was the son of a baker, and he was drawn to subjects close to ordinary life portrayed realistically, often with quiet suggestions of a religious or spiritual dimension. His Hurdy-Gurdy Player (right) and Old Peasant (opposite) both date from 1618–20.

'Saying Grace' by Nicolaes Maes (c. 1655) is still in the tradition of peasant piety. In some ways these paintings idealize poverty and labour – the woman is old and tired and the meal is a humble one. But details like the still-life of food in front of her and the cat clawing the table-cloth show close observation of real life.

The benefits of greater longevity were not shared equally by men and women. More women than men lived into old age and they also tended to live longer than men. Part of the reason for women's greater ability to survive, if not thrive, in old age was the steady and uninterrupted nature of their employments. They did not have to change the nature of their work with age, as men did. They did not find themselves without gender-appropriate occupations, nor have to establish themselves in new occupational networks. This consistency of the female experience helped to produce this greater longevity. But the relative dearth of aged males can also be explained by their general inability to navigate the challenges of old age. It seems that men could not manage well on their own or cope with a loss of independence.

Quattrocento Venice, however, contradicts this norm, with men outliving women.[26] This anomaly, while of an earlier date, bears particular importance as Venice was the home of the Commedia dell'Arte and the birthplace of Pantaloon. The pattern in Italy throughout the Renaissance was for older men to marry – and remarry – much younger women: the creation of Pantaloon can thus be understood as an expression of the resentment of youthful males. It can also just as readily be seen as underlining the importance of women to the survival of men in old age.

Life in 17th-century Europe presented many obstacles to reaching a ripe old age; disease, war and accident all played a role in ensuring that most marriages ended with the early death of a spouse. Remarriage and blended families were much more common then, despite popular ideas to the contrary today. When it came to marrying for the second or third time, gender and age played an arguably greater role than wealth in determining success. More widowers than widows remarried and did so at an overwhelmingly faster pace. The cultural commonplace of the husband-hunting widow reflected the nature of the marriage market, if not the actual sentiments of the women involved. In Austria, there were proportionally twice as many widows as widowers. In 1632, 4 per cent of all men were widowers, while 8.7 per cent of all women were widows. In 1671, this ratio was 3 per cent of men to 7.6 per cent of women. Looking ahead, the figures for 1779 show no abatement to this trend: 3.6 per cent of men were widowed, while women were nearly three more likely to remain unmarried, with 10.5 per cent of their number remaining widowed.[27] In the 17th century in the Netherlands, gentry widows remarried more often than in the 16th century, but the overwhelming trend was to remain widowed and to function as independent householders.[28] In 17th-century Rheims, men and women remarried at remarkably similar rates: 31 per cent of the men and 32.2 per cent of the women. This may well be a function of the city's business-based economy, which left many widows with desirable assets and so increased their remarriage prospects. Yet, even in such urban settings, men found remarriage easier: 63.4 per cent of the men remarried within the year, while only 30 per cent of the women did so.

Dutch gentry women, as well as artisan widows from Rheims, appear to have preferred to spend their old age as widows, heading independent households, something that they could more easily do as urban than rural widows. Here too age mattered. All widows between 35 and 50 years of age headed their own independent households in Rheims during the 17th century, even when they had adult children. But as they aged and declined physically, their dependence on others increased. Of those widows aged between 70 and 74, only half were still in independent accommodation. This does not mean that they moved in with their adult children: as these women aged, they found that fewer and fewer of their children were in close physical proximity and that other household structures were necessary. Nonetheless, the urge for autonomy was keenly felt and 40 per cent of widows still lived alone. As widows aged, their ability to re-establish married households decreased correspondingly. After 50, remarriage was a slim prospect and widows comprised the bulk of the aged female population. In short, particularly in the cities, 'once a widow, always a widow'.[29]

This state of affairs, with eagerly remarrying men and increasingly unmarriageable women, has traditionally been understood by scholars to demonstrate the patriarchical nature of 17th-century society, one that held men to be so desirable that even the old had no trouble marrying a young maid. In the same vein, old women, past childbirth and of diminishing beauty, were considered redundant to family formation and irrelevant to society. Recently, however, ideas about 17th-century society have begun to be revised. Perhaps men remarried so quickly because they fared poorly without the aid of a wife, who provided not only emotional support and companionship, but also very real housewifery and child-rearing skills. Men knew how to make money, but they did not necessarily know how to manage life within the private sphere. The following late 16th-century English example underlines a husband's need of his wife. In a petition to the overseers of the poor, it was explained that, 'whereby his wife is barred from his society and comfort, and hath been so barred this quarter of a year and upwards whereby he hath not that attendance and looking unto which a man in his case ought to have but is in great misery, his bed having never been made since the taking away of the stairs, nor none ever been above with him'.[30] Women, to follow this same line of reasoning, were better able to maintain themselves as independent householders, having already spent a lifetime combining housewifery and paid employment. Consequently, the large number of widowers who remarried – and promptly – may have done so out of a felt need.

Tied to this phenomenon in ways that are still not fully understood was the concomitant rise in numbers of never-married individuals, both male and female. As with the confirmed widow, north-west European towns possessed a disproportionate number of never-married women who presumably migrated there after their rural marriage prospects were exhausted, drawn to the city by its wide range of female employments and the greater ease of female self-sufficiency. Single women over 50 years of age accounted for more than 15 per cent of all women in towns such as Lyon or Rheims, while their rural counterparts were less plentiful but still common. Women headed roughly 24 per cent of all urban households, of whom only 7 per cent were married women, with the remainder single. Of the remaining female-headed families, widows made up 51 per cent and never-married women accounted for 42 per cent. In the Italian city-states and in the Iberian peninsula, unmarried women and men were incorporated into their extended families or found lives within religious orders. While single women were a not insignificant part of southern Europe's urban landscape, they were a commanding proportion of its elderly population.[31]

Among the intellectual elite of northern Europe, the 17th century – that 'age of reason and licentiousness' – experienced what a number of contemporary social critics termed 'bachelor-mania'. Leading lights, such as Boileau, Voltaire, La Bruyère and Corneille, were all confirmed bachelors. Worry nibbled at the edges of saloon society and tongue-and-cheek – and not so flippant – proposals were tendered to avert depopulation, including a tax on bachelors. Whether drawn there by high-minded enlightened principles or economic necessity, a sizeable number of old and single individuals were concentrated in the growing urban centres. Yet that did not mean they were isolated from friends and family, unloved and unwanted.

The place of residence and condition of tenure of the elderly had far-ranging consequences for the particulars of their lived experience. First, we must debunk the idea that the extended household, incorporating several generations and housing the aged, was Europe's universal norm. It was not, although it did exist. Given the realities of Europe's diverse geography and climate, its range of cultures and preoccupations, it is not surprising to find a variety of household types within its boundaries. The three-generation household predominated in Russia, the Baltic and the Balkans. Italy's sharecropping families

The family could be, but by no means invariably was, a tight-knit unit in which the old people had a natural place. The study of middle-class but poor households by the Le Nain brothers shows the three generations living happily together, the grandmother obviously in an honoured position.

also favoured this structure, and Spain employed a variation on it by rotating the care and accommodation of poor and aged parents between siblings. Independent, nuclear households were the norm in northern Europe. France, which straddled north and south, was neatly divided between the two tendencies.[32] Some Italian, German and French areas also formed extended households based on brothers, the *frèreche,* rather than on parents or grandparents.

The pre-industrial family of 17th-century Europe was far from a fixed institution, although each region had its traditions. And while certain areas favoured particular household structures, there remained much variation within the locality, as well as among families. Children were born, aged parents moved in, children left and family members of every age died, in a constant, fluid reconfiguring of daily living arrangements. The power of the elderly within family and household peaked and waned in relation to the structure of these living arrangements. It was as shifting as their household's composition.

When did the labouring poor retire? Never. Those who depended on skill rather than strength were lucky. The Danish painter Bernhard Keil's 'Lacemaker' could continue working into old age. Keil was a pupil of Rembrandt and later migrated to Rome. He specialized in genre scenes.

Jacopo Bassano was notable for introducing realistic scenes of contemporary life into his religious paintings. In his 'Adoration of the Shepherds' the old man (detail) has come straight from the fields of his native North Italy.

To be old and poor, as the Psalms so movingly remind us, was a fate to be feared and a state to be avoided. The lifestyle of the poor was physically and mentally demanding even for those in the pink of health. Begging, as was widely recognized at the time, took strength, stamina and mental agility. The labouring poor – day labourers and piece-workers – also faced similar demands on their physical and mental resources to patch together enough paid employment to feed themselves and their families. In both cases, scraping together the small sum required for each day's sustenance was an uncertain and unpredictable business. For those more advanced in age, the problems were compounded by the increasing fragility of their bodies.

BRIDGET HOLMES

Seventeenth-century Europe experienced a set of cultural changes that redefined what it meant to poor, as well as what society thought an appropriate response to the problem. Traditionally, the poor had been divided into the worthy – the aged, widows and orphans – who were poor through no fault of their own, and the unworthy – those who were poor because they chose not to work. Starting in the 16th century and finding its mature voice in the 17th, European society found itself placing a greater and greater emphasis upon this division among the poor, and the catchphrase 'discriminating relief' came to stand for a new intensity in winnowing out the good from the bad. The reasons behind this cultural preoccupation are clear. The 16th century bequeathed to the 17th a population problem begotten of years of exponential growth. It also passed on an economy beset by bouts of inflation and recession, and a fledgling and underdeveloped cash-based economy. A result of this economic conjunction of falling real wages, rising prices and unsettled economies was the emergence of a new category of poor: the labouring poor. These individuals were healthy, active, inclined to work or indeed working, but were nonetheless poor because they could not find jobs or the employment they did manage to secure was not adequate to meet their needs. For the first time Europe faced unemployment and underemployment. The distinction between worthy and unworthy poor consequently took on critical dimensions and shaded the world through which the aged poor had to navigate. Fortunately for them, they were unquestionably viewed as worthy of relief by virtue of their years, but the level of aid remained uncertain.

Bridget Holmes was a servant in the Stuart royal household who was still working hard at the age of 96, a distinction that brought her the honour of having her portrait painted by John Riley in 1686. Riley enjoyed painting working people (e.g. James II's nurse) but there is also an element here of parody of the formal Baroque portrait.

'The old couple' by Pietro Quast, who made a speciality of low-life scenes and beggars. Sympathetic as they may be, a hint of caricature is not far away.

An old peasant is still living with his children and grandchildren, and may still be the head of the household. David Teniers shows him being visited by a doctor for treatment to his foot. Research has shown that old women frequently lived alone, whereas old men typically continued to enjoy the comforts of family life.

Within this swirl of economic change, the indigent elderly tended to live out their final years in much the same way as they had always done – by hard and constant work, or depending on the kindness of others, and as the heads of their households, no matter how poor. The structure of their household could differ significantly from that of wealthier counterparts and was not confined to traditional family groupings. For example, old women sometimes lived with small orphaned or poor children in arrangements that benefited each party economically and socially. Alternatively, elderly women and widows might cluster together in all-female households, pooling resources and sharing responsibilities in their common drive for survival. Old women also lived alone. Old men, no matter how poor, typically lived in, and frequently headed, a household.

Some elderly people lived out their final years within the families of their adult children. However, this often proved to be a mixed blessing for those involved, as the younger generation were typically poor themselves and overburdened by children, leaving little food or money to spare for an aged parent. Barbara Ziegler, from Bächlingen in south-western Germany, described what the 1620s had been like for her: 'I stayed with my son for four years, but the food was bad and [he] supported me only with great effort.' It was not unusual in either city or countryside for poor families such as these to share a single room 'with an earth floor, mud walls, a thatched roof, a hole in the wall for a window and another for smoke to escape from the open hearth'. In 17th-century Bordeaux, 75 per cent of the labouring poor were crammed into such spaces, while in rural France things were not significantly better, with two or three families sharing an area of under 20 square yards. In cases where these arrangements lasted a number of years, it was a question of sharing poverty rather than wealth.[33]

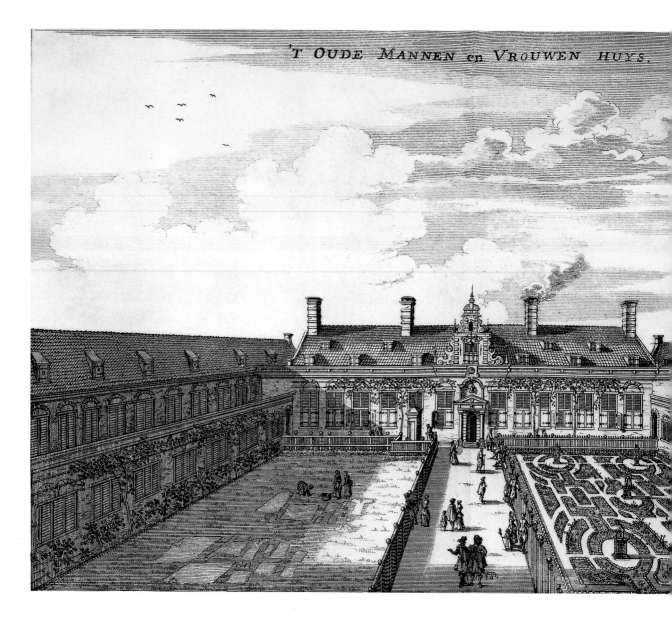

'T OUDE MANNEN en VROUWEN HUYS.

Care for the aged poor, which in the Middle Ages had been
in the hands of the monasteries, had by the 17th century, in
Protestant Northern Europe at least, been taken over by the
secular authorities. Many poorhouses were on a lavish scale,
such as this one for 'old men and women' in Amsterdam.

It is not surprising that even the best-intentioned families could crumple or dissolve under the strain of such conditions, casting the aged out to depend on their own resources. At such times, rather than attempting to reconstruct a household unit, the elderly could apply for a place in one Europe's hospitals. The medieval hospital had long and deep roots by the 17th century. These structures were originally designed to offer Christian charity to short-term occupants, such as 'pilgrims, travelling clerics, itinerant workers, travellers and migrants', in addition to a few long-term sojourners, 'the chronically ill, the aged, abandoned or orphaned ill'.[34] There, sharing a bed with whoever else needed one, the destitute elderly lived out their final years. To this medieval structure, the 17th century added a further layer of institutional support, as part of a pan-European effort to differentiate between different groups of the poor and a widespread drive towards the centralization of government and poor relief. Seventeenth-century hospitals were to specialize. The idle poor were to be confined and set to work in *Zuchthäusers*, *tuchthuis* or workhouses, as they were variously known. The aged poor were to have a place of their own. In fact, while increasing in size (yet rarely exceeding 20 beds) and number (even the biggest cities seldom boasted more than six), Europe's hospitals and institutions were rarely able to dedicate themselves to the relief of a specific group of people, including the elderly, but remained a chaotic jumble of people, problems and pestilences.

Despite a strong preference to remain at home and independent, the competition for a bed in such places was fierce. Seventeenth-century Brunswick had only 23 beds for every 1,000 inhabitants; Rheims had 24.94 per 1,000; and in Marne they were particularly scarce, with just 2.77 beds per 1,000. Furthermore, the elderly were only one of many eligible groups vying for accommodation, although they were privileged under the Danish Poor Law of 1683: 'the aged, sick, and infirm should be the first to be admitted to hospitals.' It has been suggested that 74 per cent of all applications were denied.[35]

Dire as their living conditions were, the elderly were still expected to be self-supporting in all but the most impossible circumstances. For those unable to work, friends, family and informal charity combined to provide for their barest needs. First and foremost, the aged poor were to work. As suggested earlier, this may have been easier for women than men. Begging – although repeatedly outlawed or licensed – was an option for the mobile elderly. Pawning clothes and household goods, selling possessions and borrowing money against some future windfall also complemented the day labouring and piecework that formed the critical, albeit insufficient, core of the aged's 'economy of makeshifts', to use Olwen Hufton's evocative phrase.

When poor relief failed – as it did for over half of those who needed it – there was nothing to do but beg. Beggars' lives were made more difficult by harsh laws that compelled them to move from parish to parish. Two such are portrayed in this engraving by Jacques Callot.

In the Catholic south charity to the poor was a religious duty. The haggard form of Murillo's beggars, most of whom are poor and disabled, highlight the shining sanctity of S. Diego of Alcalá, who has brought a cauldron of food. The tall man on the far right is a poor nobleman, whose code of honour forbids him to take up a trade but who sees no shame in begging.

Overleaf:
The inmates of a hospital in Utrecht solicit the charity of the public, a strangely moving group by Jan van Bijlert, c. 1630. Bijlert had trained in Rome and was influenced by Caravaggio before emphatically rejecting idealism in favour of realism and truth to nature.

Private charity in the Netherlands was supervised by boards of
governors, themselves advanced in years. Frans Hals painted a
number of group portraits to hang in the hospitals as reminders
of their pride and responsibility. These ladies are the governesses
of the Old Men's Almshouse of Haarlem. At this time, 1664,
the artist himself was in his 80s and poor; he received his fee in the
form of money and fuel.

Yet this was often not enough. At this juncture the elderly had two possible routes to obtaining public poor relief, depending on whether they were in the predominantly Roman Catholic and decentralized south or in the religiously mixed and governmentally centralized north. In countries such as Italy, religiously inspired and directed aid came from confraternities (for the lucky few), hospitals, parish funds and the Monti di Pietà, the commercial pawn shops that lent money at very low rates of interest. Less steady, but still important, were the gifts of money and food associated with religious rites, such as funerals and holy days.[36] In the north, such funds had been secularized and systematized in the 16th century; by the 17th they were under the auspices of some sort of overseer of the poor, who distributed them at weekly intervals. While considered worthy of relief, the elderly were not guaranteed it in either northern or southern Europe. Those aged individuals who found themselves with public or church-based assistance had to work hard to secure the support of bureaucracies. Poor relief, under any guise, was not for the idle.

The gap between those in poverty and those in plenty was gaping, but so too was the divide between the hard-working farmer and the idle noble. Despite the differences in comfort and style, each group shared the goal of transferring wealth and independence to the next generation, from the old to the young, and the same means of doing so, property and wealth in exchange for support.

Old-age support, for those below the very highest levels, could come in the form of bed-and-board contracts in which the farm or estate would be turned over to an adult child in exchange for specific provisions. Sometimes the elderly individual or couple was to be housed within the younger family's home, typically given the use of a specific room and rights to a certain amount of food. For those with multiple residences, a particular house could be designated for the ageing parents. Should, for example, Eleanora Bentivogli, the widow of Marquis Luigi Albergati, not remarry she was to have 'the free use of the apartments in the palazzo that she currently has the benefit of, for her own private use and for the use of the family both in summer and winter'.[37] Alternatively, and particularly towards the close of the 17th century, the aged would be supported with cash payments from the heir or from an annuity investment. Thanks to the developing cash economy, particularly in northern Europe, this sort of arrangement became increasingly common both in terms of its usage and the broader social base of people – middling farmers and merchants – availing themselves of it. In northern Europe, which placed a particular value on nuclear-family household independence, this appeared to have been an especially attractive option as it allowed elderly people greater freedom to choose their place of residence.[38]

Such exchanges, it has been suggested, normally took place roughly at age 60. They certainly coincided with the marriage of the heir or the illness or death of a parent.[39] In fact, the formation of the younger household was often dependent upon such a generational stepping-down. The moderately wealthy continued to be independent and to maintain household authority until they could no longer physically run the farm or chose to step aside. The timing of the transfer was in the hands of the older people and it placed them in a powerful position. Among the very wealthy and noble, power, authority and the family's wealth were controlled by the patriarch often long into old age. Reliant upon mental agility rather than a strong back, he felt no pressing need to relinquish headship at the first sign of physical decline.

When infirmity struck, the very wealthy could be tended by their adult offspring, hired nurses or by distant relatives who exchanged their own upkeep for care-giving. In Roman Catholic areas, such as the Italian and Iberian peninsulas, the very wealthy also drew upon a long tradition of paying a convent or monastery to act as their old age home.[40]

These contracts and arrangements are the clear antecedents of modern retirement. What set them apart from modern forms was their timing: at a moment of the elderly's choosing, very late in life and frequently close to death. (The Austrian term *ableben*, 'to die', was also used at this time to mean 'retirement'.)[41] In this way, the elderly were not forced to leave their economic and political spheres at a (relatively young) set age. Instead, by having the power to choose when to hand over wealth, power and authority, they maintained a significant amount of self-respect, as well as a continued presence in the running of farm, village, town or state. For the marginally prosperous, as well as for the fabulously wealthy, there was a shared Europe-wide ethos that valued autonomy and self-sufficiency – the very same values that we saw among the poor. Yet, except in a few most unusual cases, such as Charles V's mid-16th-century abdication as Holy Roman Emperor, retirement as we now know it was very rare. It developed slowly, and incompletely, among the elites at the end of the 17th century. This appears to have been tied directly to the developing economic culture that challenged property-based wealth as the only means of garnering respect and acknowledged the status and rewards that money could buy.

Widows were often dependent on the sons who inherited their husbands' property, although a widespread custom guaranteed them a third of his wealth. But that was by no means certain. In Louis Le Nain's 'Visit to Grandmother', (opposite) she clearly enjoys authority and appears to live comfortably.

In the family of the Dutch artist Jan Steen the same happy atmosphere reigns. Historical records about financial customs can tell us little about the emotional ties that bonded the generations together.

This self-determination was afforded only to privileged, 'male' old age. Old age for wealthy women took a distinctively different tint. While their husbands were still living, they shared the full weight of his continued authority. As widows, these women remained unquestionably privileged, possessing an inherent authority and independence based on rank. As we have seen, most elderly widows preferred to remain unmarried and exercised even greater freedoms as mistresses of their own households. Yet, except for female monarchs ruling in their own right, wealthy widowhood in old age was still a 'dependent' state. Widows stepped away from their traditional roles neither of their own free will nor at the moment of their choosing, but as determined ultimately by their husbands' decisions or deaths. And, while widows could be extremely rich, often that too was out of their hands. Their very maintenance provisions had been dictated by their husbands or fathers. In other words, the amount of power and wealth they wielded, as well as the comfort of their surroundings, was primarily – despite the well-established 'widows' third' that guaranteed them one-third of their husband's estate – provided by the generosity of their husbands and the foresight of their fathers. Because of typical marriage patterns, with wives younger than husbands, widows could face a period of many years without an established role within household or society. What was acceptable, as Lady Sarah Cowper vividly recorded, was a withdrawal – a 'retirement' – into contemplation and piety.

While parents certainly loved their children, and children their parents, the very nature of much of 17th-century Europe's transfer of wealth engendered a fair amount of inter- and intra-generational hostility. Choosing one child to receive the bulk of the patrimony was a well-known source of trouble, acknowledged by all concerned: 'I implore each of my sons,' wrote the Marquis of Yerre just after the close of the century, 'to believe that I love them as tenderly as the oldest, even though I have not been able to make them heirs along with him, but have resolved to appoint a single heir for the good of the family.'[42] The main heir's good fortune was not without its disadvantages. An aged parent's continued control over both house and estate left the adult son in a state of prolonged dependency, either unable to marry at all or placing both him and his spouse in submission. In late 17th-century Upper Provence, for example, until the death of his father, the heir was 'completely subservient to his father economically, socially and legally, just as though he were still a child'.[43] He could not, without his father's permission, buy, sell, trade, make a will or complete any legal contract. Trouble arose repeatedly as a consequence.

Early exchanges of wealth were discouraged. Ballad, tale and proverb all warned the aged man of the dangers of relinquishing control. He, it was promised, would soon find himself living worse than the servants. We have already met the proverb 'To sit on the children's bench is hard for the old'. Another peasant proverb is more direct still: 'To hand over is no longer to live.'[44] Mature men might find themselves at the foot of the table, and mature housewives could find themselves without a house to run. The potential for problems was as varied as the individuals involved, but it does not mean difficulties were never resolved and that there was no love or affection between the generations. As Lady Sarah's description of the 'kind fraud' of the quilt counters so clearly shows, a liveable and loving solution could often be found.

Among the many misconceptions about old age in the past is the idea that few individuals lived long enough to see their grandchildren or to know their own children as adults. This we now know to be false. Generally speaking, in the 17th century a 33-year-old individual would have a 64.3 per cent chance of having at least one parent still living, and 73 per cent of them would also have young children of their own.[45] Clearly, people did live long enough to know their grandchildren. Indeed, by the end of the 18th century, just over half of the children in Vernon, France, could expect to have their grandparents alive at their birth; one-third of them at age ten; and just over 10 per cent at age 20. The eldest grandchild had the greatest potential interaction with a grandparent. Europe's marriage patterns, typically involving a younger wife, meant that the maternal grandmother (usually the youngest of all four grandparents) had the longest opportunity of interacting with her grandchildren.[46] Indeed, the existence of three-generation households alone tells us that the demographic grandparent existed in 17th-century Europe.

Natural affection does not change from century to century. Rembrandt's sketch of an old woman with her grandchild could have been made today.

Only at the end of the century does the social, 'spoil-the-child', modern-looking 'grandparent' appear. Apart from acting as conduits of wealth, the elderly, particularly women, were actively engaged in child-minding and education, as witnessed by the 'Dame Schools', as they were called in England. Grandparents were also invaluable when their adult children were facing a crisis. Repeatedly during times of sickness, they, again particularly women, became substitute spouses and care-givers, running the household and nursing the sick. Nowhere does the grandmother's reconstituted role of mistress of the home come more forcefully into view than at the death of an adult child and/or child's spouse. When grandchildren were orphaned and a grandparent was still alive, a new household of grandchild/parent was formed in an arrangement that proved beneficial to both generations. Quick and nimble arms and legs could be as useful to the old as a bed and roof were to the young. While these relationships could be warm and loving, as well as mutually rewarding, they were not quite the sentimental relationships of the modern West.

Yet, as with the notions of modern retirement, the modern social role of the grandparent was just beginning to develop at the end of the century, among the same type of people, and for related reasons. The shift to a new definition of what it meant to be a grandparent may have been a direct result of the growing acceptance and use of this 'retirement', particularly among the wealthy, combined with the well-embedded notion that those who could spend their final years free from labour should spend it withdrawn from active society, in the contemplation of their life and readying themselves for coming death. Old age, traditionally viewed as a period of social isolation, was being experienced by greater numbers. Having been used to the affairs of household and state, many found it difficult to relinquish authority while still physically active. In other words, the idea of the sentimental grandparent arose as part of a search by active and leisured elderly people to find 'a positive, active and integrated' role for themselves in a stage of life that had previously been viewed as socially marginalized.[47] It was the very wealthy who could first afford this type of old age; it was also women who were most likely to experience it; and, consequently, it was grandmothers who first redefined its meaning.

What is striking about the old-age experience in 17th-century Europe is what it shares with that of the elderly of other centuries, including our own. And while the details and particulars are certainly different, the over-arching themes – the worries and preoccupations, the desires and dreams – can immediately be recognized over much of Western history. The elderly worried about losing their health, and with it their financial and household independence. They worried about becoming a 'burden' to their friends and family. The rich worried about becoming poor, while the poor worried about survival. Death and their spiritual state preoccupied many aged individuals, as did the preservation of their self-respect in the face of physical and mental decline. Consequently, they desired the respect of others, credit for hard-earned wisdom and a meaningful existence. They dreamed of the wellbeing of their children and grandchildren. These traits may be a universal part of the human condition.

There are, however, aspects of 17th-century old age that do not resonate in the modern West. The staggered and strongly idiosyncratic onset of old age does not sit well against the contemporary world's mandatory age of retirement or the onset of age-indexed pensioning. Also distinctive to the pre-modern world were medical definitions of old age, based on the four humours, which portrayed the elderly as drying up and wasting away, while post-menopausal women were viewed with suspicion, if not fear. Religion dominated early modern life and, consequently, Christianity's understanding of a good old age went far in shaping society's expectations of the elderly and the elderly's expectations of themselves. The 17th-century stage, elite literature and the sayings of peasants belittled and mocked the old in ways that few groups are targeted today. Finally, and most significantly, elderly men held very real power within their own households, as arbiters of inheritance for both their wives and children. These are some of the key components that made the 17th-century experience of old age distinctive. But despite these differences, especially in the constructed understanding of old age, it becomes clear that while the elderly were perceived differently in the 17th century, the contours of their lived experience are hauntingly familiar today.

We have not yet discovered all the aspects of old age about which we are curious or that shed important light on our understanding of the 17th century. In some areas we already have a finely crafted picture of the lives of elderly people, images that are as sharp, crisp and detailed as a still life by one of the great Northern Masters. Other topics are rendered in a much more allegorical framework, more prescriptive than descriptive, reminding us of Italian paintings of the Renaissance in their telling of stories and fashioning of truths. The image that emerges, still incomplete in many ways, is of a 17th-century old age comprising a full and vibrant range of activities and interests, needs and concerns, and pleasures and pursuits.

The Age of Reason brought a shift in popular attitudes
to old age. There is much less emphasis on religion
and preparation for death, and more on sympathy and
understanding. The old woman in Daniel Chodowiecki's
engraving of 1758 no longer reads a work of devotion
but a book of poems and songs.

5

DAVID G. TROYANSKY **THE 18TH CENTURY**

The 18th century appears to have been a transitional era in the history of old age, as in so many areas of life. Long-term demographic trends, though still relatively consistent, already showed some signs of change, as adult life expectancy increased. The socio-economic order began to experience some of the alterations associated with modernity, and modern political culture emerged in both revolutionary and non-revolutionary contexts, with important consequences for the aged. Most noticeably, particularly in France, old age underwent changes in cultural representations which had their own impacts on how people lived their lives. They included a shift from the religiosity of previous centuries to greater worldliness, and a literary and artistic turn from comic derision aimed at aged characters to greater respect and senti-mentality. By contrast, in England cultural continuity persisted across the century. English sources suggest that a great variety of cultural representations, both 'positive' and 'negative', coexisted.

Some population shifts occurred in the period, but not the demographic ageing that would take place in the 19th and 20th centuries, when fertility rates began to decline. In the 18th century, the age composition of European populations remained roughly what it had been throughout the early modern era. Those aged 60 and up constituted anywhere from 6 to 10 per cent. In France they averaged 8 per cent, while English figures clustered around 9 or 10 in the early part of the century and dipped below 8 towards the end, when fertility was on the rise.[1] But some rural pockets were older as a result of out-migration of younger people in search of work. Moreover, when one sets aside the large contingent of youth, one recognizes that those over 60 could represent 13, 15 or even 18 per cent of all those over 20 in the second half of the 18th century. The aged were present, and they were visible.

Despite the fact that the percentage of the aged in the overall European population was not yet increasing, there is evidence of greater survival of adults into old age. Life expectancy of those surviving childhood increased, and average age at death for adults also went up. From the 1740s to the 1820s, the share of French 20-year-olds reaching 60 went up from 41.9 per cent of men and 43 per cent of women to 59 and 58.1 per cent respectively, while female life expectancy at age 20 increased from 34.2 to 40.2 years.[2] At the same time, women in some parts of Europe were having their last child at earlier ages, thus increasing their own chances of surviving until all their children were grown. But socio-economic differences mattered. Elites had more of an experience and expectation of old age. No wonder literary and artistic representations of the aged became so common, and they often distinguished between the more comfortable experience of elites and the greater challenge for the poor.

Demographic and historical study of the aged in the 18th century tends to focus on those over the age of 60. Much prescriptive literature of the period uses 60 as the onset of advanced age, but historians have debated where to place the threshold. One argues that people entered old age earlier then, that physical decline often set in before the age of 60. He tries to identify when mature adults had, on average, either five or ten years to live and considers those ages as possible thresholds of old age. With a threshold in the 50s, the proportion of the visibly aged in the population was greater than historical demographers usually presume.[3]

Some social change has been observed in the 18th century, but there is no simple way of describing the impact on older people of proto-industrial development or urbanization. Small-scale industry in some parts of the countryside permitted earlier marriage and the creation of independent households outside the authority of elders, and the growth of cities meant greater individualism at all ages. But throughout Europe, much remained of traditional intergenerational relations, whether in terms of occupational inheritance or transmission of property. The key themes of participation, wellbeing and status functioned together.[4] Except for those who had sufficient wealth to withdraw if they chose, the aged tried to maintain their wellbeing by continuing to participate in economic affairs; they thus held their status as long as possible. Focusing on autonomy, responsibility and authority,[5] we find that many achieved a good old age, an independent situation as defined by contemporary norms, with harmony between the ageing individual, their family and the wider community. Autonomy was a general goal, at least in western Europe, and responsibilities were shared among immediate family members, kin and communities. But the idea that the old required care applied only to the very old, the infirm and the poor.

North-western Europe was characterized by the predominance of nuclear households, the establishment of new households at marriage and the maintenance of independence as long into old age as possible. The English historical record indicates a particularly strong ideal of independence. Independence, however, was relative. Try as they might to maintain autonomy, older people were enmeshed in familial and community networks, and they might call on those networks as physical decline set in. Ever since the 16th century, English communities had made arrangements through the Poor Law to support the neediest elders, at least in a minimal way.

As some women achieved greater independence the fortunate could reasonably aspire to a 'good old age' – naturally the richer the better. Louis de Carmontelle was a perceptive observer of French upper-class manners before the Revolution in both words and pictures. His portrait of Madame Doublet conducting legal business with her brother the Abbé Legendre is a sly comment on the comforts of self-satisfaction.

The English 'system' differed from continental European arrangements. The latter depended largely on religious and sometimes royal institutions, whereas:

> *The Old Poor Law provided pensions to the dependent elderly and occasional payments in cash and kind to those who were not yet fully decrepit... Once a community decided to pension an older individual, it was, in effect, making a life-long commitment to that person. As his or her needs changed, the parish altered its relief to meet the requirements of that individual. Moreover, the parish's support for its aged residents was based both on the legal framework of the poor laws and the cultural principle that a community was obligated to give economic aid to those who were old, poor, and unable to earn their own living. Throughout the country, the elderly were seen as particularly deserving of economic assistance not merely from their families but also from their communities. A number of elderly men and women must have received relief from their families, but between 15 and 33 percent of the aged people in each of the communities studied here relied on their parish for some assistance, and often this assistance was so extensive that it must have been their main source of income.*[6]

In feudal areas of Europe, landlords could dictate transmission of authority from older to younger peasants, but in general such matters were in the hands of families themselves. In eastern and southern Europe, household arrangements varied, with more extended and complex households and greater co-residence of aged parents and married children than in the north and west. Pre-mortem transmission of property and retirement arrangements existed in northern and west-central Europe, but in Hungary older people maintained status as heads of extended and multiple family households.[7] Different customs and legal systems determined which child co-resided with aged parents and whether peasant 'retirement' occurred. Where it did, it could come at the expense of the younger adult generation. Thus, tension was focused on intergenerational relationships within the family. But we know about such tension only when conflict spilled into the legal arena or when notarized documents sought to prevent antagonism from developing over control of property.

One of the most researched areas in which generations notarized their relations was southern France. A classic study of 18th-century Languedoc claims that parents had to lure children into respectful behaviour while maintaining authority as long as possible but that when they could no longer exercise that authority they were poorly treated, marginalized and, in some cases, poisoned.[8] Further east, in Provence, a stem-family system seems to have existed in which the marriage of children offered an occasion for the older generation to look ahead.[9] Marriage contracts laid out a plan for an eventual transmission of property, but elders made sure they were guaranteed support. Such documents spelled out rights to particular houses or rooms, precise amounts of grain and wine, even the right to continue walking in one's old fields to pick grapes. Retired parents might collect payments from several children or might migrate from house to house. Sharecropping arrangements might include old-age pensions in kind.

Some historians, looking at high cultural sources, see a reduction in tension in the 18th century. The fate of King Lear in the play's reworkings after Shakespeare's death is exemplary. The classic representation of intergenerational tension and the folly of pre-mortem transmission of property was turned into a celebration of familial piety, complete with happy ending. There was even a peasant version of the play.[10] But on the land the problem remained. Notarized contracts spelled out retirement arrangements. Parents passed on ownership but retained use of their property. Reading those contracts poses a problem. To what extent did they spell out real roles or prevent abandonment? To what

Some professions were inevitably dominated by the elderly, since it took a lifetime to rise to senior positions. This was particularly true of the law. Hogarth's engraving called 'The Bench' (1758) satirizes pomposity and mental decline. Two of the judges are fast asleep.

extent did they just guarantee support and civility? Peasant proverbs continued to warn against placing too much trust and authority in the younger generation: 'One father can support one hundred children, but a hundred children wouldn't know how to support one father.' 'To hand over is no longer to live.' 'To sit on the children's bench is hard for the old.' 'Do not take your clothes off before you go to sleep.'[11] Some of the historical literature takes maintenance contracts as descriptive of reality; some see them as a form of insurance. But the key is that such intergenerational tension operated within the family, not at the level of society at large, where change occurred relatively slowly. Only later would intergenerational conflict occur at the societal level, while families maintained a new-found domestic solidarity in the face of historical change.

Some historical literature has begun to look at relationships that skip generations. In other words, we have the history of grandparenthood. And the first large study of the topic sees the late 18th and 19th centuries as crucial. Grandparents played a larger role in their grandchildren's households in southern France than in the north, thus emphasizing the impact of different residential patterns and inheritance practices. A new representation of grandparents can be recognized in French culture in the late 18th century, preparing the way for the great stereotype of 19th-century grandparents spoiling their children's offspring. Whether in memoir or fiction, grandparents began to loom large in the world of children, and the very terms for grandfather and grandmother referred less to lineage and more to the particular relationship with grandchildren.[12]

The happy family became a popular subject in 18th-century art. The critic and philosopher Diderot urged painters to show domestic and moral scenes rather than those featuring power and sensuality. This led to a wave of sentimental pictures, from Chodowiecki (right) to Jacques-Auguste-Catherine Pajou (opposite), where the artist represents himself in the 1790s, standing at the back with his father the sculptor Augustin Pajou, and his wife and baby son, who is admiring himself in the mirror. Behind them is the artist's sister Catherine Flore, once married to the sculptor Clodion. The portrait at the back is of Martin Pajou, the father's father, so four generations are represented.

At a lower social level, sentimentality had to yield to realism, but there is still an element of sweetness in Italian artist Giacomo Ceruti's 'Peasant Family', worn down as they are with toil. Is the old man the father or grandfather of this sad little family?

The analysis of wills also reveals attempts by spouses, particularly husbands, to ensure the maintenance of their partners. Increasing poverty at the end of the 18th century seems to have led spouses to seek to help each other more effectively, although awareness of greater need doesn't necessarily indicate an increase in sentimental attachment.[13]

Some cultural representations marginalized solitary older women, but there were also much more positive realities.

> *Single women… were the women best positioned to enjoy a positive old age… in seventeenth- and eighteenth-century England, old single women of middling status experienced later life as a period of autonomy, activity and authority. As they aged, these women gained more residential and economic independence, increased their economic, religious and civic activity, extended their familial and civic authority, and continued the social relationships that were significant to them.*[14]

This constitutes a period of relative strength in women's lives.[15] In 18th-century Toulouse, women are found lodging together and helping each other maintain their autonomy as well as sharing friendship.[16]

In 18th-century England, the ideal was to be independent in the later years; the aged were felt to have a *responsibility* to be autonomous. Relations between adult generations were more often characterized by help from older to younger than the reverse. As on the European continent, goods flowed down the generations. In England, close family, kin and communities shared responsibility for the weakened aged, but there is little evidence of legal requirements that children provide help to aged parents. Elsewhere, however, such responsibilities were enforced, as in early modern Rome, where 'a game of mutual manipulation by individuals and institutions over the collective circulation of resources mobilized to help the needy. The end result of this game was a social system wherein welfare responsibilities and welfare provisions belonged to both the family and the collectivity.'[17] In such a place, the locus of tension remains strongest within the family, but oversight has extended to the community.

More 'modern' ways of managing old age emerged with the development of public service pensions in England, France and German-speaking territories. Pioneers in that area were English customs workers and French tax farmers. Gradually others were offered such benefits, with major developments in central Europe by the late 18th century. Pensions still only affected minorities, but they took the issue beyond the setting of family, household and local community to that of an entire society. Pensions, which had developed originally out of individual arrangements, were evolving into more formal manifestations of the growth of the state. By the late 17th and 18th centuries, states studied their own populations and economies. Texts in the genres of political arithmetic and public administration began to speak of age groups, and early statisticians prepared the way for the more sophisticated demographic studies of the 19th century.[18]

Grandparents play an increasingly major role in family life and therefore in art too. Trained in Paris, Antoine de Favray spent most of his long life (1706–92) in Malta, where he painted this engaging portrait of Veneranda Abela with her grandson Pietro.

The ideals of the French Revolution, which go back to the *philosophes* and such writers as Rousseau, exalted the virtues of the family and the brotherhood of man. This 'Fête de la Réunion', typical of many such festivals held in rural France in the 1790s, centres not only on brotherly love but also on the elders of the village. On the right an old couple are enthroned under an inscription 'Respect à la Vieillesse', while on the left a very old woman is helped by her children and grandchildren to join the celebrations.

At the end of the 18th century, new regimes sought to anchor themselves and create continuity by appealing to elders, and elaborated new ideas of entitlement. The founders of the American republic were cast as founding fathers in an attempt to stabilize a new regime, but whether the important emergence of youth as a challenge to the authority of elders took place in the revolutionary era or much later in the 19th century is debatable.[19] A comparison with the political imagery of the French Revolution yields an appreciation of American representation of a founding generation that loses little power as it ages. Not so in revolutionary France, which has been characterized as a world of founding brothers rather than fathers. Indeed, one influential study employs a psychoanalytic framework to portray those brothers as parricides.[20] Nonetheless, revolutionary France also tried to legitimize itself through patriotic images of elders, and sought to provide assistance to the needy aged.

The French Revolutionary *fête de la vieillesse* was one of a series of secular holidays that sought to anchor society in such natural phenomena as the seasons and the ages of life. In villages, towns and cities, French authorities in the 1790s, particularly in the second half of the decade, organized celebrations of local elders, praising them, parading them through the streets, decorating their residences, singing secular hymns and generally trying to root republican legitimacy in an idea of natural authority and honour.[21]

For example, in the city of Metz, a broadsheet announcing the festival described how republican old age was to be treated: 'Ancient republics had placed at the rank of a citizen's duties respect for old people; the French nation is the only one whose legislators established a public ceremony, a national festival, uniquely devoted to solemnly honouring old age.' The municipal administration announced the events of the day. Four healthy individuals, two fathers, aged 75 and 68, and two mothers, aged 75 and 83, possessing the best reputations for probity, patriotism and virtue, were singled out. At 7 a.m., ten young people gathered at the town hall and, accompanied by National Guardsmen and National Guard musicians, went to the old people's homes to decorate their doors with wreaths. After returning to the town hall, the young people, accompanied by musicians, a delegation of others over 60, the municipal authorities and Guardsmen, formed a cortège at 9 a.m. to meet the four honoured elders and accompany them to the town's esplanade, where speeches were delivered, the elders were honoured and the orchestra performed patriotic music. Later in the day there were artillery salvos and children's foot-races. The next year, the festival was an occasion for awarding prizes to the best students in the German class in the local secondary school.[22]

In a Parisian festival, an administrator named Moussard praised the city's elderly, admiring their physical characteristics and calling them both judge and seer.

> *It is with the eye of wisdom and experience that you judge the past; more initiated in the secrets of nature, you embrace the future; this future, you know, is that of peace, of recompense, of immortality. The benefits you will have spread about you, the virtues you will have cultivated, will perpetuate themselves in the hearts of your families, of your friends, of your disciples; you will always live in the recognition of beautiful sentiments; the memory of good never dies.*

He concluded, 'Love live the Republic where old men preside.'[23]

The festivals were attempts to ground the French republic in a humanist and classical soil. They were occasions to lament revolutionary excess and to call for prudence and moderation. As another Parisian administrator put it,

> *To honour old age solemnly is in a way to consummate the great work of universal morality; it is to enlarge the spirit, make tender the heart, stir up humanity, make those who are about to quit life taste it again, and consecrate the life of good people; it is finally to sow upon the earth the seed of the most essential social qualities, paternal love, filial love, patriotism, and consequently bravery. When one sincerely loves his family and his country, he is ready to defend them day and night.*[24]

Revolutionary social welfare legislation also expressed a desire to honour the aged. It emerged as French social thinkers moved the debate from ideas of religious charity to ideas of the social good, thus developing themes that had emerged in the Enlightenment. Proposals for old-age assistance for dependants of soldiers, former priests, workers and peasants proliferated, some suggesting aid at home, others hospitalization. Because of military demands on the national treasury, little was actually accomplished. Nevertheless, the outlines of a modern system of social welfare were already in place, and legislation addressing old-age security in the modern period often referred back to the Revolution as an era of unfulfilled promise.[25]

More successful was the attempt to provide old-age protections for civil servants. Strengthening of national bureaucracy was one of the results of the Revolution, and mechanisms for providing pensions provided a model for modern-day social security. Eighteenth-century states had begun working out formal careers for their civil servants; state development in Revolutionary Europe quickened the pace. Pension schemes emerged independently in different government ministries. They would be brought together and standardized in the 19th century. Then they served as a model for the rest of the population in an era of social security.

A far bleaker picture of old age is offered by Giuseppe Zucchi: 'What is the point of wanting something if you can't have it?' One old man has found consolation in religion, the other still wants to enjoy life.

An early old-age pension was awarded by Napoleon in January 1807 to a Pole called Nerecki. The act was generous, although in view of his age — allegedly 117 — not perhaps unduly expensive. The painting is by Jean-Charles Tardieu, who made a career immortalizing Napoleon's greatness.

HENRY JENKINS of *ELLERTON*, in *YORKSHIRE*,
Who lived to the Surprizing Age of 169
Which is 16 Years longer than Old Parr

The state certainly played an important role in preparing for modern ways of organizing old age. So did the medical profession. Medical texts specializing in the diseases of the aged or defining some ailments by age group began to appear with greater frequency. They coexisted with publications that still told traditional tales of exceptionally long life. Thomas Parr, the 152-year-old Shropshire peasant, supposedly born in 1483, was still written about in the 18th century, when other long-livers were compared to him. Aged Germans who grew new teeth were the object of popular fascination. Annibal Camous, the so-called Marseilles Socrates, who supposedly died at 121 in 1759, was a figure of local legend.[26] Despite such tales, guides to ageing well referred less and less to fantastic tales and spiritual matters and concentrated more on disease, diet and health. Jean Goulin, writing on the ailments of old men, mentioned 'gout, rheumatism, weakened eyesight, weakened legs, catarrh, torpor, apoplexy, heartburn, lethargy, paralysis, diarrhea, scurvy, and the drying-up of seminal fluid and tears'.[27] His book on women's medicine claimed that the menopause resulted in great benefits.

ANNIBAL CAMOUX DE MARSEILLE .

mort en 1759, agé de 122 ans

A la raison toujours fidele
Pour compagne il eut la gayeté,
Pour recompense la Santé.
Voulés vous vivre heureux? prenés le pour modele

LE
SOCRATE
MARSEILLOIS,
OU
PARTICULARITÉS
INSTRUCTIVES
ET
INTÉRESSANTES
POUR L'HUMANITÉ.
Au sujet du fameux ANNIBAL
CAMOUX de Marseille, décédé
il y a environ 12 ans à l'âge de 122.

ORNÉ DE SON PORTRAIT.

A MARSEILLE.
Chez JEAN MOSSY, Imprimeur du Roi & de
la Marine, & Libraire, au Parc.

M. DCC. LXXIII.
AVEC PERMISSION.

'**The Marseille Socrates**', Annibal Camous, who died in 1759,
was said to have lived to be 121. 'Always faithful to reason,
he had gaiety for his companion and health for his reward.
If you want to live happy, follow his example'.

Just as medical texts were identifying the illnesses of particular ages, so medical institutions began a process of specialization. Reformers desired to distinguish between the aged, the poor, the unwanted and the sick; all had traditionally been deposited together. Institutions for the aged ranged from large hospitals to smaller hospices. They were still often associated with religious orders, but their medical role became increasingly important.[28]

Scientific literature emphasized the physical reality of ageing. The most influential text was that of Buffon, in which he explains how life ends by degrees.

As one advances in age the bones, cartilage, membranes, flesh, skin, and all the fibres of the body become more solid, harder, and drier, all the parts recede and contract, all movements become slower, more difficult, the circulation of fluids is accomplished with less freedom, transpiration diminishes, secretions are altered, the digestion of foods becomes slow and laborious, the nourishing juices are less abundant, and not being able to be received in most fibres that have become too weak, they no longer serve for nutrition; these too solid parts are already dead, for they cease to nourish themselves; thus the body dies little by little and by parts, its movement diminishes by degrees, life extinguishes itself by successive changes, and death is only the last limit of this succession of degrees, the last nuance of life.[29]

Those who never retired could belong to all walks of life, from Betty Dick, the town-crier of Dalkeith (left), who was 85 when she died in 1778, to Thomas Guy (opposite), the philanthropist who spent his large fortune on charitable causes, including the foundation of Guy's Hospital, London, and who lived to be 81.

Within the illustration:

A Table of Interest.

Plan of the Hospital

Memorandums for making
my last Will sometime or other.
To my Son Ⅱ I give £ 5 0 p. an.
To my Daughter as long as she
keeps single £ 20. p. an.
To building & endowing an Hospital & erecting my Statue
£100.000.

'**To show virtue as pleasing**, vice as odious, to expose what
is ridiculous, that is the aim of every honest man who
takes up the pen, the brush or the chisel', wrote Diderot.
No painter followed these precepts more obediently than
Jean-Baptiste Greuze. His 'Dame de Charité' is a fine
example. Here a young mother and her daughter visit an
elderly bedridden couple and the little girl is urged to
present a purse. The scene is made all the more touching
by the others waiting their turn, a nun and two youths.
The old man has been a soldier, as we see from the sword
hanging on the wall.

Scientific and medical literature, whatever its validity, attempted to demystify the process of growing old. The medicalization of old age was part of a larger story that was related to the general secularization of European culture. One of the great themes of 18th-century historiography in France is that of dechristianization, which played an important role in the story of old age. It was a key element in the history of death — testaments referred less frequently to the Virgin Mary, demanded fewer masses and made smaller religious bequests. Books of advice, religious practices and literary representations also reveal significant changes. Rather than focus on the next world, a more secularized culture paid attention to the last years in this one. The image of the patriarch or matriarch was softened and had an impact on representations of both old age and death. Scenes of interaction between grandparents and grandchildren as well as of gatherings around deathbeds became newly sentimental.

The literature on old age in 18th-century France emphasizes a philosophical shift from an earlier religious, Augustinian view of old age to a more secular Ciceronian one: that is, from religious retreat to retirement. In the 16th and 17th centuries, religious texts had emphasized the challenge of death rather than that of old age. The aged body served as a symbol of worldliness, sin and decay, an obstacle to salvation, while the soul was thought of as more youthful. Such ideas continued to appear in some religious texts that encouraged disgust for life and a yearning for death. Thus, a 17th-century book on scorning life and wishing for death entered a fifth edition in 1713 and continued to devalue old age: 'What advantage will we find in living longer? Do not old age and the infirmities that accompany it render us insupportable for others and for ourselves? Consider an old man overburdened with years, his spirit dejected, his body exhausted, his face lined with wrinkles, his eyes half closed, his voice trembling, his head bent toward the earth as if seeking a sepulcher in which to throw himself: is not this a kind of monster in nature?' Bishop Bossuet, writing at the end of the 17th century but read for decades afterwards, referred to old age as 'ordinarily... soiled with the filth of avarice'. Still in the 1730s a text on sin and salvation could belittle earthly longevity: 'What good does it do Adam, Methuselah, or Noah to have lived each nearly a thousand years: are they any less dead? What difference is there between their life, long as it might have been, and that of those who have only lived forty or fifty years? For there remains for the ones and the others only the thought of having been.'[30]

By the middle of the 18th century, texts on growing old evoked such religious themes less commonly. A Ciceronian tradition looked back to the *On Old Age* of classical Roman literature, which described the good old age of the officer class. It responded to common complaints about old age and argued in favour of continued activity and eventually the possibility of retirement from office. A more secular view of ageing focused on the body. Baron d'Holbach described the last stage of life: 'in old age, man fades entirely, his fibres and his nerves stiffen, his senses become dull, his eyesight gets cloudy, his ears become callous, his ideas become disjointed, his memory disappears, his imagination is muffled; what then becomes of his soul? Alas! it gives way at the same time as his body.' He compared religious views unfavourably with 'natural' ones: 'Nature tells children to honor, to love, to heed their parents, to support them in old age; religion says to prefer the oracles of their god and to spurn father and mother when it is a matter of divine interest.'[31] His emphasis was on reciprocity between the generations.

Cicero's text appeared in multiple translations and editions, and lines from the work turned up in ordinary writings on old age, even in unpublished autobiographical texts.[32] Cicero, after all, had been part of the humanist curriculum. At the start of the 18th century, the French writer and patron of letters Anne, Marquise de Lambert produced a version for women that appeared in print only at mid-century. While others repeated notions of older women becoming less feminine and more masculine, Lambert described a distinctive process for women. The idea that women were defined by their sexuality was hardly original, but it can be argued that Lambert's idea of a woman's plan for life was.[33] A certain ambiguity, however, persisted in the contrast between her emphasis on retreat and avoidance of passion and her own continued sentimental life and organization of an important Parisian salon.

At the turn of the 18th to the 19th century, there appeared a number of texts expressing ideals that combined Enlightenment concern for this world with a spirituality free of the older prejudices against old age. J.H. Meister, for example, wrote of the continued creativity of older people, accepted continued sensuality as natural and claimed that the present moment belongs equally to people of all ages. He recommended a Ciceronian semi-retirement and described the joys of grand-parenthood. Similarly the Prussian philosopher J.H.S. Formey wrote of the bliss an older person would experience in reflecting on the past of family life, and Madame Necker, wife of Louis XVI's finance minister, praised the interaction of old age and youth.[34]

Lack of vanity brought a certain notoriety to the German painter Anna Dorothea Therbusch when she was admitted to the French academy, and she painted herself (opposite) as she really was. She was short-sighted and the odd lens suspended from her forehead was to remedy this. It could be argued that absence of vanity does not rule out pride.

L'Age de Maturité

L'Age de Discretion

L'Age Declinant

L'Age Viril

L'Age de

La Jeunesse

L'Ado‑
cence

50 Ans

40 Ans

Le Cours
de la Vie de
l'Homme ou
l'Homme dans ses
differens Ages

60 Ans

30 Ans

70

20 Ans

L'Enfance

10 Ans

LE JUGEMENT UNIVERSEL

L'Age de Puerilité 4 Ans

The familiar saga of the Ages of Man,
and Woman, follows the same pattern
as in the past. Decade by decade:
Infancy and Childhood, Adolescence,
Youth, Manhood, Discretion, Maturity
(aged 50); then Decline, Decadence,
Old Age, Decrepitude and finally
Imbecility and Childishness (100).

'The Pedlar of Ribbons, Shoes and
Thread.' But the old man is not what
he seems. 'Mouches' was slang for
'police spies'. 'When they see me
coming, they say "Watch out for flies".
I pretend to be deaf and dare not open
my mouth. For I am by nature a spy,
a thousand times more to be feared
than a scorpion.'

Artistic renderings of the ages of life repeated old stereotypes, but they too became more secular. And they eventually came to resemble the social experience of ageing more realistically. The 'ages of life', *degrés des âges* or *Lebenstreppe* offered a stepladder representation of the life course, rising from the left in ten-year intervals to a peak of 50, and declining to the right to 100. Their legends appeared in Latin, Italian, French, German, Spanish, Dutch and English. Versions of the 16th and 17th centuries had emphasized flames of judgment beneath the ladder, but by the 18th and 19th centuries such prints were more concerned with drawing attention to the social experience of maturing and growing older.

The faces of the old, full of mature experience and knowledge, began to dominate 18th-century painting, dwelling upon the realities of this world rather than the hopes and fears of the next. Right and opposite, two typical examples: 'The Old Woman', by Françoise Duparc; and the same subject by Joachim Martin Falbe.

Images of the aged took various forms. Emblem books of earlier ceturies had used older people as allegorical figures, representing grief, suspicion, malice, parsimony and calamity, but also wisdom, experience and penitence. Some 18th-century artists continued those traditions, but increasingly they focused on the realities of old age. Dutch and Flemish painters of the 17th century and their counterparts in the rest of Europe in the 18th depicted honoured elders surrounded by family members or juxtaposed with children. Some illustrated proverbs and others simply portrayed families upon ceremonial or critical occasions. Portraits depicted the dignity of elders and the accomplishments of a lifetime. They ranged from images of nobles, officers and magistrates to depictions of middle-class and working-class elders. Religious images had emphasized the approach of death and hopes for the next world; now artists described the realities of this one. It had become common for artists to demonstrate their abilities by painting old faces and heads: the body was a great focus. Genre paintings depicted the aged poor, the most dignified and deserving of the needy.

It would be wrong to present the evolution of artistic images of the aged as moving in one direction only. Yes, there was a secularization exemplified by shifts in subject matter from aged saints to aged philosophers, and there seems to have been a growing interest in depicting the elderly of various social strata. Moreover, several artists, such as Reynolds, Liotard and Chardin, turned seriously to self-portraiture in old age, thus providing visual models of long experience and continued work. But beyond that, it probably makes sense to say that artists were drawn both to strong elders and to the weak aged, 'green' old age and decrepitude. Whatever aspect of old age they portrayed, they seemed keen on maintaining older persons' dignity. Critics now had a difficult time with the traditional theme of 'Roman charity', in which a daughter breastfed her aged father. Filial piety was one thing; such a scene was more difficult for 18th-century viewers than it had been for those of the 17th.

Self-portraiture is confession or autobiography. Sometimes the artist presents himself as he wishes to be seen, sometimes as he knows himself to be, sometimes to discover who he is. The Swiss pastellist Jean-Etienne Liotard (1702–89) was a self-conscious eccentric who spent his whole life travelling – Italy, Greece, Constantinople (where he lived for four years and acquired the habit of wearing Turkish dress), Austria, France, England and Holland. The portraits for which he is famous are realistic studies of his sitters' personalities, but his own, in spite of painting fifteen self-portraits (here aged about 70), is curiously elusive. He seemed to assume different roles, perhaps as a sort of disguise. The fact that he had a twin brother may or may not be relevant. He lived to be 86.

No fantasy comes between Jean-Claude Chardin (below left) and the truth. This self-portrait is as objective as the still-lifes that were his favourite subjects; here he is 72. And Joshua Reynolds (below right, aged 65), happy to paint his aristocratic sitters in classical or mythological roles, had no use for them himself.

Eighteenth-century critics and art consumers appreciated images of active old people. Wrinkled faces and gnarled hands were symbols of experience and work. Embroiderers, sewers and weavers embodied expertise and the dignity of skilled labour. Active servants, including cooks and gamekeepers, and street vendors showed what could be done in old age. Philosophers, like those painted by Fragonard and David, represented the wisdom of the aged. At the same time, artists portrayed the infirmities of old age: toothlessness, blindness, paralysis.

Artistic representations had often depicted literary scenes, and a general shift in literary representation of the aged from ridicule to respect may be detected. Poems and plays in the early part of the century often depicted old people as blocking the progress of youth, even as repulsive. Comedies commonly involved competition between older and younger men for the love of the same woman or the continued efforts at seduction by an ageing woman. Such behaviour was held up to ridicule. In France, by the second half of the 18th century, the mood had shifted. Aged characters had become more dignified, a shift that can be tied to secularization and a more social and deferential view. A similar evolution may have occurred elsewhere on the European continent. In Germany patriarchal authority emerged strengthened after the Thirty Years' War in the 17th century and evolved into something softer and more sentimental in the 18th.[35]

On the other hand, the continuing negative image of 'man-hungry spinsters, gigolo-hunting crones, and sex-crazed widows' in 18th-century England demonstrates the survival of a very old theme long after it had fallen from popularity across the Channel.[36] Images could be used and reused. Contradictory representations coexist, negative ones in, say, *Gulliver's Travels* and more positive ones in the writings of David Hume and Adam Smith.[37] But how do we combine fictional representations in Jonathan Swift with old age as described by two philosophers?

Gnarled fingers could still retain their skill. Despite appearances, it seems certain that the old lady is Turkish, partly because Liotard was in Constantinople when he drew her in 1778 and partly because of the technique shown. She is embroidering leather with metal strips in a way that the Turks had inherited from Byzantium.

'Folly Dresses Decrepitude in the Adornment of Youth' is a French satirical print of 1745. The amorous pretensions of both old men and old women had long been the stuff of comedy.

In 18th-century France women writers measured their own experience against common cultural representations and created their own ways of growing old. In her correspondence, the Marquise du Deffand made use of both the real-life character of Ninon de Lenclos, famed *vieille amoureuse* in the late 17th and very early 18th centuries, and well-known fictional characters from the novels of Crébillon to explore the sentimental life of the maturing old woman, including her own.[38] In many of her surviving letters Voltaire's friend Madame de Graffigny explores the experience of an ageing woman writer, her friendships, her health, her loves, even a first orgasm at age 48, indicating perhaps a new-found freedom and comfort.

> In her final years, [the letters] are a sometimes horrifying record of illness, documenting in stupefying detail the pain of growing old. Graffigny knew indigestion, sore throat, headache, toothache, colds, coughs and fevers. She had a breast cancer scare. She spat blood; she was bled, despite her scorn for the procedure. She was subject to palpitations and convulsions, and plagued with oozing skin eruptions, incrustations and running sores in her ears and on her scalp (she was grateful that her coiffure concealed most of them). She suffered from swollen ears and cheeks, haemorrhoids, rheumatism, diarrhoea, constipation and cramps. She was often too weak to walk and — increasingly as she aged — had dizzy spells and blackouts. For her various ailments she consulted doctors who gave her concoctions and contradictory advice. But the weakness became chronic, while the blackouts grew progressively more frightening. Then death intervened.[39]

From ridicule to respect: 'Catherine Warman' (left) might almost be one of Swift's Struldbruggs, whereas Christian Seybold's 'Old Woman with Green Scarf' of 1794, perhaps nearly as old, has dignity and beauty.

Graffigny's old age was one that she endured, but also one she enjoyed and invented, so it is hard to reduce her experience to something clearly representative of the period. There was no simple pattern. We have already met Lady Sarah Cowper (1644–1720), who kept a diary between 1700 and 1716 which she used to explore the mental universe of one self-consciously ageing individual. It is a record of her reading of the Bible and the periodical press, her spiritual reflections, her sociability and her experience as a widow and mother of grown children. She even engaged in political commentary, particularly in relation to the careers of the men in her family.[40] A study of older women on both sides of the Atlantic also indicates a continued religious concern, an enjoyment of family life and an attempt to balance detachment with involvement.[41] The world of ageing women seems distant from the secularizing world of the Enlightenment. Yet both are parts of the history of old age in the same era.

Old age in the 18th century can be captured in a remarkable variety of sources. They range from the demographic and social to the religious, scientific, artistic and literary. Within particular genres and aspects of life, we can detect some patterns: a shift from the religious to the secular, from retreat to retirement, from a literature of ridicule to one of respect. But there is also considerable diversity, and generalizations are increasingly difficult to make. Judgments have to be based on reading ageing women's diaries or letters, examining individual and family portraits, and observing intergenerational transmission of property. A history of old age must take account of both continuity and change.

Nonetheless, longer lives meant greater opportunity to play the roles associated with the aged. The image of the latter seems to have softened. Life experience was valued, not just as a preparation for death, and political and economic change announced a world in which people might identify with an era and a demographic cohort. The growth of a consumer culture also meant that people would begin to associate particular dress or economic behaviour with particular generations. Those who engaged in politics were presumably more conscious than others of change over time. As Europe entered the 19th century, experience of events of the 1790s and the subsequent Napoleonic Wars encouraged awareness of the passage of time. Revolutionaries spoke of an *ancien régime*, and those who had reached maturity in that era would be the old of the 19th century.

The stern morality of 18th-century America made no concessions to vanity. In 1770 the naive artist Winthrop Chandler painted Martha Lathrop, only 55 years old but from her expression quite ready to meet her maker.

The years seem to make no impact on men like the British prime minister William Ewart Gladstone, who tried to retire in 1875 at the age of 66, but was called back by irresistible public demand. He became prime minister again in 1880, remained in office (with intervals) until 1894 and died in 1898, aged 88. This photograph shows him on the campaign trail in 1885, when he was 76, making an election speech from a train window. That is itself significant. The railway had brought everyone in the country within a few hours of each other, and the voice of Gladstone, one of the great orators of his time, was heard by unprecedented numbers.

6

THOMAS R. COLE AND CLAUDIA EDWARDS

THE 19TH CENTURY

Although the experience of growing and being old is always a personal one, some consideration of the factors that determine the life chances, status and behaviour in old age collectively is necessary to understand what might have been different in the 19th century from previous times.

The big changes transforming Europe and North America were first and foremost those of industrialization, urbanization and population growth. These were helped by, and in turn promoted, better transportation, which led to greater availability of diverse goods and the diffusion of ideas through trade, travel and migration, and changes to the labour market including, at the higher-skilled end, professionalization (of for example medicine) and, at the other end, 'proletarianization' and de-skilling of workers through the emergence of large-scale and mechanized production. New economic realities also brought about social and political change accompanied by fresh intellectual, cultural and religious expressions.

Most of these big changes occurred first in Britain and took time to encompass all of continental Europe and North America. Thus, any generalizations are marred by imprecision, time lags and different national paths to economic development and social change. Even within countries, industrialization took place in a patchy manner, with modern and traditional sectors and regions coexisting for long periods of time and with old and new production methods existing side by side in the same localities. Nonetheless, change would ultimately impact on every community and those least able to adapt to new challenges were affected most adversely. The elderly, and we will consider here foremost the elderly poor, experienced the big changes in their working lives, family and local community, their health and life chances, access to local services, and socio-economic status. A consulting physician, P.M. Roget, expressed a familiar pessimistic view in 1833: 'Need we pursue this "strange eventful history" to the last melancholy chapter of man's existence, and contemplate the wreck of those exalted faculties which ennoble his nature, and of which the deprivation lowers his condition far beneath that of the beasts of the field?'[1]

Industrialization and structural change affected the working lives of older people in different ways. In areas where the agricultural sector was shrinking, young people who moved to the towns and cities in pursuit of industrial and urban-based employment left behind an ageing rural workforce. In regions experiencing 'proto-industrial' activity (where a merchant put out raw materials to local villages for production of finished goods to be sold on distant markets), working opportunities existed for the old as domestic outworkers, generally alongside other family members, for example in the textile sector as weavers or knitters. While this might have been seasonal and low-paid (supplementary) employment only, the pace and hours of work could at least be determined by the worker, which facilitated the productive contribution of the elderly to the household. This safeguarded their economic role in household decision-making, with respect to consumption as well as production.

On the other hand, factory workers who lost their strength or became infirm or chronically ill, and who could no longer keep up with the pace of the machine and the length of the working day, had to find new ways of earning an income. Workers in the artisanal trades, for example shoemakers, bookbinders and engineers, enjoyed greater independence, support and bargaining power given their possession of valuable assets (knowledge, tools, premises) and connection to the guild or working men's associations. But organizational changes, such as piece-working, and technological change demanded greater speed, flexibility and constant adaptation of skills and, in some cases, the application of machinery reduced the requirement for skills or replaced the worker altogether. Generally, people attempted to continue in their occupation for as long as possible, and then moved into 'lighter' or more menial jobs, including charring, sweeping and street-cleaning.

The old crossing-sweeper interviewed by Henry Mayhew for his book on the London poor (1851) told him a tale that must have been common to thousands of working-class men and women who had nothing to support them in old age. After marrying she had been in service with a rich household and the couple lived comfortably. Now a widow and no longer able to work she shared a squalid room for which she paid a shilling a week and swept the street crossing in return for the occasional tip.

THE CROSSING-SWEEPER THAT HAS BEEN A MAID-SERVANT.

The lucky ones were those who had a skill and could go on working at home. In his early years Vincent van Gogh was deeply concerned with the life of the poor in the Netherlands. This painting of a weaver beside his loom (opposite above) dates from 1884. Below: an elderly Hungarian couple spinning and weaving in their cottage in the 1890s.

Family relationships and household structures can vary enormously across space and time. They are determined by customary practices, economic status and demographic factors. Even where values or tradition idealized an inclusion of older people in the household, economic and demographic realities often precluded the attainment of such ideals. With gains in mortality only slowly materializing from greater industrial wealth, the availability of kin for support in advanced old age was a constraining factor. Arguably, the availability of (proto-) industrial jobs for the young enabled their earlier (material) independence and thus weakened family ties, while the availability of child labour (in combination with falling adult wages) could establish greater intergenerational dependence. Cooperation between generations was also witnessed when aged parents provided child care for English mothers working in the early cotton mills.[2] A more hard-headed point of view was held by Thomas Jefferson, writing in 1815: 'Nothing is more incumbent on the old, than to know when they shall get out of the way, and relinquish to younger successors the honours they can no longer earn, and the duties they can no longer perform.'[3]

In a French vineyard an old labourer rests, 1869. Jean-François Millet was one of those artists who drew attention to the plight of those for whom ceasing to work meant either penury or charity – something that most were reluctant to accept.

Van Gogh identified strongly with the poor. In 1881, when he painted his 'Old Peasant by the Fire', he was just as poor himself. His approach, however, was more religious than social.

Patterns of cohabitation, and material and psycho-social support for older family members were also influenced by migration. Depending on who migrated and why, the impact on the family could be very different. Whether young women took up employment as domestic servants or, as in areas of France, Italy and North America, they went to work in factories with employer-run dormitories, they would have temporarily left their parents behind.[4] However, when whole family groups migrated together to fast-expanding towns and cities, then lack and high cost of housing forced the generations to crowd together.

Where economically weak members were abandoned or economic resources could not stretch to their support, the community had to shoulder greater responsibility for looking after the old, the sick, the widowed and orphaned. Community support might then have to fill the gap in the form of public relief (either as a poor law 'pension' or in an institution), religious or private charity, or through almsgiving.

The plight of the old who ended their days in a workhouse is movingly
apparent in this illustration to Pierce Egan's 'Life of an Actor' of 1825.
A successful actor visits an old colleague who has fallen on hard times.
It is a red-letter day for the other inmates, all thin and poorly dressed,
one of them on crutches.

Bad urban living conditions would have disproportionately affected the very young and recent in-migrants with low resistance to disease rather than elderly survivors, but the latter's health and life chances would have been importantly influenced by their access to, especially material, support. Where such support rested on local initiatives – thus on local wealth – either through taxation or charity, demand and supply could be seriously out of balance. The spatial segregation of towns into wealthy and poor areas, and the disparate fortunes of industrializing and declining rural districts meant that welfare services were often least available where they were most needed and where competition for support between claimants of all age groups would be greatest. Even where services were dedicated to the elderly, such as almshouses, their availability did not necessarily keep up with population growth, and other types of welfare often became more popular.

Were the elderly poor considered less deserving over time? Were they increasingly unable to appropriate resources due to the loss of status in society? Industrialization and proletarianization – that is, the creation of a workforce that was dependent on wages and therefore suitable for the discipline of factory work, but in consequence also extremely vulnerable to loss of income from business fluctuations, poor health and infirmity – developed in a capitalist economy that glorified devotion to work and gauged its success by the amount of profit earned and reinvested. To maximize such profit, an abundant, cheap and healthy workforce was of paramount importance, providing justification for targeting health services at younger people who were part of the productive workforce. The mechanisms for the spread of infectious diseases were ill understood and, in accordance with utilitarian principles, medical practice and research prioritized potentially curable conditions in the population of working age.

In the following pages we will examine aspects of the welfare of older people during the 19th century in three key areas: socio-economic, physical and spiritual. Their distinction is clearly artificial, but it enables a more focused discussion and reflects the fact that the interests of researchers and methods of investigation have also been different in these three areas.

Distinguishing between different aspects of welfare also highlights how change with respect to the old was not a linear process that affected all areas of life to the same degree or in the same direction. Recent research drawn from qualitative investigations has emphasized the weaknesses of generalizations based on social-science models that regard the elderly as victims of economic change and that do not incorporate wider cultural aspects of ageing, the meaning of old age and the values held by elderly people themselves.[5]

Modernization — while challenging old customs and beliefs and changing social and economic constellations — was not of necessity synonymous with poorer life chances or reduced intergenerational support and contentment among the old. It did, however, force individuals to make more complex choices and, then as now, the ability to choose depended keenly on one's material position, physical health, mental capabilities and ability to build interpersonal relationships.

By combining different methodologies the myth of a 'golden age' for the elderly prior to industrialization and urbanization can be debunked, as previous chapters have already shown. At the same time, research also points to some of the gains for elderly individuals from the emerging middle classes that were available in increasingly wealthy societies able to supply greater welfare provision and autonomous living for their elderly. Tolstoy, for instance, admittedly a member of the privileged class, found much to enjoy in old age: 'Don't complain about old age. How much good it has brought me that was unexpected and beautiful. I concluded from that that the end of old age and of life will be just as unexpectedly beautiful.'[6]

For the middle classes the prospect of old age was by no means threatening. On the contrary, it could be the crown of a prosperous life when men and women could enjoy their reward in the shape of leisure and comfort. Three paintings all tell the same story across countries and social strata in Germany, Denmark and Switzerland. Left: Carl Spitzweg's 'Cactus-loving Priest' of 1856. Below: C.W. Eschersberg's 'Madame Schmidt' of 1818. Below right: Albert Anker's 'Countryman Reading a Newspaper' of 1881.

Bearing in mind the economics of the fine arts, it is not surprising to find their output strongly biased towards portraiture of the wealthy and towards landscape and narrative paintings acceptable to the morality and ideals of that same elite. Nevertheless, a different choice of subject matter, ordinary people in ordinary places experiencing ordinary events, was promoted by the proliferation of magazines and periodicals in the pre-photographic reproduction age which used wood engravings to illustrate topical stories and news items.[7] Such 'ordinary' people included the poor and the old, captured in workhouses and backstreets, enduring hardship or enjoying too much drink. With the widening artistic gaze, previously unexplored moments of the social and economic reality of the less fortunate, but more numerous, members of society became part of our documented past – open to interpretation by future as well as contemporary observers, but nonetheless a powerful reminder of life at its least desirable, but unavoidable for many.

Here, we look not at the wealthy few who left comparatively ample historical records behind, but on the many elderly whose material existences have to be pieced together from our leaner knowledge of what made up their 'economy of makeshifts', that is, the constantly changing amalgam of sources of practical, pecuniary and material support. While for those still able to work employment would be the most important source of support, for the remainder a combination of money, meals, clothes, shelter, household help, to name but the most important, from either family, charity, the state or any combination of these would provide such support.

Historians have examined demographic patterns for clues to changing perceptions of the aged's role in the family and society, but often with inconclusive results. In the USA, the percentage of those aged over 60 years increased from 4 per cent in 1830 to 6.4 per cent in 1906,[8] while in France this age group made up already 8.7 per cent in 1801, rising to 12.6 per cent in 1906.[9] In England their share stabilized at a low 6–7 per cent by the end of the 18th century and remained at around that level until the early 20th century.[10] Yet despite the differences in the proportion of elderly, and thus their presumed burden on the young, in none of these countries were the elderly exempt from experiencing poverty and dependence.

Even if elderly people were only a small proportion of the population, demands on kin for their care could still be significant, either because of competition with other dependants, especially children during times of high fertility, or because of smaller numbers of younger kin remaining, in particular from high rates of mortality or migration.

Support from kin could take the form of providing accommodation, sums of money, meals, contact, nursing or housekeeping duties. The English Poor Law Report of 1834 was not unduly optimistic about the situation:

> *The duty of supporting parents and children, in old age or infirmity, is so strongly enforced by our natural feelings that it is often well performed, even among savages, and almost always so in a nation deserving the name of civilized. We believe that England is the only European country in which it is neglected.*[11]

While cohabitation is assumed to be a sign of strong family ties, its absence is not necessarily proof of neglect of the elderly. Indeed, many studies of Western societies now reveal the preference of elderly people to maintain their independence for as long as possible and for young people to set up their own households after marriage even in pre-industrial Europe, particularly in England.[12]

Home ownership can be seen as an indication of independence for the elderly, since homes, in addition to providing shelter and security for borrowing, can also be used to yield income from rent or taking in lodgers. During mid-century, home ownership among Americans peaked in late middle age, but, from the late 19th century, it peaked at the end of the life course.[13] Already in 1900, some 65 per cent of urban and 71 per cent of rural 70-plus-year-olds owned their home in the USA.[14]

'**Homeless**': Gustave Doré's graphic image of 1872 needs no commentary.

'The Golden Wedding' by the Italian painter Luigi Nono suggests that
rural poverty was easier to bear than urban. Peasant life in Continental
Europe was relatively unaffected by the industrial revolution and the old
were better integrated into the community.

Household composition of the pre-industrial rural West was certainly regionally diverse. On the one hand, northern and urban France, North America, and in particular England were characterized by very low proportions of large and complex households. On the other, southern France, northern Italy, parts of Hungary and Austria, and especially Russia displayed very different rural household patterns that support the notion of greater complexity and several generations living under one roof.[15] A study of different Hungarian villages shows the importance of regional and ethnic variation even within one country, and thus highlights the difficulty of drawing any conclusions from small numbers of case studies.[16] Also, in times of crisis, even in England households could be large, incorporating living-in (rural) servants, (urban) lodgers or grown children due to the availability of (urban) wage-labour employment near to home.

However, industrialization and urbanization, and profound changes in the economic relationships between family members as well as growing individualism, privacy and domesticity (the segregation of work from home), increasingly made for smaller households, composed only of the nuclear family.

It can be postulated that, if custom or emotional ties are too weak to guarantee familial support for the old, then the elderly's bargaining power over the bequest of land, tools and other economic assets, as well as trade skills, will safeguard their comforts until death. The growing availability of industrial wage-labour in urban areas, however, removed parental control over children and took the bargaining power away from the aged; it also created an elderly proletariat that had nothing to bequeath to its offspring. That such reduced intergenerational dependence created smaller households appears to be true, but whether it also led to declining support in general is much more difficult to show.

Two bourgeois families: 'The Berlin Household' by Eduard Gärtner (second quarter of the 19th century) exemplifies Biedermeier taste and manners, the children well trained and well behaved, the old grandmother proud and content. William Powell Frith's 'Many Happy Returns of the Day' (1856) shows a more relaxed English occasion. It is the baby's birthday. She sits under a celebratory wreath. The father watches approvingly as his elder daughter offers a glass of wine to her grandfather.

All ages mingle in the market square in front of Les Halles in Paris, a painting by Victor Gabriel Gilbert of 1880. The older people here are no doubt obliged to go on working. There is no suggestion that they are discontented, but the painter does not conceal a look of resignation in the faces of the two women in the foreground.

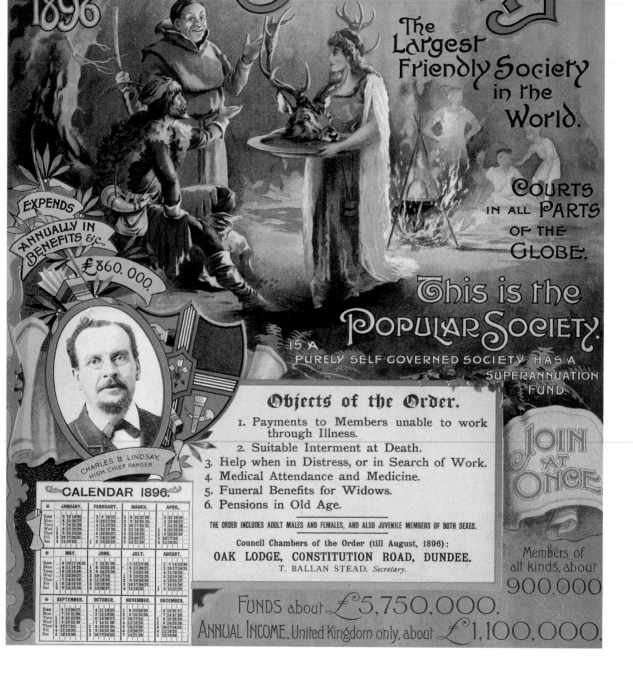

Ancient Order of Foresters

1896

The Largest Friendly Society in the World.

Courts in all Parts of the Globe.

This is the Popular Society.

Is a Purely Self-Governed Society. Has a Superannuation Fund.

Expends Annually in Benefits &c., £860,000.

CHARLES B. LINDSAY,
HIGH CHIEF RANGER.

Objects of the Order.

1. Payments to Members unable to work through Illness.
2. Suitable Interment at Death.
3. Help when in Distress, or in Search of Work.
4. Medical Attendance and Medicine.
5. Funeral Benefits for Widows.
6. Pensions in Old Age.

THE ORDER INCLUDES ADULT MALES AND FEMALES, AND ALSO JUVENILE MEMBERS OF BOTH SEXES.

Council Chambers of the Order (till August, 1896):

OAK LODGE, CONSTITUTION ROAD, DUNDEE.

T. BALLAN STEAD, *Secretary.*

Join at Once

Members of all kinds, about 900,000

CALENDAR 1896.

*	JANUARY.	FEBRUARY.	MARCH.	APRIL.
Sun	5 12 19 26	2 9 16 23	1 8 15 22 29	5 12 19 26
Mon	6 13 20 27	3 10 17 24	2 9 16 23 30	6 13 20 27
Tues	7 14 21 28	4 11 18 25	3 10 17 24 31	7 14 21 28
Wed	1 8 15 22 29	5 12 19 26	4 11 18 25	1 8 15 22 29
Thur	2 9 16 23 30	6 13 20 27	5 12 19 26	2 9 16 23 30
Fri	3 10 17 24 31	7 14 21 28	6 13 20 27	3 10 17 24
Sat	4 11 18 25	1 8 15 22 29	7 14 21 28	4 11 18 25

*	MAY.	JUNE.	JULY.	AUGUST.
Sun	3 10 17 24 31	7 14 21 28	5 12 19 26	2 9 16 23 30
Mon	4 11 18 25	1 8 15 22 29	6 13 20 27	3 10 17 24 31
Tues	5 12 19 26	2 9 16 23 30	7 14 21 28	4 11 18 25
Wed	6 13 20 27	3 10 17 24	1 8 15 22 29	5 12 19 26
Thur	7 14 21 28	4 11 18 25	2 9 16 23 30	6 13 20 27
Fri	1 8 15 22 29	5 12 19 26	3 10 17 24 31	7 14 21 28
Sat	2 9 16 23 30	6 13 20 27	4 11 18 25	1 8 15 22 29

*	SEPTEMBER.	OCTOBER.	NOVEMBER.	DECEMBER.
Sun	6 13 20 27	4 11 18 25	1 8 15 22 29	6 13 20 27
Mon	7 14 21 28	5 12 19 26	2 9 16 23 30	7 14 21 28
Tues	1 8 15 22 29	6 13 20 27	3 10 17 24	1 8 15 22 29
Wed	2 9 16 23 30	7 14 21 28	4 11 18 25	2 9 16 23 30
Thur	3 10 17 24	1 8 15 22 29	5 12 19 26	3 10 17 24 31
Fri	4 11 18 25	2 9 16 23 30	6 13 20 27	4 11 18 25
Sat	5 12 19 26	3 10 17 24 31	7 14 21 28	5 12 19 26

FUNDS about £5,750,000.

ANNUAL INCOME, United Kingdom only, about £1,100,000.

Before the advent of state-funded old-age pensions, most elderly people had to continue to work until they were no longer able to. Employment, although not the only, was certainly the most important element in the aged's economy of makeshifts. From data on wages and earnings we know that ageing workers tended to move into less secure, lower-skilled and lower-paid casual jobs, or jobs in declining industries, and were the first to become unemployed during economic downturns. An article in an American newspaper of 1913 painted a gloomy picture of the older worker's predicament:

> *In the search for increased efficiency, begotten in modern time by the practically universal worship of the dollar… gray hair has come to be recognized as an unforgivable witness of industrial imbecility, and experience the invariable companion of advancing years, instead of being valued as common sense would require it to be, has become a handicap so great as to make the employment of its possessor, in the performance of tasks and duties for which his life work has fitted him, practically impossible.*[17]

In 1890 North America, circa 60 per cent of gainfully employed men aged over 65 years worked in agriculture, fishing and mining compared with 42 per cent of men aged 15–45.[18] Older workers were also over-represented in traditional industries and handicrafts, and underrepresented in the emerging industry-based sectors of the economy.

By the turn of the 19th century, males aged 65 years and over in England and Wales were overrepresented in agriculture, service, clothing, the professions (the only highly paid sector), and as labourers.[19] In 1861, just under a quarter of London's female workforce was over 45 years old, but almost half of its laundresses and charwomen came from that group.[20] Work carried out by the old could be degrading, especially for those previously employed in higher-skilled occupations. It was often also exhausting, for example road-mending or dock work, and it was usually marginal, casual and poorly paid.[21]

Arguably, these shifts in employment were not only due to the failing physical strength, stamina, speed or eyesight of workers, but also to the introduction of scientific management techniques, new technologies and competitive pressures to raise the efficiency of the modern capitalist economy.

Those lucky enough to have enjoyed a sufficiently high and constant stream of wage income and prudent enough to have joined some kind of workmen's association, could also benefit from drawing sickness pay when no longer able to work for medical reasons.[22] Yet despite growing coverage in England, many – including the most vulnerable – were probably excluded from such benefits.

Friendly societies were early forms of insurance and pension schemes. At first privately financed by their members, their functions were quite soon taken over, beginning in Germany, by the state. In 1896 the Ancient Order of Foresters had 900,000 members and capital of over five million pounds. It covered sick pay, burial expenses, unemployment, medical treatment and old age pensions. But of course these benefits were available only to those able to pay into the scheme in the first place.

In America, occupational retirement pensions and old-age annuities sold by mutual benefit societies emerged after the Civil War, but probably provided financial support to less than 1 per cent of workers before World War I.[23] A pioneering old-age insurance scheme for Prussian miners was set up as early as 1854 and other large German employers offered social benefits to workers in an attempt to secure labour supplies and thwart state interference.[24] Social insurance legislation for invalidity and old age began in 1889, but old-age pensions were modest and only benefited workers of 70 and over.[25] Pensions were, of course, also available to European and American war veterans and civil servants, but for many recourse had to be made to other sources of support.

Estimations of the relative importance of charity are more often underpinned by political rhetoric than by historical investigation. The main problems underlying charitable assistance are its small scale, the localized and lay nature of its activity and its arbitrary choice of selection criteria for beneficiaries. This leads to small amounts of cash being made available for distribution to needy individuals, an inability to accurately gauge claimants' needs, and poor and unequal spatial coverage. Thus, while some elderly no doubt benefited from the voluntary giving of the rich, for many it remained an inaccessible or at least unpredictable source of income.

The organization of relief in Amsterdam, Holland, during the first half of the 19th century may serve as an example here.[26] The largest relief institution was the Reformed Church, but Roman Catholics, Ashkenazi Jews and Lutherans were also active in providing charitable support to the sick and infirm, the elderly, widows with children and workers with large families.[27] This support was mainly granted in the form of outdoor relief and, during 1829–54, over 40 per cent of those aged 70 and over benefited from it. However, the sums distributed were always only a fraction of what was needed for the individual's survival, suggesting that it was understood that recipients, elderly or not, needed to rely on other sources of support as well. As regards charitable institutions, only 4 per cent of Amsterdam's relief funds were directed towards almshouses and elderly homes during 1800–50.

The deserving poor – especially old soldiers and sailors – had long been provided accommodation by the state in many European countries. The material standards were indeed high, but as Max Liebermann's painting of the Old Men's home in Amsterdam in 1880 shows, the atmosphere was melancholy and the inhabitants were generally perceived as living nostalgically in the past.

In America, institutional provision for the elderly before the Civil War was extremely limited, but improved with the setting up of many private homes for the elderly, especially after 1875.[28] By contrast, the importance of almshouses in Britain continued to diminish over the 19th century as new endowments for them failed to keep pace with population growth. Instead, British voluntary giving became dominated by *inter vivos* subscription charities, mainly for schools during the 18th and for hospitals and dispensaries during the 19th century.[29] Yet, while British almshouses catered specifically for the

elderly, general and specialized voluntary hospitals did not. In fact, the rules and procedures for admission automatically discriminated against the elderly, who would encounter greater difficulties in obtaining letters of recommendation and whose medical conditions were often chronic and incurable and thus not eligible for treatment.[30]

In times of medical as well as material need, then, many elderly people turned to the public sector for support. Again, the Western experience is characterized by vast geographic and time differences. In Britain, the 'generosity' of public support amounted to between 0.8 per cent and 2.4 per cent of national income during the 18th and 19th centuries,[31] with cyclical variations in the fortunes of particular groups of recipients such as the elderly.[32] In addition, because poor relief was organized and financed through local taxes, it was also subject to geographic variation. British relief for the elderly poor came either in the form of regular cash benefits or through admission to the workhouse or its infirmary ('indoor relief').

There is not space here to discuss the nature of these institutions in any detail; may it suffice to say that for most they were considered their final choice as it involved a complete loss of autonomy, of personal belongings, contact with friends and family (they might even be separated from their spouses in the same institution), and life in often crowded and unsanitary conditions, with little means of distraction, poor or nonexistent nursing arrangements and monotonous diets.

Yet, institutionalization in the dreaded workhouse increased between the mid- and late 19th century for both men and women; by 1901, almost 10 per cent of English men and 6 per cent of women aged 75 and over were in workhouses.[33] In London, already in 1851, one in eight women of this age lived in a workhouse.[34]

This contrasts sharply with the American experience, where public funds were increasingly channelled into the building of asylums and other institutions catering specifically to certain groups of society other than the aged with the consequence that the proportion of old people in almshouses went up, but overall never surpassed the low and stable level of 2 per cent of 60-plus-year-olds living in them.[35] In Prussia, institutional provision multiplied over six times between 1846 and 1913, but the prioritizing of curable cases led to the increasing marginalization of the infirm and chronically diseased old.[36]

Looking for crime, the policeman's lamp lights up only misery: a painfully vivid image from Gustave Doré's illustrations of London in 1872. It was to eradicate such scenes as these that the major programmes of social reform were initiated in most European and North American countries during the last quarter of the 19th century.

Emphasis on suffering, not only
of the old but also of the infirm and
the mentally ill, was of course not
new to Western civilisation but it
was now divorced from the religious
dimension and the solutions proposed
were entirely secular. It is easy to find
such socially committed works of
literature in all languages. Artists
too sought to awaken the consciences
and compassion of the public, as
Géricault does in his haunting
'Mad Woman'.

French *hospices* were reserved to cater for the old, but did in reality also admit disabled patients of all ages and incurable children, rendering statistics more difficult to interpret. Nonetheless, it appears that every year perhaps only 2.1 per cent of the population aged 75 and over resided in a *hospice* during the 1860s and that no more than 11 per cent of French elderly were ever admitted to a *hospice*.[37] During the second half of the 19th century, the percentage of the population aged over 60 to become inpatients actually decreased, except in Paris where hospitalization rates went up markedly after 1875. Also, while *hospices* were dominated by men in the 1850s, the situation reversed so that in the 1920s the majority of inpatients were women.[38]

In conclusion, the social and economic realities of growing old in the 19th century were diverse and changing, but a common thread was the precariousness of people's existence and, most probably, their preference for independence and thus the continued importance of income from work.

One contemporary social investigator found that, in England and Wales towards the end of the 19th century, about 55 per cent of elderly people managed to support themselves through earnings and personal means; however, 5 per cent relied exclusively on parish provision, another 5 per cent exclusively on relations, and only 10 per cent received their main income from charities, the remainder (25 per cent) struggling on a combination of all sources.[39]

Material welfare in old age was clearly shaped by the availability of public, private and familial provision, but it was mainly a function of health and thus the ability to work. We will examine the elderly's physical welfare next.

The medieval hospital at Beaune in France had been performing the same service for centuries, but in the name of God rather than the state. In this very early daguerreotype of c.1848 one of the Sisters of Charity, a religious order, wearing a habit that was to become the nurse's uniform, brings food to an elderly patient.

THE

Friendly Societies'

MONTHLY MAGAZINE.

(FOR THE SOUTHERN COUNTIES.)

No. 8.—Vol 1.] NOVEMBER, 1889. [Price 1d., by Post 1½d.

(ENTERED AT STATIONERS' HALL.)

NOTICES.

Secretaries, and others, will oblige by sending accounts of meetings, or newspapers containing such accounts, not later than the 27th of each month ; before if possible.

Communications for the Editor should be addressed to him at 15, Fraser Road, Southsea.

Orders and advertisements should be addressed to the Secretary, at the same place.

EDITORIAL NOTES.

The half-yearly report and accounts of the South-Western District, Ancient Order of Foresters, which we summarise in another column, evidence a state of well-being that is highly satisfactory. The District has made immense strides during the last decade. Thanks largely to the well-directed zeal and energy of several District Chief Rangers, new neighbourhoods have been opened up during that period, and Country Courts established which are now doing well. At the present time the District comprises no fewer than 122 Courts, with a total of 20,166 contributing members, as compared with 20,095 in June last. The various funds are in a healthy condition, and by the establishment of a District Investment Fund most of the surplus money is out at good interest and with ample security. A foremost part is being taken by the District in the constitutional agitation against the tax on the transfer of bonds, which has not inaptly been described as "a tax on poor men's providence." The D.C.R. (Bro. H. B. Rohss) and the D.S. (Bro. A. J. Dyer), recently accompanied the H.C.R. and the H.S.C.R. of the Order, with the Parliamentary Agents of the Foresters and Oddfellows, as a deputation to Mr. Goschen, the Chancellor of the Exchequer. In the name of the two great Friendly Societies which they represented, the deputation laid their protest before the Right-Hon. gentleman, by whom they were courteously treated. We regret to learn, however, that they came away with but faint hopes of any amelioration in regard to the tax, being told that as the Friendly Societies had become capitalists and investors they must expect to pay the toll which the State charges on these transfers. This is poor comfort, indeed, and the protest which the Committee raise against the hard-earned savings of the industrial classes, contributed as a provision against sickness and adversity, being placed on the same basis as the money of the private capitalist is worthy of serious consideration on the part of those with whom the adjustment of the incidence of taxation lies.

The Ancient Order of Foresters of America has taken the place of the Subsidiary High Court of the United States, and no coloured people need apply. It was surely a joke, though, of the delegates who met at Minneapolis and drew up the high-sounding "Declaration of Independence," to introduce the phrase—"While we recognise that all men are free and equal before the law, and do not seek to deprive any of their rights and privileges to which they are entitled, we claim the right heretofore granted us, and inherent in all men, to legislate for ourselves upon questions so vital to our welfare and prosperity." It was, then, to accentuate the equality of all men, and to see that none were deprived of their rights and privileges, that the delegates resolved secession from the High Court of the Order! Happy delegates, to be contented with such logic !

Look on that picture, and then on this—it is hardly a companion one :— A New York correspondent states that the senior class of Harvard College has chosen for orator on Class Day one of its two negro members. He is named Clement Garrett Morgan, and his father was a Virginian slave, set free by Lincoln's Emancipation Proclamation. The Orator is always chosen by the vote of the whole class, and to be selected is regarded as the highest mark of favour a student can receive from his fellows. The present class numbers 275, and Mr. Morgan was chosen over all his white competitors by a large majority. He has unusual gifts of oratory, having won the Oratorical Prize last year. " The incident," writes an editorial commentator, " shows in a striking manner the progress made in America since the War in overcoming race prejudice." Humph !

We are glad to give prominence in another column to the meeting and entertainment held at Landport on the 23rd ult., in honour of Mr. Jackson, Vice-President of the Board of Directors of the U.A.O.D., who was on a visit to Portsmouth. The gathering—which was convened at very short notice—was interesting as an evidence of the friendly feeling that exists between members of the different Orders in the town, and of their general readiness to recognise the services rendered to any particular Society by one holding high office therein. The introduction on such an occasion of references to the proposed establishment of a Friendly Societies' Council in Portsmouth was most opportune. From information lately to hand we have reason to believe that the matter will not be allowed to end in talk, but that some practical steps are about to be taken towards achieving an object which appears to be desired on all hands.

A true story comes from British Columbia which shows that the Foresters there have caught the spirit of fraternity that is a guiding principle of their own and other Orders. In May last a member of Court " Pride of Finsbury," No. 1681, who was at Vancouver for the purpose of improving his position and regaining his health, met with an accident which necessitated his removal to a hospital. During his few weeks' stay in the town he had discovered a recently-established Court in the vicinity—namely, " Pacific," No. 7267—and had made himself known to the brethren. What followed, as soon as they heard of his accident, is best told in the grateful sojourner's own words : "When in the Hospital many of the members visited me three times a week. They brought me fruit and flowers, and most specially urged me to send to the C.R. or Secretary if I required anything, and it should be procured. I have been laid up a month through the accident, and if I had not been so kindly treated the cost would have been very severe to me. The doctors here charge five dollars a visit, and no medicine. An ordinary prescription costs one to three dollars. The Court Surgeon attended me four or five times per week. The Hospital treatment cost five dollars per week." Bravo, British Columbians !

For some time past the Druids have been thinking that they are under some disadvantage in having no official journal or magazine, such as other Orders possess.

The risks to health and welfare emanating from the profound transformations of the 19th century did not, of course, affect the elderly alone, but some of the private and institutional initiatives developed in response to them were much less accessible to this age group, such as hospitals, and to the poor in particular, such as friendly society benefits.

For the individual, health during the later stages of life had always been a function of genetic disposition and lifestyle factors that determined resistance to disease, and occupational and environmental factors that determined exposure to harmful substances and pathogens of infectious disease.[40] Arguably, the accumulation of insults to health from material and psycho-social adversity increased for many from the stresses that industrialization, migration and urbanization posed. These would include occupational hazards, greater work intensity, crowding with poor sanitation, poor diet and lack of social cohesion.

As far as the first industrializing nation is concerned, and considering such indicators as income per head, height, life expectancy, or literacy and political freedom, British living standards appear not to have markedly improved until after mid-century.[41] So what of the physical welfare of the elderly?

A variety of sources can be considered, but none provides a wholly satisfactory answer.[42] The most commonly used indicator of (poor) health is age-specific mortality. The higher death rates for older people indicate poorer health relative to younger population groups. This trend is mirrored by available statistics on the ability to function: disability (e.g., percentage blind) rose with age, as did absence from work due to sickness (e.g., as recorded in friendly society data).[43] Information on other aspects of health, such as depression, fitness or self-rated well-being, survives only as anecdotal evidence from diaries, biographies or visual representations. These provide valuable insights into individual experiences of health and suffering, but do not afford reliable or representative evidence of trends in health status for different age groups over time.

Nonetheless, despite this lack of hard data, we may be willing to accept that health did deteriorate with age and that, correspondingly, older people had greater needs for support to ameliorate or overcome the problems posed by disability, infirmity, disease, pain, isolation and mental illness. While support might have been forthcoming via different agents (orthodox medical practitioners, healers and other fringe practitioners, lay carers, counsellors/clerics) and services (mutual association, church, friends, family, mainstream and fringe medical services), it is possible that none was proportionate to the need of the elderly.

'I have been laid up a month through the accident, and if I had not been so kindly treated the cost would have been very severe to me': one of the comforting stories told in the Friendly Societies' Monthly Magazine of November 1889. These societies sought to stamp out prejudices of all kinds. The middle column tells how a black student at Harvard had been chosen as class orator, quoting an editorial comment: '"The incident shows in a striking manner the progress made in America since the War in overcoming race prejudice." Humph!' One wonders what 'Humph!' means.

English hospital records show that the elderly were grossly underrepresented as inpatients relative to their higher (medical) need compared with younger age groups (except children, who were often excluded from voluntary hospitals), and compared with fee-paying private patients of a similar age but higher social class.

While rates of use of charitable and public medical services thus cannot reveal the relative or absolute need of older people, they still allow us some idea of the type of diseases and conditions suffered in old age and the degree of success with which they were treated. Medical opinion on the whole was fatalistic and generally offered little hope of improvement: 'In old age the powers of the system undergo slow but steady decay; loss of the teeth, followed by impairment of the digestive powers, paves the way to imperfect nutrition of the blood, enfeebled action of the heart, fatty and atheromatous degeneration of the arteries, loss of generative power; and finally, impairment of the function of all parts of the nervous system, death taking place in a large number of cases from apoplexy, and from pulmonary and cardiac affections.'[44]

One study of the disease structure of older people admitted to hospital suggests a very varied intake of cases, but in the most commonly admitted categories of respiratory and musculo-skeletal diseases two conditions clearly stand out: bronchitis and rheumatism.[45] The workhouse infirmary also housed patients suffering from generalized old-age debility and decay. Given the infirmary's willingness to admit patients whose mental and physical capabilities were clearly expiring, it is not surprising that its death rates were over twice as high as in the voluntary sector. Yet, this can also be explained by the much-higher background mortality of the local infirmary population compared with that of the voluntary hospital.

The study also found that the public and private sectors treated many more young and middle-aged people than elderly, but that the private sector was particularly adept at minimizing admission of older patients, especially of the very old, and at keeping hospitalization periods roughly the same length for all admitted irrespective of age. Although the underrepresentation of elderly patients might be explained in part by hospital admission rules which sought to exclude sufferers least able to benefit from treatment (e.g., chronic and venereal disease), it appears also to have been rooted in patients' illness behaviour: fewer elderly people sought admission as outpatients.

In public institutions, older people managed to stay indoors for longer compared with the private sector and compared with the young. However, over the course of the 19th century, length of hospitalization was dramatically curtailed. So while access to hospital beds improved at both types of institution over time, in the public sector this came at the expense of the ability to stay for long periods of time.

The workhouses set up by new legislation in the 19th century were intended to be – at least for the 'deserving' among the aged poor – benevolent institutions. But they were not always sensitively administered, and many of the elderly poor came to fear them as much as the prospect of starvation. One of the features most resented was the segregation of men and women. Two photographs of London workhouses – St Pancras in 1895 and Marylebone in 1900 – still give a chilling impression.

The coming of photography in the 1840s made it possible to document the lives of the very old with an authenticity that can still take us by surprise. William Colley, 'The Jersey Patriarch', was aged 102 when this photograph was taken about 1848.
To live a hundred years and still enjoy bodily and mental health was an event to be celebrated. Michel-Eugène Chevreul was an eminent scientist born in 1786. His fame rests on his work as a chemist (animal fats) and his influence as a colour-theorist. His hundredth birthday, when he was photographed by Nadar (opposite), was a national occasion. He lived to be 103.

J. lith. de Delpech.

L. Boilly 1825

Les époux assortis.

Increasing the use of medical facilities by the British elderly to address their greater medical need was a slow process that began in the 19th century, but continued well into the 20th, with pockets of discrimination and ageism still in existence today.[46] However, apart from urban outliers, this process probably started later on the European continent, as research on Germany and France suggests.[47]

Why did supply of institutional medical services for the elderly increase so slowly, in particular with respect to specialized staff, research and facilities? One answer is economic in nature: while British bedside medicine was about care and advice, its institutional counterpart was driven by a need to produce positive, publishable results in the form of cures; voluntary hospitals were accountable to their subscribers, public institutions to taxpayers. Ageing and the diseases specific to old age did not lend themselves to quick cures, so in Britain their study and the attention to their sufferers had to wait until the late 19th century.

In France, by contrast, medical research into old age flourished during the 19th century, although its 'innovative quality' deteriorated after the 1870s despite an increase in the quantity of geriatric research output.[48] This was probably due to a combination of factors, including the continued pessimistic views on possible treatments by French medical researchers, their narrow focus on old-age pathology (especially post-mortem examination of degenerated organs), rather than on systematic linkages of pathological discovery with patient histories of symptoms or treatment regimes, as well as their reluctance to explore novel avenues of, for example, biological research or animal experiments.

Notwithstanding the alleged later failing of French geriatric medicine in terms of research and its earlier failing in terms of ability to produce improvements in elderly patients, the large *hospices* of Paris (notably the Bicêtre for men and Salpêtrière for women), with their high annual death rates of circa 20 per cent, represented perfect training grounds for physicians;[49] the works of Reveillé-Parise, Durand-Fardel and Charcot among others were important sources of knowledge for doctors throughout Europe and North America, and were considered superior to the work of their German and British counterparts such as Carl Canstatt and George E. Day.[50]

While elite French medicine may have developed new insights into the pathological changes in old age, ordinary doctors could draw on little new to alleviate or cure the old. This would explain why many elderly people simply did not seek any contact with orthodox doctors even when terminally ill: French vital statistics for 1859–60 for males aged over 60 reveal that 41 per cent of deaths had no recorded cause.[51]

'The Well-Matched Couple'.
Mockery of the infirm and disabled took a long time to die. A grotesque print after a drawing by Boilly of 1825 ridicules a man with a false eye and his wife with false teeth.

In Germany, during the second half of the 19th century, when disease nomenclature in official statistics became more sophisticated, the cause-of-death category of 'age-related infirmity' for the elderly actually increased, suggesting that doctors, and presumably patients too, were quite happy with the concept of a natural, unavoidable death. Also, entrenched notions of the untreatability of old-age illness served conveniently as an apology for the neglect of the elderly in medical institutions where German doctors were not to squander time and resources on incurable cases.[52]

Late 19th-century American doctors viewed growing old as a pathological process, where organic alterations inevitably led to decay and disease. However, unlike their German counterparts, they endeavoured to bring the elderly under their control, to make them submit to the expert physician's 'custodial care', consisting of appropriate treatment of age-related afflictions and of special regimens, most easily administered in an institutional context.[53] The lack of effective therapeutics and the certainty of the incurability of old-age diseases did not deter American practitioners from attending elderly patients and from caring for any aspect of their needs.[54]

In Britain, the paucity of research output in comparison with France bears witness to the relative neglect of the study of advanced age by the medical profession. Nonetheless, professional and lay attitudes towards old age, ageing and disease underwent important modifications over the course of the 19th century. The idea that nothing could be done to alleviate the drawbacks of age was beginning to be challenged. Daniel Maclachlan, for instance, wrote in 1867: 'Their [the aged's] diseases and infirmities have been too much regarded as inseparable concomitants of advancing years, the inevitable consequences of the progressive, natural decay of the organism and decline of the vital functions generally, and therefore but little if at all within reach of the physician.'[55]

Entries in medical dictionaries and the few medical textbooks[56] available increasingly divided the ageing process itself into 'morbid' and 'normal' degenerative alterations. For example, while the wasting of muscle or the brittleness of bone was considered normal in advanced life, thrombosis from a fibroid thickening of the arteria was consider morbid. As more and more natural states of decay were medicalized by labelling them states of disease instead, at least in theory more and more were also thought to be avoidable and/or open to cure. In addition, after 1850, Anglo-American medics with a special interest in old age slowly replaced cautious approaches to treatment and the principle of non-interference with growing confidence in the powers of medicine to combat disease and alleviate suffering.[57]

The truth of photography in the mid-19th century comes across with such immediacy partly because the medium was still new. This American war veteran and his wife have not been taught to pose for their portraits, and certainly no one has asked them to smile.

British concern with longevity and with averting bodily decline as long as possible ultimately replaced the chronological stages-of-life model and produced a preoccupation with behaviour and lifestyle that was extensively explored by lay writers on the subject. One of those who took a more optimistic view of what medicine could do for the elderly was Barnard van Oven, who published a book on 'the best means of attaining a healthful old age' in London in 1853:

> *I do not hesitate to assert that the duration of the period of maturity is greatly within our control; and that, although the termination of the journey of human life is absolute and certain, yet that not only the length of that journey, but the manner of its division into various stages, and the degree of ease and pleasure with which we may travel, depend essentially on ourselves.*[58]

He goes on to observe that

> *it is from the class of physicians and surgeons who have the care of large hospitals that we must expect such works as will alter and improve the practice of medicine... The position of the physician and surgeon, whose labours are devoted to private practice, is widely different... It is his duty to use as skilfully as he can all known appliances and means of cure, but not to employ new ones, however well he may think of them, until repeated experience and observation have proved their fitness and value.*[59]

As regards doctors, the aspiration to prolong maturity and to delay and compress the period of decrepit old age justified and further encouraged their focus on middle life and its diseases. The growth of the medical marketplace (including voluntary hospitals, public medicine and friendly-society doctors), the professionalization of its orthodox practitioners and the slowly rising use of institutional services by the elderly did little to bring 'old-age medicine' into the mainstream. Whether or not we believe that 19th-century medicine had much to offer in the way of improving health and life chances of (elderly) patients is beside the point: welfare is not merely about outcome, it is much more about process. As long as elderly patients found themselves excluded from medical care, this discrimination would have impacted negatively on their perceived, and thus actual, wellbeing.

Generalizations are always fraught with problems, but none more so than in the field of investigation which is called here 'spiritual welfare'. Even if we agreed on some narrow religious definition of the term, problems of spatial and longitudinal differences in the experiences of the elderly are compounded by the complexities of faith: there are different denominations within one faith, different religious practices among members of the same denomination depending on the abilities and convictions of the religious leader, the group and the availability of meeting places and resources.

'Eventide'. The title that Herbert Herkomer gave to his painting of a scene in the Westminster Union workhouse, London, in 1878 is more sentimental than the picture itself. Advances in geriatric medicine meant that many more people were living into extreme old age. In 1853 it was admitted by the medical profession that 'the degree of ease and pleasure [enjoyed by the elderly] depends essentially upon ourselves'.

'I remember when I was a child': another painting by Angelo Morbelli,
whose work we have already seen (page 11), of his favourite subject,
women in an Italian old people's home. Here he imagines the kind of
conversation that must have been commonplace. It became a cliché,
no doubt not without substance, that old people thought of nothing but
the past. The implication is unavoidable that those who spent their last
years at home in familiar surroundings had less to regret than those in
public care. This detail (right) is from L.A. Ring's large painting of 1898
showing an old couple being visited by their grandchild.

In addition, religious messages – which might be reconstructed from recorded sermons, letters or diaries – need to be interpreted and integrated into a person's individual thought-processes to generate spiritual growth and wellbeing. We are therefore unable to measure or truly ascertain any elderly person's spiritual welfare; all we can attempt to do is study some key components conducive to generating such welfare. These include – for the narrow religious sense of the term – people's access to religious texts for their personal consumption, dialogue with or instruction from other believers, and their exposure to the thoughts of religious figureheads through, most notably, sermons.

As regards access to religious texts, two developments were of importance. First, growing prosperity among the middle classes and, towards the end of the period, also among the working classes allowed for the increased purchase of books, including religious publications such as the Bible. Second, data on school enrolments and other indicators of literacy suggest that this trend was complemented by growing proportions of populations being able to read, albeit with male literacy rates above female ones and with countries displaying very different rates of achievement: around 1860, 85 per cent of Austro-Hungarian men remained illiterate compared with 40 per cent in Belgium, 18 per cent in the Netherlands, less than 7 per cent in the USA and 5 per cent in Prussia.[60] This suggests that more and more elderly people should have enjoyed access to religious reading material in their own homes and that larger numbers were able to read them or have texts read to them by family, friends and neighbours.

Something of the flavour of their missionary efforts can be gathered from a few sample quotations. A primary assumption was that standards of morality did not decline with age. 'The moral faculties,' wrote Dr Benjamin Rush in 1812, 'when properly regulated and directed, never partake of the decay of the intellectual faculties in old age, even in persons of uncultivated kinds.'[61] By the same reasoning, a virtuous life was a guarantee of a contented old age: 'The retrospect of a well-spent life is a cordial of infinitely more efficiency than all the resources of the medical art' (Sir Henry Halford, 1831),[62] or, in the words of Henry Ward Beecher, 'There is something beautiful in the thought of a man leaning upon his own staff. In youth we are cutting the staff that you are to lean upon in old age.'[63] And even an unhappy old age could bring spiritual benefits, since it was all part of God's plan. 'You must believe,' according to Sir James Stonhouse in 1824, 'that He has *merciful Designs* in afflicting you. He observes what Influence this *Affliction* has on your Mind.'[64]

Religious texts were certainly also freely available in the main institutions that catered for the needs of older persons, including voluntary hospitals and poorhouses. In these institutions, all inmates were also increasingly exposed to the reformative zeal of benefactors and volunteers, in particular middle-class women who took it on themselves to regularly visit and comfort the sick, inspect and fundraise for establishments, administer charitable donations and 'dispense large doses of Scripture to patients in waiting-rooms' and at the bedside with the view to convert, indoctrinate and instil moral and religious values.[65]

One popular English booklet, written by a physician to the General Infirmary in Northampton, 'for the use of the sick belonging to the Infirmaries, as well as Out-Patients, as those within the House... and of equal Service to every sick person', elaborates on the dual roles of medical institutions as places for the restoration of bodily health and prolongation of mortal life on the one hand, and as promoters of spiritual welfare and as aids to help save immortal souls on the other.[66] For these roles to be successfully carried out, patients were advised to be grateful to the doctor, comply with the methods of cure, respect and give little trouble to their carers, and to 'do good' by comforting and reading to others, and by using the opportunity of retirement from labour to contemplate their past failings and to practise their Christian faith. This called for daily reading from the Bible, praying, attending sermons and taking spiritual guidance from a clergyman.

How old age ought to be. Conditioned by the sentimental taste of the time, photographers could abandon documenting real life and construct a fake reality in the image of art. This is a posed photograph that challenges painting – Henry Peach Robinson's 'When the Day's Work is Done', 1877.

Minutes taken by the Weekly Committee of the Bristol Royal Infirmary, an English institution heavily patronized by Nonconformists, and especially Quakers, illustrate the working relationship between churchmen and hospital administrators. In May 1849, the duty of nurses to advise the matron immediately of any patient wishing to see a minister of religion or chaplain, and to encourage seriously ill patients to see such as person, was reiterated.[67] This might have followed on from a complaint in September of the previous year by a Catholic priest who claimed that the final sacrament could not be given as nurses and patients did not alert clerics in time. However, in this case, the committee also felt that the Catholic priest abused his visiting rights and directed him to adhere closely to the infirmary rules with respect to the visiting of patients.[68] Equally indicative, though not so serious, is the following edict issued by the Royal British Infirmary Committee in 1872: 'The committee having heard that it has been the practice of the Chaplain to solicit donations from the patients for missionary purposes, desire that the chaplain be informed that such donations are unauthorized by the committee, and that collecting for any purpose, without their authority, be discontinued.'[69]

The relationship between English voluntary hospitals and churches can easily be described as symbiotic. Hospitals provided grounds for evangelizing activities and churches grounds for the recruiting of subscribers and other supporters. In May 1860, the same Bristol Royal Infirmary Committee resolved to cooperate with a rival hospital in the effort to obtain from the clergy and ministers of Bristol collections in their churches and chapels on the second Sunday in January in each year for the benefit of their institutions.[70] A year later, churchwardens of all parishes were urged to help canvass the city to liquidate the hospital's accumulated debt of £5,626.[71]

Undoubtedly, the spiritual welfare of the sick, infirm and dying, as well as of other disadvantaged members of society from prostitutes to paupers, from orphans to the elderly, was a key consideration to those patronizing, administering and supporting charitable and public institutions. Spiritual welfare, attainable through religious belief and moral behaviour, was not merely the individual's responsibility, but was considered an integral part of any service delivered to those receiving material and physical support. To facilitate this, voluntary hospitals boasted their own chapels and resident clergymen; lesser institutions were frequented by female visitors and paid working-class missionaries. Whether we label these actions self-interest or benevolence, indoctrination or moral support, responsibility for the body was combined with the opportunity to save the soul; together, they made for a holistic approach to welfare that is no longer of concern to most providers of the present day.

If the spiritual welfare of the elderly was a recognized objective, then what were the messages of different clergymen to this age group? As these would have varied infinitely by faith, community and over time, a case-study approach will be taken here to illustrate how a particular set of preachers treated the issue of ageing, the meaning of old age and the role for the elderly in society, and how some of these ideas were reflected in contemporary art. The case study is based on the teachings of Romantic evangelicals of the north-eastern United States during the middle third of the 19th century, and on a series of paintings by Thomas Cole entitled *The Voyage of Life*.[72] This part of the Western world provides a good example of a region undergoing the changes necessary to becoming a modern capitalist, urban-based, industrial economy, and it is thus illuminating to examine religious developments during those times.

'The Last Muster' by Herbert Herkomer, 1875. In the chapel of Wren's Royal Hospital at Chelsea in London, one of the pensioners looks with alarm at his neighbour. The old man has died during the service.

For this purpose, we study sermons given by a number of eminent ministers who took a new 'Romantic' direction in their teaching of evangelical Protestantism to redress internal dynamics within their church and to make their church a more accessible and safer sphere for Christians to withdraw to from the pressures of the profane world. These ministers included Henry Ward Beecher, Phillips Brooks, Horace Bushnell and Theodore Parker. It is likely that their congregations were made up predominantly of women and old men,[73] so would have included the elderly and their main carers at home.

The Romantic label derives from a focus on nurturing Christian sentiment, on evoking emotions in religious followers. Instead of a rationalized emphasis on sin, guilt and self-loathing, these ministers impressed on their parishioners the love of Christ and the importance of such qualities as forgiveness, humility and gentleness. The earlier painful process of conversion through repentance and obedience to a sovereign God was replaced with the notion of a tranquil journey where, under Christ's guidance, lifelong personal, moral and spiritual improvement was possible. The emotive messages of the Romantic ministers were underpinned by the use of images and music and were well suited to an audience heavily dominated by women and the old. However, the elevation of human qualities that were culturally considered female, while providing a clearly delineated sanctuary from the real world, did much to drive out young and middle-aged men and to shape a view of older people, including old men, that associated them closely with the feminine sphere. The language of the Romantics did not fit with the aggressive overtones of the masculine worlds of power, production and business. Women and old men existed outside of the competitive struggles for wealth, status and worldly pleasures.

Even if elderly men accepted their removal from worldly pursuits to a life of passivity and piety within the safe haven of the church, what did ministers preach to further their spiritual growth and wellbeing? It appears that, in spite of the make-up of their congregation, ministers concentrated more on the preparation for old age than on old age itself. In a sermon on the topic, Henry Ward Beecher focused on giving physical advice to his younger listeners, using capitalist metaphors of adding to, through temperate behaviour, and subtracting from, through sinful living, the physical stock of vitality.[74] Other Romantic ministers echoed these messages with images of the deprived, dependent and wretched old sinner who abused his body during youth and manhood (and, very rarely, also womanhood).

Lifelong preparation for old age also involved the secular, especially in order to ensure (financial) independence from one's children, and the spiritual, that is developing a strong Christian character. By the time old age arrived, spiritual preparation for death was already to have been completed — the elderly had no further preparations to make; after a lifetime of laying foundations, the benefits of a beautiful old age could be reaped and, after a natural death, heavenly treasures enjoyed. Yet, the Romantics' emphasis was not on making ready for eternal life, but on preparing for a long life. Given the correct physical, secular, intellectual and spiritual preparation, premature death and an ugly, dependent, sick and painful old age could be avoided, suggesting that those suffering the negative realities of disease, poverty and dependence in old age could expect little in the way of consolation, comfort and support for spiritual growth from attending sermons by Romantic ministers.

However, the ideal of a healthy, productive and independent long life, followed by a passive, kindly and nostalgic old age culminating in a pain-free, quiet and anticipated natural death, was just that: an ideal. An ideal, firstly, that could elevate the elder onto a pedestal of moral achievement and respect through righteous living, albeit at the cost of ostracizing others who displayed self-inflicted decay and misery. This has been labelled the 'dualistic' vision of old age and was similar in spirit to the preoccupations of British moralists with the issue of lifestyle, where health and longevity might be regarded as worldly rewards for proper conduct, while infirmity and old age would represent punishment for intemperance and undesirable behaviour. Secondly, the Romantic evangelicals' ideal of a long life, ripe old age and natural death held the promise of a predictable and secure life course for those struggling with the secular realities of economic uncertainty and social change.

A good life would lead to a good old age without the need for excessive religious devotion. Eunice Pinney was a self-taught American artist whose 'Cotter's Saturday Night' was painted about 1815. The emphasis is on quiet faith. In the family's plain living room grandfather reads the Bible in preparation for Sunday worship.

THE COTTERS SATURDAY NIGHT

Such an orderly life course was illustrated in the four 1842 paintings of Thomas Cole's *The Voyage of Life – Childhood, Youth, Manhood* and *Old Age* – which enjoyed great popularity in the USA. The paintings' vast natural scenery and nautical theme matched the American context of a richly endowed but sparsely settled frontier country where self-made individuals sought to tame and tap the country's resources. They also incorporated the traditional association of different life stages with different seasons of the year and times of the day, as well as the symbol of the hourglass. However, the older (European) representation of the life course as a rising and falling staircase was replaced with the notion of an upward journey, culminating not in middle-aged worldly success, power and prosperity, but in a serene old age spent peacefully awaiting immortal life. Cole's voyager faced his challenges during middle life, but his unwavering faith allowed him to navigate safely along the river of life towards the ocean of death and immortality.

Cole's work conveyed with certainty that spiritual preparation would lead to a good old age and to eternal life. Physical preparation, as elaborated in the sermons of Romantic ministers, was of no concern here. But while Cole's work emphasized the importance of spirituality and faith, and portrayed the orderly succession from one life stage to the next, it left unresolved the question of exactly how individuals were to achieve spiritual growth and self-improvement in the face of the all too common adverse realities of material deprivation, physical suffering and social isolation.

The economic and social realities towards the end of the lifecycle were shaped by class, gender and personal wealth, ability to work, access to kin and availability of communal resources for support, and were reflected most obviously in one's place of living, appearance and scope for social interaction. At one end of the spectrum, emaciated, infirm and isolated elders lived out their last days in a public institution, separated from family and friends, deprived of personal belongings, autonomy and dignity. At the other end, well-to-do heads of family commanded respect and maintained control over their personal wealth, surrounded (if not necessarily cherished) by a circle of family, staff and acquaintances, living out their last days in their own homes, retired from work and with sufficient time, energy and intellect to prepare for the inevitable.

'The Voyage of Life' by Thomas Cole is a series of American allegorical canvases in which he explores the history of man in America in 1842. They are a novel version of the traditional diagram of the Ages of Man. Life is a river flowing through a vast landscape which also reflects the seasons of the year and the times of day. 'Childhood (Spring, Morning)' depicts the beginning of the voyage, the baby in a boat navigated by an angel. In 'Youth (Summer, Noon)', man takes over the boat himself and the angel bids farewell from the bank.

'Well, Betty,' said th' doctor, 'heaw dun yo get on?
I'm soory to yer 'at yo'n lost yo'r owd mon:
What complaint had he, Betty?' Says hoo, 'I caun't tell,
We ne'er had no doctor; he deed of hissel.'

'Ay, Betty,' said th'doctor, 'there's one thing quite sure;
Owd age is a thing that no physic can cure:
Fate will have her way, lass, – do o' that we con, –
When th' time's up, we's ha' to sign o'er, an' be gone.'
(Edwin Waugh, *Owd Enoch*, c. 1870)[75]

The images presented in this chapter usefully remind us of the economic extremes experienced by the elderly, but they have also contributed to perpetuate the myths and black-and-white perspectives we hold on existence itself in old age. For the majority of the elderly, of course, lived in between these extremes of opulence and poverty, of cosy homes and cold institutions, of family devotion and desperate isolation, of recreational activity and degrading work, of spiritual preparation and mind-numbing boredom, and of autonomy and dependence.

Nonetheless, what the extreme views on the socio-economic realities of old age combine with the shades of grey in between is the representation of the physical decay in old age in actual or implied juxtaposition with the beauty, virility and strength of youth. Whether idealized or feared, old age was defined foremost by loss: the loss of good looks, of health and of strength. The contrasts of young and old are explored in pictures of institutional life (old inmate, young carer), in family scenes and in the stages of life. Physiological and pathological changes, although never emphasized, are best illustrated in portraits, whether of the wealthy patriarch or the decrepit crossing-sweeper. Physical ability rather than chronological age determined one's material and social position. The neat division into stages of life where physical utility and social roles changed in tandem became increasingly less tenable in a society driven by new utilitarian ideals and (later) scientific possibilities. As life expectancy increased in the West over the 19th century, work 'opportunities' for the elderly decreased and social roles were redefined. Yet the core themes of diversity of experience within old age, of competition and cooperation between generations, and of the physical hardships of old age continue unabated.

In '**Manhood** (Autumn, Evening)', man is alone at the mercy of the current, swept along through dangerous rapids. With 'Old Age (Winter, Night)' he drifts calmly towards death, watched over once more by the angel. It is a deeply religious allegory, painted at a time when Cole was going through the experience of conversion. Its climax is not worldly success but resignation.

THE LIFE AND AGE OF WOMAN.

Stages of Woman's life from infancy to the brink of the grave.

LIFE AND AGE OF MAN.

Fear God, and keep his Commandments

STAGES OF MANS LIFE FROM THE CRADLE TO THE GRAVE.

Resist the Devil and he will flee from you.

Until the first Five years be spent, the Child is lamblike innocent.

At Ten, he goat like skips and joys in games & sports and foolish toys.

At Twenty, love doth swell his veins and eagle like untamed remains.

With bull like strength to smite his foes. At Thirty to the field he goes.

At Forty might his courage quails but with wit fox like he helps to manage it.

Strength fails at Fifty, but with wit fox like he helps to manage it.

At Sixty, oft by stealthy ways, wolf like he tries his wealth to raise.

At Seventy news he'll hear and tell, but dog like loves at home to dwell.

The cat keeps house and loves the fire. At Eighty we the same desire.

At Ninety every trifling care becomes a burden hard to bear.

If we should reach the Hundreth year The sick of life the grave we Fear.

Perhaps the most profound change has been the gradual abandonment of concern for the spiritual welfare of the elderly. While paintings of Bible reading, of the journey towards heaven and eternal life, of the constant reminder of death in the lifecycle stages, and of quiet contemplation of the meaning of life were universally familiar and essential images during the 19th century, the increasing focus on the extension of middle life and the avoidance of death has all but crowded out public concern for spiritual welfare.

The German chancellor Otto von Bismarck was among the first to see adequate provision for old age as a state responsibility. Speaking to the Reichstag in March 1884, he said:

> *The social significance of a general insurance of the propertyless appears immeasurable to me; it is essential to generate a basic conservative conviction amongst the vast majority of unpropertied people through the feelings that come with the right to a pension. Why should the soldier of work not have a pension like the soldier of the civil service? That is state socialism, that is the legitimate operation of practical Christianity.*[76]

The welfare of older people depends at all times on economic, social, physical and spiritual aspects and is characterized by huge diversity, but the big transformations begun and developed in the 19th century have altered their relative importance and the variations possible within each category. The accumulation of wealth in the Western world opened the possibility for assured material comfort and retirement in old age, but this did not eliminate the concept of a burdensome generation and our fluid views on the appropriate social role and status of the elderly. Better living standards and advanced medical science have increased life expectancy without necessarily raising our sense of wellbeing, and while the possibilities for entertainment and intellectual distraction have certainly augmented, guidance and enthusiasm for spiritual development have arguably much diminished. Choice of themes in the fine arts and their rendition represent one important way of illuminating our ever-changing views of old age and its occurrence in our Western world.

In contrast to Cole's gloriously romantic picture of the ages of man, the popular graphic artists Currier and Ives revived the traditional scheme in the mid-century, a scheme based very solidly on mundane reality. Interestingly, Woman goes through fewer and less distinctly defined ages than Man. (Interestingly too, the artists seem undecided whether the peak of his career is military or civil.)

7

PAT THANE   **THE 20TH CENTURY**

'Old age' has always been the most diverse of all age categories. As we have seen, for centuries it has been defined as including people from their 50s, or even younger, to past 100, a range far wider than those ascribed to 'youth' or 'middle age'. It embraces some of the richest and the very poorest in all societies, people who are highly active and the severely decrepit. In the 20th century this diversity grew more than ever before. During this period in all the societies on which this volume has focused, and in others, for the first time in history it became normal to grow old. Although, as we have seen, survival to old age was more common in earlier centuries than is sometimes thought, it was only during the 20th century that, overwhelmingly, most people born in these regions of the world lived to old age. Death in childhood, youth or middle age became unusual and shocking. More people lived to very old age. In Britain at the beginning of the 20th century an average of 74 people a year reached 100; by the end of the century 3,000 did so. In Japan even in 1960 there were only 144 centenarians; in 1997 there were 8,500. In Britain expectation of life at birth in 1901 was 51 years for men and 58 for women. In 1991 it was 76 and 81, respectively. In general women outlived men. There were similar experiences in most 'developed' countries, with the exception of Russia and some other former Communist countries of Eastern Europe where male life expectancy fell at the end of the century, after the fall of Communism.[1]

Elsewhere, men and women not only lived longer but remained healthy and active until later in life. This was something people had dreamed of for centuries: the prolongation of active life. It was the outcome of unprecedented improvements in living standards, especially in income, diet and hygiene. Only a little less important were the great leaps in medical knowledge and techniques during the century. Curiously, though, this achievement was generally received not with joy but with concern and pessimism about the 'burden' that growing numbers of older, supposedly dependent, people would impose upon a shrinking younger population. This was partly because the rise in life expectancy coincided with a fall in the birth-rate, internationally. Consequently,

'Crabbed age and youth cannot live together', said Shakespeare. But in the 20th century they could...maybe. In John Held's 'Life' cover (1926) a dashing young flapper is teaching an old dog new tricks.

older people not only increased in numbers, but as a proportion of the population, as the numbers of younger people fell. Fears grew that populations were failing to reproduce themselves: they were ageing and declining. These fears were first evident in the 1920s and '30s and led, particularly in Nazi Germany and Fascist Italy, to largely unsuccessful attempts to bribe women to have more children and to penalize the unproductive, by such means as bonuses and medals for mothers of numerous children and tax penalties for celibacy. Elsewhere, particularly in Britain and France, the response took the form of panicky predictions of the decline of the international power of the West as they aged, while Asian and African countries had high birth-rates and youthful populations. The ageing of populations symbolized the decline of nations.[2]

Such fears diminished during and after World War II, when birth-rates turned upwards again. They returned at the end of the century, as births fell once more. Once again, from the 1980s doom-laden predictions of the adverse social and economic effects of the ageing of populations were issued by such institutions as the World Bank.[3]

Ageing occurred at a different pace and with different effects in different countries. France experienced a low birth-rate much earlier than other countries. Nine per cent of the French population were aged 60 or over as early as 1836; 18 per cent had reached this age by 1976. Sweden did not reach 9 per cent of over-60s until 1876, but its age structure changed faster and it reached the 18 per cent point by 1962. The United States, which sustained relatively high birth-rates throughout the 20th century, largely due to its high rate of immigration, did not reach 8 per cent of over-60s until 1935 and is not expected to reach 18 per cent before 2008. The pattern for Australia, another immigrant nation, was similar. In all these countries, most old people were female, since women have long tended to outlive men.[4]

What were the effects of the ageing of individuals and societies in the 20th century? Of course, some people ended their lives in states of sad physical and/or mental decline, though only a minority experienced long periods of dependency. The incidence of conditions such as Alzheimer's rose, partly because more people survived the diseases which had ravaged younger people in previous centuries, such as tuberculosis, to die of sicknesses of old age. The 20th century did not find the secret of eternal youth, though, as we shall see, the search for it continued.

Modern societies found a new language to describe the stages of ageing. A term coined in France, and wisely used elsewhere, described the period of active old age as the 'third age', following the 'first age' of childhood and youth and the 'second age' of adult maturity. The later, less active and independent phase of life was the 'fourth age'.

The 'threat' of an ageing population troubled the nations of Europe in the years between World Wars I and II. The standard remedy was to encourage larger families, so strong public appeals were made to women to produce more children. The French poster of 1919–21 urges them to join the National Alliance against Depopulation, with the slogan 'No children today, no France tomorrow'. Germany under the Nazis (1935) puts motherhood on a level with patriotism. An older woman shakes the hand of a young mother of three children under the words 'For young women, work means motherhood.'

Most older people throughout the century inhabited the 'third age'. But the very definition of the age boundaries and characteristics of this age group changed over time as did the language describing them. As we have seen in earlier chapters, subjective and everyday definitions of who was 'old' and when 'old age' began had long been variable and dependent more on the appearance and physical capacities of individuals than on chronological age. At the same time, over many centuries, internationally, official definitions of when people became 'old', too old for example for public service, were remarkably stable at around age 60.

Old people queue at a German post-office to collect their state benefits, a drawing of about 1890. During the previous ten years legislation had introduced insurance against illness, accidents, disability and old age.

This disparity between official and popular perceptions continued through the 20th century and became, if anything, more stark. This was driven partly by another important change: the introduction and spread of pensions provided by the state, and by employers or non-government organizations. By the 1960s a pension of some kind – not necessarily a generous one – was the normal expectation of older people in all developed countries. Pensions were payable, most commonly, from age 60 or 65, sometimes 55 or 70. The first state pensions were introduced in Germany in 1889 for, mainly male, workers aged 70, or earlier if they were permanently incapacitated. Denmark followed suit in 1892 with pensions targeted at the poorest people, mainly female, from age 60. New Zealand introduced similar pensions in 1898, payable from age 65, closely followed by Australia, then, in 1908, by Britain, where the pensionable age was 70, reduced to 65 in 1925 and, for women only, to 60 in 1940. The United States and Canada were slower to introduce comprehensive pension schemes. These emerged gradually in the US from 1935 and in Canada from 1927, in both cases payable from age 70. By the 1970s the minimum state pension age varied across countries from 55 to 70. It was most commonly 65.[5]

Increasingly, at least in non-Communist countries, the pension age became the normal age of voluntary or involuntary retirement from paid work. In the Communist countries of Eastern Europe, especially in the USSR from the time of the Bolshevik revolution of 1917 to the fall of Communism in 1989, unlike in capitalist countries, strenuous efforts were made to avoid linking pensions and retirement.

'Are you over 50? Don't miss the seniors' train!' This poster of 1996 is a little misleading. It is not offering cut-price railway journeys for the elderly, but announcing the fact that a special 'Train des Seniors' would be calling at certain specified stations and standing there from 8 in the morning to 8 at night. They will contain a collection of 'ideas, products and services specially intended to be useful to you in your New Life'.

Elsewhere, the prevailing pension age became, in popular as well as official discourse, the boundary between middle and old age, defining it by age more rigidly than before. This change was evident in everyday language. In Britain, by the middle of the century 'old-age pensioner' ('age pensioner' in Australia) had become a synonym for 'old person'.

Yet no sooner were such usages established than people became uncomfortable with them, as defining older people negatively, as dependent on the state or on the young: that is, for what they were not – no longer productive workers or citizens – rather than for their positive qualities. In the search for a more positive language, 'senior citizen' became common usage in the US and 'the elderly' in Britain, until by the 1980s this had also come to be seen as pejorative and was replaced by the ambiguous 'older people', a term also used in the United States.[6]

Such changes were driven by perceptions of the disparities between a language which constructed people above a certain age as helpless and dependent and the visible reality that increasing numbers of them were not. Change was encouraged by articulate older people them-selves and also by professionals in the internationally growing field of gerontology. This was a creation of the mid-20th century, a response to the increasing numbers of older people, designed both to study ageing and old age and to serve as an advocate for older people when required.

The changes in language which effectively resisted negative, pejorative references to old age conflicted with another widespread international trope: assertions that old people were less respected in modern societies than in 'the past'. We have seen in earlier chapters that this conviction of ever-diminishing respect for age is as old as recorded Western discourse. At no time has it had much substance, not least because 'old people' have never been an undifferentiated group and social attitudes towards rich and poor, male and female, active and inactive, nice and nasty older people have varied greatly at all times. The ongoing search in the 20th century for a language of respect for age, at least in English-speaking nations (comparisons with other languages would be instruc-tive), and the ready adjustment of language suggest that this is no more true of the 20th century than of earlier times.

Not only language, but also the experiences of old people shifted in unprecedented and not always predictable ways. An important change, as already suggested, was in the experience of work. At the beginning of the century, as for long before, in all societies those who could afford to do so chose when to retire. State officials and high-status employees in the private sector often had secure pensions and fixed retirement ages, generally lower than the state pension age. This was 60 in the British civil service from the mid-19th century, in the United States by the mid-20th century it varied from 55 to 62 depending upon length of service. Sixty was a common starting age for public-service pensions.

One of the few professions fully open to the old was fortune-telling (opposite). Here at least the appearance of old age, with its attributes of wisdom and experience, was an asset rather than a liability. This Finnish painting, 'The Fortune-Teller', of 1899 is by Juko Rissenen.

Poor people (who were the majority in all societies) worked to support themselves for as long as they were able, sometimes to very late ages, generally at increasingly degraded tasks with diminishing incomes. In largely rural Finland, as in most other countries at the beginning of the century, old women worked as laundresses, cleaners, hawkers, labourers or hod carriers on building sites. Men took more or less casual jobs as labourers on building sites or in road construction, work which disappeared in the long Finnish winter and was seasonal everywhere. With unemployment normally came destitution.[7]

Overleaf:
For Otto Nagel art was a political weapon. He was an ardent Communist, and his painting of four lonely people, 'The Park Bench, Wedding' (Wedding in a suburb of Berlin where there was an old people's home), is an indictment of the way capitalist society treated its aged poor. It was painted in 1927, six years before Hitler came to power. The Nazis condemned Nagel's art as 'degenerate'; he spent time in a concentration camp and over twenty of his canvases were destroyed. Their ideological message, however, should not blind us to his understanding of and sympathy for human unhappiness.

The fate of poor older people was similar everywhere. They had no alternative. If they had surviving families, as many did not given the high death-rates of the early 20th century, these were likely also to be too poor to give older relatives more than minimal support. Public welfare support, everywhere, was minimal and generally deliberately stigmatizing. Better-paid, mainly male, skilled workers often belonged to pension savings schemes, but they were a minority of poorer people. The first state pensions were designed to diminish this degradation and to raise the status of people whose poverty, often after a long life of toil, was not their own fault. But pensions were rarely enough to enable old people to give up work, nor were they intended to be. They did (as was intended) assist children to support ageing parents, or supplement personal saving to enable some individuals to retire.

In capitalist countries in the 1920s and '30s occupational and private pensions and retirement at around ages 60–65 spread through the lower levels of (mainly male) 'white-collar' workers. Poorer manual workers also increasingly gave up permanent paid work at earlier ages than before, but for different reasons. An effect of the high unemployment of these years was that older workers were often unable to find other jobs once unemployed. It was thought desirable, for example by the International Labour Office (ILO, a division of the League of

Nations), for older people to retire when jobs were scarce, leaving work for the young. The ILO advocated state pensions at a level sufficient to support retirement. This was nowhere the reality at this time, though in the United States unemployment among older male workers, including many in the middle classes, led to the Social Security Act of 1935. For the first time in American history old people were assured of a regular income.[8]

But nowhere did a state pension provide more than a very basic income. The reality for very many older people who were no longer able to support themselves by work was poverty. Men, especially, often ended their lives in workhouses or other institutions. George Orwell described a private lodging house in northern England in the 1930s where unemployed, and even some employed, men lived four to an overcrowded, squalid room. They included 'two old age pensioners' who handed their weekly pensions over to the proprietors 'and in return got the kind of accommodation you would expect for ten shillings; that is a bed in the attic and meals chiefly of bread-and-butter'. One was dying of cancer and only left his bed once a week to collect his pension. The other, 'called by everyone Old Jack, was an ex-miner aged seventy-eight who had worked well over fifty years in the pits'.[9]

State pensions varied from country to country; first Germany, then Denmark, then New Zealand had introduced them before 1900. By the 1920s, hardly any old people were left penniless. At first fairly meagre, payments did increase as the result of demand. Just before World War II, in 1939, old age pensioners militantly demanded a rise.

Soup kitchens were long needed for retired or unemployed men who did not qualify for official benefits. But they were regarded as humiliating to the old. From 'L'Assiette au Beurre', 1903.

LA SOUPE
En attendant les retraites ouvrières...

Soviet Russia, priding itself on its care for the workers, was in the forefront of pension schemes. But it was a poor country and every effort was made to keep people at work as long as possible. This photograph tells an exemplary tale. Mikhail Vorobyov retired in 1974 at the age of 60, but he was unhappy without work and voluntarily returned to the factory, where he was always welcome (second from left). He was also a member of the Vocational Orientation Council at the plant.

The story was different in the Soviet Union, which was committed ideologically to the valorization of work and workers and to exhibiting the long-lived vitality of which workers had become capable in a workers' democracy. The country also needed maximum employment if it was to expand the economy; and it could not easily afford to pay pensions to large numbers of people. Hence it had a strong incentive to keep people at work until as late in life as possible. In 1935 Stalin proclaimed the importance of exploiting to the full the experience of older workers. One of many exhortatory stories of the time was of a 96-year-old former Red Partisan and collective farmer who moved to Moscow, where he was given a room and a pension, but who still refused to give up work, finding employment as a watchman. In the Soviet Union, unlike other countries, by the 1930s 'pensioner' was a respectable identity, implying age and seniority rather than dependency. The social-security system was designed to encourage people to work to as late an age as possible; to turn them into welfare dependants, it was said, would rob them of full participation in Soviet society. Thus, as they became unfit for their accustomed jobs, they were transferred to lighter employment, though with consequent loss of earnings. A skilled electrician might become a watchman, a carpenter a toilet attendant – as he might also in the West, without the accompanying ideological rhetoric. A difference from the West, though, was that old people were officially represented as citizens of a distinctive and in some ways privileged kind.

Older Soviet workers were more likely than their capitalist counterparts to remain employed in the 1920s and '30s and to receive greater rhetorical valorization, but their conditions of life were often considerably worse, though, in a still very poor country, this was also true of younger workers. After World War II pensions improved somewhat for Soviet citizens who were too old to work, especially for professionals and those who were deemed to have given distinguished service to the USSR, but pressure on older people to keep on working remained strong.[10]

Their political leaders practised what they preached, if in somewhat greater comfort – and if they survived the purges and rivalries among the leadership. Stalin himself died in office in 1953, aged 74, as did Brezhnev in 1982, aged 76. Khrushchev retired in 1964, aged 71. It was not only in the Soviet Union that politicians (and indeed other professionals) worked longer than their poorer contemporaries. Winston Churchill had reached the state pension age of 65 in 1939 when World War II began and he sustained a punishing workload as war leader for the next six years. He became prime minister again in 1951, aged 77, though by then he was in poor health; he retired, reluctantly, four years later. F.D. Roosevelt died in office in 1945 at the relatively young age of 63, the age at which Dwight D. Eisenhower assumed the Presidency of the United States in 1953. He remained in office for eight years. Charles de Gaulle became President of France in 1958 aged 68, and remained in office for 11 years. Old men dominated the politics of many states in the mid-20th century, sometimes, especially dictators, outstaying their capacities for the role, as with Francisco Franco, who gave up control of Spain reluctantly when he was close to death at age 83 in 1975. By the end of the century, however, most states had younger leaders, elected in their 40s or 50s.

World leaders never retire, and their age is rarely seen as a disqualification for high office. This was particularly true of the years after World War II. When Charles de Gaulle, President of France, aged 72, visited Germany in 1962 he met Chancellor Konrad Adenauer, aged 86.

Irony ends in pathos in Saul Steinberg's 'Untitled, 1954', a version of
the traditional diagram of the Ages of Man. The successful man rises
from infant, through boy scout, academic, business man, tycoon to...
playboy on a beach in Florida, retired, relaxed, happy but – useless.

It was only after World War II, especially from the 1950s, that improved pensions were introduced in all Western capitalist countries and retirement at 60/65 became normal for most people, more quickly in some countries than others. However, simultaneously, the International Labour Organization, supported by many governments, including those of Britain and France, reversed its previous attitude to retirement and argued that earlier retirement should be discouraged. It was believed that the shrinking numbers of younger workers, due to the low pre-war birth-rates, necessitated older workers staying in the workforce to sustain the now buoyant post-war international economy.

Nevertheless, retirement at 60/65 gradually became almost universal. Workers wanted a period of rest between a long working life and the onset of physical decline, understandably since manual workers who were in their 60s in the 1950s might have been working since they were 12 or 13. Nowhere did their pensions make them rich but they enabled them to survive without working and, as living standards improved, more were helped by their children. But the sudden experience of limitless leisure late in life was not always easy. British carworkers and shipbuilders retiring in the 1970s 'seemed worn out and despairingly lost, cut off from former workmates. They wept on their last day at work [and said] "I felt terrible". "It seemed as though you were suddenly cut off from life". They lay in bed in the morning "puzzled about how to fill me time in".' Yet a group of miners was so sustained by the community network of neighbours and relatives that giving up work seemed a positive blessing. 'When a person's been underground for so many years it's a new lease of life. It's just a grand feeling.'[11]

Employers were generally not persuaded of the value of older workers except in traditional marginal jobs and, increasingly, modern technology provided efficient alternatives to ageing cleaners or frail watchmen. Employers compensated for the shortfall in younger workers by employing more women and immigrant workers.

So, at the very time that most people were living longer and remaining fitter to later ages, instead of working later in life they left the labour market at earlier ages than ever before. This became particularly evident in the 1980s, when the recurrence of high levels of unemployment internationally again led to earlier retirements. By the late 1990s almost one-third of West European workers had retired permanently from paid work by the age of 60. Some left willingly, on comfortable pensions, to enjoy relaxation, travel, consumption. A new generation of WOOPIES (Well-Off Older Persons) was identified by advertisers and welcomed by politicians. But they were a distinct minority. Others gave up work more reluctantly.[12]

It was sometimes argued that early retirement was the unavoidable consequence of changing technologies: skills and knowledge became obsolescent ever faster and older people could not keep pace. But all the evidence pointed in the opposite direction. Older workers certainly suffered from the belief by employers and others in their declining abilities and low adaptability, but, whenever it was put to the test, people, even in their 70s or older, proved themselves highly capable of learning new skills. In fact they could cope better in the high-tech labour market of the late 20th century, which required brain power rather than physical power.[13]

Rather, older workers were rejected from a shrinking labour market because they were more costly, and often less malleable, than younger people. But by the end of the century it was recognized that when they left the workplace, their experience and often greater reliability, compared with younger workers, went too. Also, enterprises and governments became concerned about the growing cost of pensions and the falling numbers of younger workers capable of paying the contributions required to fund the pensions of older people.

Much alarm was aroused by predictions that the proportions of older people, aged 60 and over, would rise from, in 1990, 15.5 per cent in Australia, 20.4 per cent in Germany, 22.8 per cent in Sweden, 20.7 per cent in the UK and 16.8 per cent in the US; to, in 2020, 18.2 per cent, 28.3 per cent, 26.5 per cent, 24 per cent and 22.5 per cent respectively; with corresponding reductions in the numbers aged 15-60 — people of actual and potential working age, as conventionally defined.[14] Such bald statistics ignored the potential effects of international migration on the age structures of wealthier countries, since migrants tend to be young; or the possibility of a future reversal of the declining birth-rates of most countries. These were the very same mistakes which had been made in the previous panic about the dire impending consequences of the ageing of populations — in the 1920s–1940s. These had been quite erroneous — both birth-rates and migration increased internationally during and after World War II — but they had been wholly forgotten by the end of the century. Nor did estimates of the cost 'burden' of older populations take account of the savings accruing from smaller numbers of children and young people requiring expensive education and other services. Equally importantly they assumed that working and retirement ages would not change, despite the clear evidence that by the end of the century people reaching retirement age were much fitter than their counterparts earlier in the century when retirement rules were introduced and were capable and often willing to remain in employment to later ages.[15] Workers, governments and employers introduced new incentives to reverse the trend of the previous half-century, delay retirement and extend the normal working life.

Against this background, however, in the 1990s workers had good reason to worry about the future security of their pensions, as governments and employers sought to cut them. Once more, this was more so in some countries than others. Both state and employer pensions were substantially cut in Britain, Australia and New Zealand. In France, Germany and other Western European countries workers were better able to defend their pensions.

At the end of the century, attitudes to and the experiences of older workers were changing, driven by social and economic change. More measured analysis of the implications of the ageing of populations concluded that the costs of supporting the immediate, large, generation of older people was easily containable by the advanced economies and that in the longer-run, even if patterns of migration and fertility did not change, changing retirement practices combined with changed patterns of saving and expenditure by individuals and governments could avert the 'crisis' which some had foretold.[16]

Rules of retirement are surprisingly varied. In some of the higher professions retirement is compulsory at 60 or 65. In more lowly jobs older workers can stay on indefinitely if they wish — as many do. Here an obviously elderly man — around the time when old-age pensions were first introduced in Britain — takes part in the cleaning and restoration of an English church.

Medical knowledge was changing too. It was only in the 20th century that medicine achieved the capacity to diagnose and cure extensively, and only since the mid-20th century have medical services been easily and cheaply available to people of all ages in most developed countries. Much of the gain benefited younger people, enabling them to survive to later ages. Research not specifically directed towards older people improved diagnosis and treatment of conditions common among them, such as heart disease, hypertension and cancers. Modern technology could also be used to keep people alive but with a poor quality of life, posing new ethical dilemmas for medicine.

Though medicine directed towards the needs of older people became firmly established, it remained low in status in the medical hierarchy. Awareness that older people posed specific questions for medical research is as old as medicine itself, but only from the beginning of the 20th century did a specialized medicine of old age, known as geriatrics, develop internationally. The term was coined in the United States in 1909 by an Austrian-born medical practitioner, Ignatz Nascher (1863–1945). Nascher believed, correctly, that doctors paid insufficient attention to the ill-health of older people: since they had not long to live, it was not thought worthwhile trying to cure them. The persistence of this belief slowed acceptance of his work and has ensured that geriatrics remains persistently marginalized internationally.

Nascher believed that the health of older people could be improved by better diet, exercise and mental stimulation. This had been recommended for centuries. Nascher demonstrated its efficacy through experiments with older people in New York in the 1920s, but his work was slow to gain acceptance in the medical world of the United States and other non-Communist countries.[17]

For unexplained reasons the Caspian republic of Georgia holds the record for the longevity of its population. It is not uncommon to find a man of 90, as here, still tending his vines.

A Georgian great-grandmother, aged, almost incredibly, 137, tells fairy-stories to her young descendants (opposite).

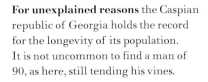

The desire to prolong active life, even, at last, to reveal the secret of rejuvenation, received stronger support in the Soviet Union, driven by the conviction that Bolshevism could revolutionize even the lifespan. Soviet gerontologists argued that humankind had the capacity to live much longer than was currently the case, to 120 and beyond, and that Soviet society could demonstrate its comprehensive superiority by bringing this about. Statistics which demonstrated that average Soviet life expectancy had improved since the revolution of 1917 were invoked to prove the superiority of Communist society, though similar or greater gains were evident in non-Communist countries. Experiments with hormones and glandular grafts to humans from monkeys were encouraged, which, it was hoped, would restore youthful vigour, even cure male impotence. The Soviet press publicized feats of longevity which allegedly demonstrated that Soviet citizens were already achieving exceptional lifespans. Such feats of superlongevity were apparently most prevalent in the Caucasus. A succession of Soviet medical researchers in the 1930s, '50s, '60s and '70s sought the secret of the apparently greater lifespans of Caucasian peasants, without success. Despite these seeming exceptions, in their determination to valorize the industrial worker, Soviet leaders were less inclined than some in earlier centuries to attribute long life to the benefits of rural living. It was believed, in the Soviet Union as elsewhere, that diet, exercise and hygiene could maintain health and extend life in any environment.[18]

Geriatric medicine became increasingly attractive in non-Communist countries as the numbers of older people, and the costs of their medical care, increased. In Britain by the 1930s large numbers of stroke patients were filling hospital beds because improvements in drug treatments kept them alive but did not restore their mobility. Increased use of physiotherapy and other forms of rehabilitation freed them from hospital in growing numbers. With the introduction in Britain in 1948 of a National Health Service providing free healthcare for all citizens, and the establishment of similar systems throughout Europe such practices became more widespread. Greater access to healthcare for poorer ageing people revealed that attention to quite mundane but disabling conditions affecting the hearing, eyesight, teeth and feet of older people could greatly improve their lives. Conditions which had long been regarded as natural features of ageing, to be endured, could now be cured.

Improvements in medical technology and drug therapy continued to the end of the century to extend active life through procedures such as implantation of cardiac pacemakers and joint and organ replacements. Hormone Replacement Therapy (HRT) was hailed as bringing the longed-for rejuvenation to post-menopausal women, though there were reports of adverse side effects. Certain causes of death in older age groups, notably heart disease, declined, though this was due above all to the age-old remedies of improved diet and exercise.

Health care for the old improves all the time, not only because of the increased availability of money but also because of medical advances. Immunisation against pneumonia and related diseases is now provided free of charge in most European countries.

As life is prolonged the pattern of fatal diseases changes. Most people now die of diseases that are specific to old age. Opposite: a CT scan of the brain of a patient with Alzheimer's Disease, showing the dark areas affected by degeneration, leading to senile dementia. Medical research is now concentrated upon conditions which in the past affected only a minority of the population.

Aged 80 or over?

Make sure you get your pneumo jab

ⓘmmunisation
the safest way to protect your health for life

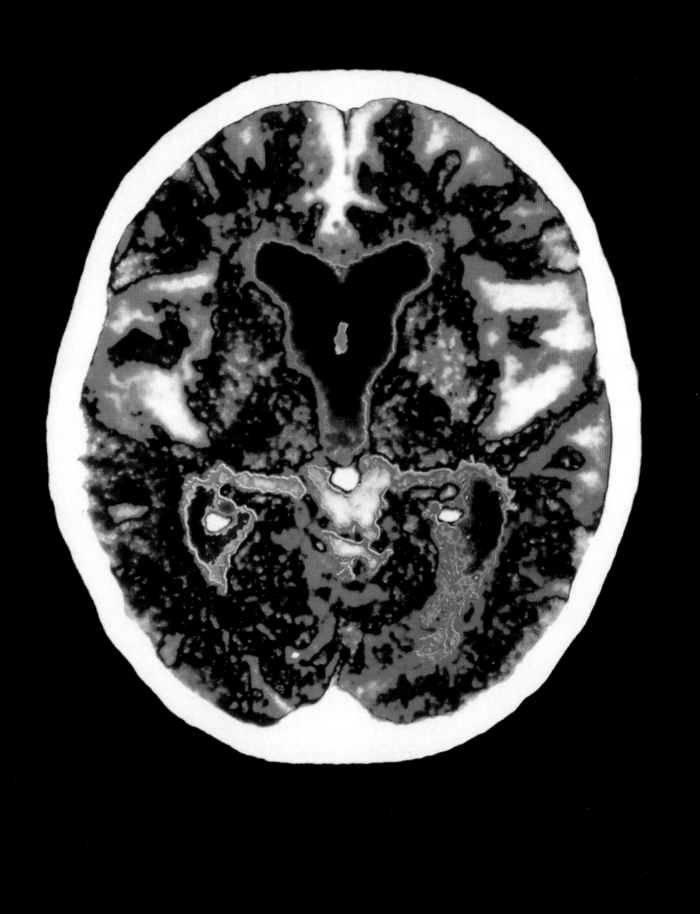

The outcome by the end of the century was the simultaneous survival of the largest numbers of fit people in their 60s and 70s ever known, and of the largest numbers of chronically ill older people ever known. Many who recovered from acute conditions which would have killed them in earlier times succumbed to chronic disorders such as arthritis, diabetes or Alzheimer's. But the majority of people surviving to their 80s and 90s at the end of the century did not suffer from acute illness and regarded themselves as in good health and capable of independent activity. For most people, even at very late ages, death was not preceded by a long period of serious dependency, though all of these experiences varied by age, class and gender.[19]

More old people lived alone in the later 20th century. This was often interpreted as meaning increased loneliness, especially when linked to the falling birth-rate, increased divorce and increased geographical mobility. Some people were old, alone and lonely. This had always been the fate of some old people. But many more younger people also lived alone and very many older people preferred independence to dependence on their children. They were in frequent contact with family and friends even when they lived alone. Family size fell over the century, but, unlike all previous centuries, overwhelmingly children survived to adulthood and old age and, although people had fewer children, more older people than ever before had at least one surviving child. Children did not necessarily live close at hand, but mobility, especially in search of work, both within and between nations had been an international fact of life for centuries. When children migrated in previous centuries, perhaps to the other side of the world, contact might be lost entirely. Improved communications over the 20th century meant that families could keep in ready contact by telephone, later by email, and get together easily by fast means of transport. Separation was not initiated only by younger people. Increasingly as affluence grew, older people in the northern United States or Europe moved far from their children to enjoy retirement in Florida or Arizona, Spain or southern France; sometimes, particularly in the US, in retirement communities which were not always welcoming to younger relatives. They might move again, closer to their children, at a later, more fragile stage of old age.[20]

Older, like younger, people changed their appearances over the century. How they were represented and represented themselves changed as their styles of life became more varied. Older people in the later 20th century tended to look younger than people of similar age in the past, not least because they were healthier and had their natural teeth rather than false teeth or none. Medical specialists suggested that 75-year-olds at the end of the century were physiologically similar to 60- or 65-year-olds at the beginning of the century.[21]

'Remind me – am I getting up or going to bed?'

Not everyone feels like laughing at jokes about the infirmities of old age, but at least they have lost the element of cruelty that characterised them in the past. This cartoon appeared in 'The Oldie', a magazine specifically aimed at older readers.

The age-specific dress codes of earlier centuries slowly disappeared, more gradually in the countryside than the towns and in poorer than richer regions. It became easier for men and women to disguise the signs of ageing, as cosmetics and hair dyes improved in range and quality and became cheaper and more readily available from the 1930s onwards. Cosmetic surgery was also more effective and increasingly used by the end of the century.

Such rejuvenation of the appearance was still widely stigmatized in the middle of the century, but less so as it became more commonplace. However, it remained controversial and far from universal even among those who could afford it. For each well-known figure who used every available artifice to seek to appear unchangingly young in appearance, into their 60s or beyond, another would make her or his ageing body publicly visible, e.g., the National Portrait Gallery portrait of Germaine Greer and the self-portraits of Lucian Freud. Painters and photographers called in question the widely held view that old age was not valued in the late 20th century through dignified depictions of older people.

For the creative artist old age need make little difference. For Lucian Freud, the fascination of the naked body never depended on youth or conventional beauty. This study of himself, 'Painter Working, Reflection' (1993), was made when he was over 70. The Australian literary historian and critic Germaine Greer likewise rejects the prevailing fashion for 'rejuvenation' in any of its forms. Her 1995 portrait at the age of 56 by Paula Rego (right) shows a woman for whom the ageing process is not a problem.

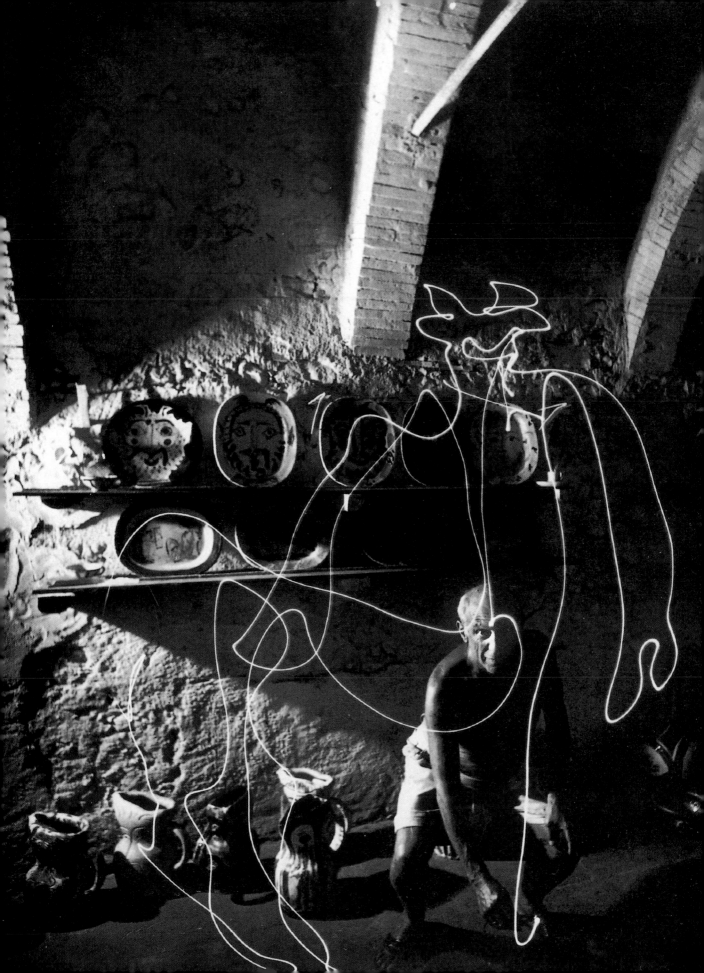

Picasso's creative energy never left him. He was already nearly 70 when he drew a wild beast in the air with a flashlight, the line being caught by the photographer's open lens. For Picasso, art itself was action, just as the wild beast in him was part of his humanity. The photo is by Gjon Mili, of 'Life', 1950.

Should they retire? The question has been asked of many powerful old men past and present. But boundless confidence, complete belief in the rightness of their cause and the loyalty of their admirers make them impregnable. Fidel Castro and Pope John Paul II are shining examples, in their own contrasting spheres, of men unwilling to relinquish power in their late 70s and 80s. Indeed, the Pope earned very wide admiration for refusing to give up in spite of being severely disabled and terminally ill.

'*High Kicks*', a photograph celebrating the vitality, though not the dignity, of old age. It was taken in 1953 on the promenade of Blackpool, a popular holiday resort in Britain. For these ladies old age holds no terrors.

Some argued that a cult of youth forced older people to disguise their ages, denying them the possibility to 'grow old gracefully' and 'naturally'. Others responded that there had been nothing graceful about the natural ageing of all too many old people in the past, and no obvious reason why at a certain age people should become less free to alter their appearance, or be bound by more rigid style conventions than the young. Rather, older people had more freedoms than ever before and age boundaries were being destabilized.

Representations of old age in literature and memoirs expressed this growing variety of experience. The energetic, committed, well-to-do British social reformer Beatrice Webb reflected in her diary in the 1930s and '40s on her own ageing and that of her husband, the Labour Party politician Sidney Webb. She oscillated between commenting on her failing powers and relief at the degree of activity of which she was still capable. She observed the variety of experiences of ageing. Her sister Rosy, who as a young woman had been a highly problematic anorexic, at close to 70 was enjoying greater independence than ever. She was *here for a week, between her voyage to the Arctic regions round about Spitzbergen and returning to Majorca for the winter… Rosy is happier and healthier than I have ever known her during her youth and prime of life… she has become a globe-trotter with a purpose – the enjoyment and picturing of nature and architecture… her husband and children are more or less dependent upon her for subsidies and she certainly is generous with her limited income – travelling third class or cheap tourist, staying at cheap lodging… the secret of her happiness is her art, her freedom to go and do as she likes and make casual friends by the way.*

But an 84-year-old friend had slipped into miserable decline:

Louise is hopelessly crippled and creeps about the house. Her mind is clear and old age and helplessness have softened her outlook on the world… but she is desperately lonely and bored with existence… The plain truth is that the aged feel what their children and some of their friends are thinking about: "If you are not enjoying life, why don't you die and be done with it". And the old person may feel that there is no answer, except that he does not want to die or does not see any comfortable way of doing it.

Beatrice Webb died, aged 85, in 1943. Her diary conveys an explicit struggle against a stereotype of helplessness, initially triumphant, but less successful as time went on.[22]

For intellectuals declining powers are harder to bear. Beatrice and Sydney Webb, economists and social critics, went on producing influential books into old age, but her diary records her growing depression. She was 84 when this photograph was taken in their London garden.

The French writer Simone de Beauvoir drew on Proust, Gide, Mauriac and others to support her relentlessly negative depiction of old age in her book of the same name (1970, in French *La Vieillesse*, in US *The Coming of Age*), written in her own, in fact active and highly productive, old age. She asked: 'Are the old really human beings? Judging by the way our society treats them, the question is open to doubt... old age is a shameful secret, a forbidden subject', reaching deeply pessimistic conclusions. De Beauvoir provided a characteristically subtle and insightful account of the problem of defining old age:

> *Hitherto I have spoken of old age as though that expression stood for a clearly defined reality. In fact, as far as our own species is concerned old age is by no means easy to define. It is a biological phenomenon... It brings with it psychological consequences — certain forms of behaviour are rightly looked upon as being characteristic of old age. And like all human situations it has an existential dimension — it changes the individual's relationship with time and therefore his relationship with the world and with his own history. Then again man never lives in a state of nature: in his own old age, as at every period of his life, his status is imposed upon him by the society in which he belongs. What so complicates the whole problem is the close interdependence of all these points of view... Lastly society takes into account the aged man's personal make-up — his decrepitude or his experience for example — when it allots him his role and position: and conversely. The individual is conditioned by society's theoretical and practical attitude towards him.*[23]

The poet Edith Sitwell, aged 75, made herself into an icon of old age. Melancholy, sensitivity, wisdom — even beauty — are all there in this self-consciously 'produced' photograph by Cecil Beaton. She died two years later.

The personal stories recounted by de Beauvoir depict lives in old age as various as those described by Beatrice Webb. In 1968 a 75-year-old former waitress lived alone in poverty in central Paris, in an attic, without gas, electricity or running water, up 'three storeys of handsome staircase, then two half-floors of steep narrow steps... "It is a nightmare for me," said Madame R. "Sometimes in winter, when I am not very steady on my feet, I stay there leaning against the wall, wondering whether I shall ever get down again"... She is not bored, she says. She walks about a great deal; she reads the headlines at the newspaper stand, and neighbours give her yesterday's paper. When she can she goes to ceremonies in Paris.'[24]

Worse still was the situation de Beauvoir found described in a realistic Dutch novel by Jacoba Van Velde (in French *La Grande Salle*) of an old woman's experience in a residential home: 'Never alone — it's dreadful. Always surrounded by people!... and they treat you as though you were one or two years old — a baby.'[25]

More optimistic were the findings of a survey of French centenarians carried out in 1959. There were six or seven hundred in France at that time, most in Brittany, four out of five of them female. They *had had a great variety of jobs... they were then living in the country with their children or grandchildren, or in some cases in institutions or rest-homes... They had very little money; they were all thin... They loved their food but ate little. Many of them were strong and well, and this also applied to the men — there was one who played billiards at over 99. Some of the women were slightly shaky, they were a little hard of hearing and their sight was dim, but they were neither blind nor deaf. They slept well. They passed their time reading, knitting or taking short walks. Their minds were clear and their memories excellent. They were independent, even-tempered and sometimes gay; they had a lively sense of humour and they were very sociable. They were high-handed towards their 70-year-old children and treated them as young people. Sometimes they complained of the present-day generation, but they were interested in modern times and kept in touch with what was going on... they... had never suffered from any chronic illness. They did not seem afraid of death.*[26]

Some novelists depicted old age positively and benignly, such as Ann Tyler in *Patchwork Planet* (1998) and Alison Lurie in *The Last Resort* (1998) — even as mischievous fun, as is the case with the ageing theatrical twin sisters at the centre of Angela Carter's *Wise Children* (1991).

Poetry also represented the variety of old age. Jenny Joseph's old woman was also mischievous:

> *When I am an old woman, I shall wear purple*
> *With a red hat that doesn't go, and doesn't suit me*
> *And I shall spend my pension on brandy and summer gloves*
> *...*
> *And run my stick along the public railings*
> *And make up for the sobriety of youth.*

While Dylan Thomas in 1951 urged his dying father to resist resignation to old age:

> *Do not go gentle into that good night,*
> *Old Age should burn and rave at close of day;*
> *Rage, rage against the dying of the light.*

Film, the quintessential medium of the 20th century, also defies simple generalizations about its depictions of old age. Some representations are positive. The Danish film *Babette's Feast* (1987) depicts an occasion of brief rejuvenation when a servant wins a lottery and spends her winnings providing a feast for a group of ageing people for whom she works. They relax, dance, are happy for an evening. In the Scottish film *Local Hero* (1983), a stubborn old man saves his community from the worst effects of exploitation by an oil company by winning over the equally elderly Texan who owns it.

Other films convey the complexities of relationships within and between the generations and the varied characteristics of older people. In the American film *On Golden Pond* (1981) an older couple are subtly represented, she (Katharine Hepburn) as active, lively, optimistic, he (Henry Fonda), a retired college professor, acerbic, introverted and raging against increasing frailty. At one point he scolds young people: 'Do you think it's funny being old? My whole goddam body's falling apart.' They negotiate and, rather too easily, resolve the tensions between the father and the younger generation.

Films also explore relations across social divisions. Krzysztof Kieslowski's *Red* (1995) depicts a compassionate young model who befriends an unhappy, reclusive old man, a retired judge. Their relationship regenerates both their lives. In the British film *Mrs Brown* (1997), the ageing Queen Victoria, grieving for Prince Albert and withdrawn from public life, regains her emotional strength through her relationship with her retainer Mr Brown. The film examines how class differences complicate the relationship. *Driving Miss Daisy* (1989) explores a similar supportive relationship between a 72-year-old wealthy Jewish widow and a black chauffeur in late middle age in the southern United States over 25 years from the late 1940s. She is excitable, spoilt, cantankerous; he calm, patient, generous. She grows emotionally as together they experience racial discrimination and intolerance, the civil rights movement and family events. In the end he is a stronger source of support to her than her children when she descends into dementia.

More negative representations of old age appear in the French two-film epic *Jean de Florette* (1986) and *Manon des Sources* (1987), in which an old bachelor causes the deaths of his only son and his nephew in his embittered determination to preserve the land on which he lives and pass it to the next generation. The American film *Lost in Yonkers* (1993) centres on Grandma Kurnitz, who is unrelentingly mean-spirited. Her personality was formed by her own traumatic childhood and has scarred her own children. This exact opposite of the stereotypical sweet grandmother is portrayed as equally unyielding with her two grandsons. The latter grow emotionally by learning to cope with their grandmother; she is too scarred by her past to grow by responding to them.

Films more often undermine than reinforce negative stereotypes of old age, representing older people as original, idiosyncratic characters, independent and autonomous. They are often more engaged with life than their middle-aged children, with whom they are depicted as having less in common than with the still-younger generation, who also resist control by the middle generation – perhaps another idealized stereotype.[27]

Film, the art form of the 20th and 21st centuries, has inevitably faced the subject of old age. 'On Golden Pond' (opposite top) of 1981 turned on the relationship between characters played by Katharine Hepburn and Henry Fonda, the one enjoying life optimistically in spite of the passing of time, the other angrily resenting the loss of youth. Below: a scene from 'Jean de Florette' (1986), which highlights the bitterness of an old bachelor as he fights to keep control of his land.

How do these representations of old age by professional writers and filmmakers compare with how old people who have no claim to fame see themselves and are seen by others?

In 1992 the British research organization Mass Observation gathered a set of writings on impressions of 'growing older'. A dominant theme among the responses was the variety of the experiences of ageing. A 65-year-old retired female local government officer summed up a common feeling: 'it's this habit of wanting to treat all people of a certain age group in the same way that seems wrong, whatever that age group is. People are no longer allowed to be individuals.' A retired female library assistant commented:

> Now that I am 67 I must consider myself to be 'elderly'. General outlook and attitude seem to be the deciding factor in placing people in age categories. The old saying 'you're as old as you feel' has some truth in it and we all know people who are old at 40 and some who are much older but have an interest in life and an awareness of all about them, who give an impression of comparative youthfulness in spite of the lines and wrinkles.

A 67-year-old housewife from Kent wrote: 'These days you aren't classed as old until you are 80. I don't feel old, with fashions very flexible you can look fashionable up to any age. My mother is 95 and she wears very fashionable clothes.' The 'flexibility' of modern fashion and the disappearance of age-related dress codes were often mentioned as central to the widely perceived blurring of age boundaries.

This was not just self-deception among the old, seeking to deny the unpleasant reality of ageing, for it was a perception shared by younger people. A female shop supervisor, who was almost 40, discussed older women in the following terms:

> I remember my mother saying 'I may be a wrinkled 57 on the outside, but I'm 17 inside', when I caught her playing hopscotch out on the pavement with my daughter. I'm beginning to understand what she meant... some people are born 'middle aged' while some old folk sparkle, are open-minded and have a zest for life.

> I find it very difficult to estimate people's ages. Indeed age doesn't seem a very important consideration in view of improved housing, nutrition and medicine... with extended life expectancy, I believe you can be considered young until the late 40s, then be at a peak until 55–66 years... then enjoy a further rewarding and active phase (perhaps this is middle age) until the physical deterioration which eventually comes with advancing years forces you to slow down into 'old age', which can still be a rewarding experience if you have your faculties and a decent standard of living. Of course, there are many factors other than chronological age which determine whether you are

perceived to be young, middle-aged or old. Good health... social and economic status... doing a job one enjoys.

As a volunteer worker for social services, I have supported women I've regarded as being a generation older than myself and suddenly realized that they are ten years younger than me. They have a poor self-image, are worn down by marital and financial problems, are in poor shape physically.

On the other hand as a member of a keep-fit association, I am often amazed when fellow-members reveal their ages. Women in their 70s with trim, supple bodies glow with vitality and enthusiasm for life and look twenty years younger.

A 44-year-old receptionist described her vision of the late 20th-century 'ages of women':

By 50 the grey hairs might be showing slightly and there might be menopausal problems, but notwithstanding she is still living life to the full. By 60 she might be slowing down, but can still keep up looking

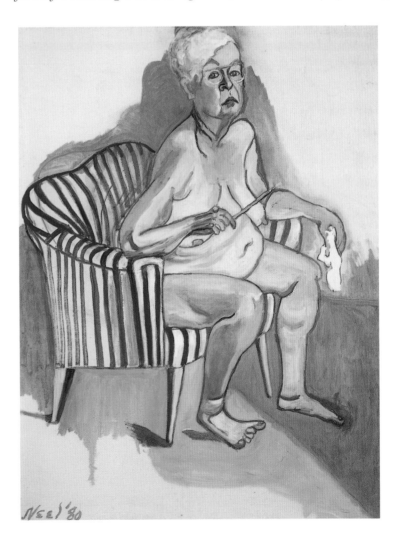

It is a measure of the acceptability of the aged body that artists can now paint themselves in the nude without either pathos or embarrassment. Alice Neel, aged 80, is as alert and active as she was fifty years before.

after the grandchildren and taking exercise. By 70 and 80 though there is a big difference, with not being as active and having a lined face.

The respondents were divided as to whether women aged faster than men, though most emphasized the negative impact of retirement on men and the benefit to women of the continuity of their working lives, because household tasks continued, and of the acceptability of cosmetics for women.

A stronger theme was the need and capacity of older people for independence. Inability to sustain independent living emerged as the most important perceived marker of the onset of old age, for women and men. A 60-year-old midwife stated that ' "old" is when you can no longer do what you want'. A widow wrote: 'although I am aged 78 I do not think of myself as old but elderly. Perhaps because I am fairly independent and can look after myself.' Several writers expressed fears that when they ceased to live independently they would be stereotyped and patronized.

A writer and counsellor living in London expressed her response to conventional stereotypes:

Yesterday I was 60. There – I have come out and said it. How does it feel? Well a whole lot better than I thought. Never, but never have I so dreaded a birthday. But why should this be such a milestone? We are indoctrinated, that's why… So I am a Senior Citizen and an old age pensioner? This is ludicrous because I feel 25 going on 18. The years I

suppose have been kind to me but no-one stays the same. Still I know my personality is as eccentric and adventurous as it ever was... is it my imagination or are people stepping outside the age categories as it becomes increasingly difficult to tell how old they are?

This optimistic woman had a good marriage to a younger man, following an earlier disastrous marriage. The ageing of their husbands influenced the outlook of many women on their own ageing. A 67-year-old retired clerk wrote:

I feel considerably older than I did even five years ago, probably because I have a husband who has Parkinson's disease and I am unable to leave him to himself for more than a week. I am not enjoying getting old and I don't believe if everyone was honest they would not agree with me.

Personality and other aspects of their environment affected individual outlooks on ageing. A 54 year old woman wrote: 'I have lived too long. I am not decrepit but I no longer think the world such a wonderful place. I live in an insular community where progress is slow.'

The writers had divided views about whether older people were respected in British society. An 'almost 65'-year-old housewife thought: 'Yes, I think most people respect the elderly. In fact some elderly don't respect the younger ones today.' A 48-year-old carer commented: 'No, I don't think as a society we respect older people en masse, but I certainly respect my older friends.' A part-Chinese civil servant aged 47 commented:

We were brought up to respect our grandparents and that attitude continues in this family (the Chinese influence) but this means that grandparents are remote. They get their own way and people running round after them but they are not their grandchildren's friends.

Several writers discussed the changing experience of old people over the century by making comparisons between their own ageing and that of their parents and grandparents, for example a retired social worker from South London recalled:

My grandparents did not do very much outside their homes whereas my elderly and old friends attend day classes (university extramural) and visit family and friends in this country and abroad.[28]

A group of older women in a writing workshop in Melbourne in 1994 revealed to the two women in their late 40s leading the workshop that they had previously stereotyped old women as an undifferentiated mass, unaware of the differences among them. The older women commented on the difference between the faces they saw in the mirror and their senses of themselves: 'below the ageing surface, a sense of

Received ideas of old age have changed dramatically throughout history, as we have seen. From ancient Greece to the end of the Middle Ages it was generally perceived as an unmitigated tragedy, to be endured only for the sake of a reward in the next world. In the 18th and 19th centuries the picture lightens, except for those who have other crosses to bear such as poverty or illness. Only with the late 20th century has old age come to be seen as a stage in life that (with luck, health and freedom) can be enjoyed on its own terms.

youthful identity is maintained, a continuous sense of the self that does not match the reflection in the mirror.' But they refused to substitute negative stereotypes with equally simplified positive ones and were adamant that 'we [should] not glorify ageing or simply reverse the binary and equate old with beautiful'. One 64-year-old complained of slowing down, aching, of not being able to do what she had done as a young woman. An 82-year-old reported her fury at receiving a badge from her daughter and granddaughter that read: 'I'm old and proud.' 'I'm old,' she said. 'One day you live to be eighty and the next you live to be ninety. What's to be proud of?' Though they were all fit, they expressed fears about the future. As one woman put it: 'As the years go on, if there is one paramount overriding fear it is that of being unable to be in control of one's life or one's bodily functions, a fear of being an enormous and rather revolting burden on one's children.'

One 69-year-old lived more joyously in the present, whether in fact or fantasy is unclear: 'She had surely let herself go. And for the first time in her life, her age collided with her youth and she felt truly free.'[29]

Forty-two women, all born in 1931, were interviewed and photographed in 2000–01 as they neared their 70th birthdays by a woman also born in 1931. They lived mostly in the United States, in Iowa where the author lived, or in New York where she grew up, a few in Britain or Germany. The author was

> delighted by the variety of experience of women who are within months of the same age... My portraits made their age apparent with the kind of shock we all experience when we catch our reflection, involuntarily in a window or mirror. We know we are seventy years old, but our mind's eye sees a different, younger, or perhaps ageless self... [yet m]ost of the women displayed few signs of vanity. Only twelve colour their hair and only seventeen seemed to have dressed up to meet me.

They were all active, independent women, even if they were battling with illness. They had had, and continued to have, very varied lives.[30]

Fifty-five interviews with older men and women, mostly working class, carried out in Britain in the late 1980s told similar stories. Overwhelmingly, when asked: 'Do you think of yourself as old?', people answered no. Only two said definitely yes. Only one, an 82-year-old woman, was firmly negative. She was active and in good health, but she hated being old. Of course, they were aware of physical changes as they aged, but 'feeling old' for them related above all to capacity for independence and to subjective feelings.[31] For all of these older people at the end of the 20th century 'old age' was not just about the number of years they had lived.

1 Introduction: The Age of Old Age

1. D. Vassberg, 'Old Age in Early Modern Castilian Villages', in S. Ottaway, L. Botelho and K. Kittredge (eds), *Power and Poverty. Old Age in the Pre-Industrial Past* (Greenwood, Connecticutt, 2002), pp. 145–66; E. Wrigley, R. Davies and J. Oeppen, *English Population History from Family Reconstitution, 1580–1837* (Cambridge, 1997), pp. 281–93.

2. E. Wrigley, 'Fertility Strategy for the Individual and the Group', in C. Tilly (ed), *Historical Studies in Changing Fertility* (Princeton, 1979), pp. 255–6.

3. J. Falkingham and C. Gordon, 'Fifty Years On: The Income and Household Composition of the Elderly in London and Britain', in B. Bytheway and J. Johnson (eds), *Welfare and the Ageing Experience* (1990), pp. 148–71.

4. P. Thane, *Old Age in English History. Past Experiences, Present Issues* (Oxford, 2000), pp. 73–4.

5. Vassberg, 'Old Age', pp. 156–7.

6. Ibid.; W.A. Achenbaum, *Old Age in the New Land. The American Experience since 1790* (1979), pp. 115–17; C. Haber and B. Gratton, *Old Age and the Search for Security. An American Social History* (Bloomington, 1994), pp. 25–6, 38–42, 86–7; Thane, *Old Age*, pp. 119–46, 287–307, 407–35.

7. Achenbaum, *Old Age in the New Land*, pp. 116–17; Haber and Gratton, *Old Age and the Search for Security*, pp. 116–42; R. Jütte, *Poverty and Deviance in Early Modern Europe* (Cambridge, 1994).

8. Plato, *The Republic*, trans. D. Lee (2nd edn, 1987), pp. 61–3.

9. A. Rowlands, 'Stereotypes and Statistics: Old Women and Accusations of Witchcraft in Early Modern Europe', in Ottaway, Botelho and Kittredge, *Power and Poverty*, p. 169.

10. E.g. R. Harris, *Gender and Aging in Mesopotamia* (Oklahoma, 2000).

11. See Chapters 2–6.

12. S. Shahar, *Growing Old in the Middle Ages* (London, 1997), pp. 25–8.

13. Ibid., pp. 114–19.

14. S. Ottaway, *The Decline of Life. Old Age in Eighteenth Century England* (Cambridge, 2004), p. 33.

15. K. Kittredge, '"The Aged Dame to Venery Inclin'd": Images of Sexual Older Women in Eighteenth-Century Britain', in Ottaway, Botelho and Kittredge, *Power and Poverty*, pp. 247–64.

16. Thane, *Old Age*, p. 85.

17. Ibid., p. 59; G. Gruman, 'A History of Ideas about the Prolongation of Life', *Transactions of the American Philosophical Society*, 56:9 (1966), pp. 1–97.

18. J. Swift, *Gulliver's Travels* (Harmondsworth, 1967), pp. 256–7.

19. J. Vaupel, 'The Remarkable Improvements in Survival at Later Ages', in J. Grimley Evans et al (eds), *Ageing: Science, Medicine and Society. Philosophical Transactions: Biological Sciences* (The Royal Society, 1997), pp. 1799–1804.

20. W. Shakespeare, *As You Like It*, Act 2, Scene 7, lines 157–66.
21. Ibid., Act 2, Scene 3, lines 47–55.
22. Thane, *Old Age*, pp. 50–1.
23. Quoted in Simone de Beauvoir, *Old Age*, trans. Patrick O'Brian (Penguin, Harmondsworth, 1977), pp. 178–9.
24. Michel de Montaigne, *Essays*, trans. John Florio, bk I, ch. LVII.
25. De Beauvoir, *Old Age*, pp. 179–80.
26. Jean-Pierre Bois, *Les Vieux de Montaigne aux premières retraites* (Fayard, 1989), pp. 285–8.
27. Goethe, *Faust*, Part II, Act V, trans. Philip Wayne.
28. De Beauvoir, *Old Age*, pp. 560–3.

2 The Ancient Greek and Roman Worlds

1. *Digest of Roman Law* 50.6.6 pref.
2. Juncus *ap.* Stobaeus, *Florilegium* 50.2.85, W.-H. 1052.1–2.
3. Isidorus, *Origines* 11.2.8, 30, following Jerome, *Comm. in Amos* 2.pr. (*Patr. Lat.* 25.1021–3 = *Corpus Christ., ser. Lat.* 76.255–6).
4. Seneca the Younger, *Consolatio ad Marciam* 21.4: 'non una hominibus senecta est.'
5. *Corpus Inscriptionum Latinarum* (*CIL*) 8.9158 = *Inscriptiones Latinae Selectae* (*ILS*) 8503: 'flos iuventutis.'
6. *Papyrus Sakaon* 40.12–13 (Theadelphia, AD 318–20).
7. *CIL* 11.137 = *ILS* 1980.
8. Seneca the Elder, *Controversiae* 10.5; one defence suggested for this action is that the old slave was useless and was about to die anyway: '*senem inutilem, expiraturum; si verum, inquit, vultis, non occidit illum, sed deficientis et alioqui expiraturi morte usus est.*'
9. St Augustine, *City of God* 15–16, utilizing Pliny the Elder's *Natural History* bk 7.
10. See the brilliant study by P. Zanker, *The Mask of Socrates: the Image of the Intellectual in Antiquity* (Berkeley, Oxford: University of California Press, 1995).
11. Herodotus, *Histories* 1.87.
12. Lucian, *de Luctu* 16–17.
13. T.G. Parkin, *Old Age in the Roman World: A Cultural and Social History* (Johns Hopkins University Press, 2003), pp. 46–51.
14. Hierokles *ap.* Stobaeus, *Flor.* 25.53 (W.-H. 642 = von Arnim, p. 58) and *Flor.* 22.1.24 (W.-H. 503 = von Arnim 53). On the subject of old-age welfare in Athenian and Roman societies, see further T.G. Parkin, 'Out of Sight, Out of Mind: Elderly Members of the Roman Family', in B. Rawson and P. Weaver (eds), *The Roman Family in Italy: Status, Sentiment, Space* (Oxford: Oxford University Press, 1997), pp. 123–48.
15. Aristophanes, *Wasps* 736–40, 1354–7.
16. See further Parkin, 'Out of Sight, Out of Mind' and *Old Age in the Roman World*, ch. 8, including for the notion that old age was a second childhood.
17. Such an exercise has been carried out by the Cambridge Population Group (CAMSIM), and its methods utilized by Richard Saller in the Roman context; see especially R.P. Saller, *Patriarchy, Property and Death* (Cambridge: Cambridge University Press, 1994).
18. There is interesting discussion in this regard in W.K. Lacey, *The Family in Classical Greece* (London: Thames and Hudson, 1968), pp. 116–18.
19. R.P. Saller and B.D. Shaw, 'Tombstones and Roman Family Relations in the Principate', *Journal of Roman Studies* 74 (1984), pp. 124–56, especially pp. 136–7. For ancient Greek grandparents, see the general account by J.-N. Corvisier, 'Les grands-parents dans le monde grec ancien', *Annales de démographie historique* (1991), pp. 21–31, part of a collection of papers on grandparents in history from a demographic perspective.
20. Further discussion in Parkin, *Old Age in the Roman World*, pp. 51–6. For comparative purposes, cf. P Laslett, *A Fresh Map of Life*[2] (London, 1996), ch. 8, and the excellent study by R. Wall, 'Elderly Persons and Members of their Households in England and Wales from Preindustrial Times to the Present', in D.I. Kertzer and P. Laslett (eds), *Aging in the Past: Demography, Society, and Old Age* (Berkeley, Los Angeles and London, 1995), pp. 81–106.
21. R.S. Bagnall and B.W. Frier, *The Demography of Roman Egypt* (Cambridge University Press, 1994), p. 62 (and cf. pp. 146–7 on three-, and in one case four-, generation households).
22. Tacitus, *Dial.* 28.4 has Messalla comment that in the 'good old days' an older female relative would have had charge over the young children of the house; now slaves take control. Grandparents, where they survived, might have had a particular role to play within the household when a child's natural parent or parents were no longer on the scene. It is in just such a situation, that involving children who have lost their parent(s), that we most commonly meet living grandparents in the ancient testimony.
23. Thomas Wiedemann provided an excellent analysis of this theme in his *Adults and Children in the Roman Empire* (London: Routledge, 1989), and it is worth quoting a few sentences (pp. 176–7): 'Classical society relegated children, together with women, old men, and slaves, to the margins of community life. While that gave each of these groups an intermediate position between being fully human and being a beast, it might also give them a position intermediate between the human world and that of the gods... The relative physical weakness of the child, the old man, and the woman, meant that these three groups were thought to require, or deserve, particular support from the supernatural... It is because they are excluded from the political process or from social influence that they have no other way to express their concerns than by reference to powers outside the political community, controlled as it usually is by "rational" adult males... It was this powerlessness that lay behind the assumption that "marginal" groups were more likely to be in touch with the divine world than were adult male citizens... The old are thought to be particularly numinous.'

24. Plato, *Laws* 6.759d; Aristotle, *Politics* 7.1329a30–34.

25. Vestal Virgins being one notable exception, whose (voluntary) 'retirement' after 30 years would roughly coincide with the menopause.

26. Maximianus was popular in the Middle Ages, not least, perhaps, because of the somewhat misogynistic attitudes he sometimes avers. His poems, heavily influenced by the Roman love elegists, are also at times quite racy, which makes his use as a medieval school text more surprising.

27. [Plato,] *Axiochos* 367b.

28. Xenophon, *Apol.* 6, 8; similarly *Mem.* 4.8.1, 8.

29. Aristotle, *Rhetoric* 2.13.

30. Lucian, *Dialogues of the Dead* 27.9. Cf. Sophocles, frag. 66 [Radt]: 'no one loves life like the ageing man', a line, incidentally, that made it into ancient collections of proverbial sayings as illustrating both a positive and a negative attitude towards old age!

31. Juvenal, *Satires* 10.188–288, and cf. Shakespeare's *Hamlet* 2.2.195–208. See further Parkin, *Old Age in the Roman World*, pp. 79–89.

32. On the health of older people in antiquity, see Parkin, *Old Age in the Roman World*, pp. 247–56, with further references.

33. Vergil, *Aeneid* 5.395–6.

34. Galen, from his work 'That the *mores* of the soul follow the *temperamenta* of the body'; Greek text in the edition of Galen by C.G. Kühn, vol. 4, pp. 786–7.

35. Seneca the Younger, *Epistles* 108.28.

36. There is an English translation of the *de Sanitate Tuenda* by R.M. Green: *A Translation of Galen's Hygiene* (Springfield, Illinois: Charles C. Thomas Publ., 1951).

37. Pliny the Elder, *Nat. Hist.* 14.8.60, 22.53.114.

38. Hesiod, *Theog.* 211–25; see also Cicero, *de Nat. Deor.* 3.17.44 and Hyginus, *Fab.* pr.1.

39. For a survey of theories of prolongevity, see Gruman, 'A History of Ideas about the Prolongation of Life', pp. 1–102.

40. See further Parkin, *Old Age in the Roman World*, pp. 257–8.

41. Cicero, *On Old Age* 38.

3 The Middle Ages and Renaissance

1. Z. Razi, *Life, Marriage and Death in a Medieval Parish* (Cambridge, 1980), pp. 109, 128; D. Herlihy and C. Klapisch, *Les Toscans et leur familles: étude du Catasto florentin de 1427* (Paris, 1980), pp. 199–201; M. Campbell, 'Population Pressure, Inheritance and the Land Market in a 14th-Century Peasant Community', in R. Smith (ed.), *Land, Kinship and Life Cycle* (Cambridge, 1984), pp. 87–134.

2. Shahar, *Growing Old in the Middle Ages*, 'Winter Clothes Us in Shadow and Pain', p. 29; Parkin, *Old Age in the Roman World*, pp. 13–35.

3. S. Shahar, 'Who Were the Old in the Middle Ages?', *Social History of Medicine* 6 (1993), pp. 313–41; Shahar, *Growing Old in the Middle Ages*, pp. 14–18, 24–7.

4. P. Dennis, P. Foote and R. Perkins (eds/trans), *Laws of Early Iceland. Gragas. Christian Laws* I (Winnipeg, 1980), p. 49.

5. B. Pullan, *Rich and Poor in Renaissance Venice* (Oxford, 1971), p. 51 and n. 82.

6. A. Luders, T. Tomlins and J. Raithby (eds), *The Statutes of the Realm* (2nd edn, 1963), vol. II, p. 657.

7. Shahar, *Growing Old in the Middle Ages*, pp. 18–19.

8. Luders, Tomlins and Raithby, *Statutes of the Realm*, vol. I, p. 307.

9. Beugnot (ed.), *Assise de la haute court. Le livre de Jean d'Ibelin*, in *Recueil des historiens de Croisades* (Paris, 1841), vol. I, pp. 362–4.

10. P. Laslett, 'History of Aging and the Aged', in *Family Life and Illicit Love in Earlier Generations* (Cambridge 1977), ch. 5; M. Mitterauer and R. Sieder, *The European Family. Patriarchy to Partnership from the Middle Ages to the Present*, trans. K. Osterveen and M. Hörziager (Oxford, 1982), 146; P. Thane, 'Old Age in English History', in C. Conrad and H. von Kondratowitz (eds), *Zur Kulturgeschichte des Alterns* (Berlin, 1993), pp. 18–19.

11. G. Biraben, *Les Hommes et la peste en France et les pays européens et méditerranéens* (Paris, 1975), vol. I, pp. 218–25; J. Heers, *Le clan familial au Moyen-Âge. Étude sur les structures politiques et sociales de milieux urbains* (Paris, 1974), p. 70 and n. 3; Herlihy and Klapisch, *Les Toscans et leur familles*, pp. 459–61; Razi, *Life, Marriage and Death in a Medieval Parish*, pp. 1, 129, 151; M. Zerner, 'Une crise de mortabilité au XVe siècle à travers les testaments et les rôles d'inscriptions', *Annales ESC* 34 (1979), pp. 571–8; R. Trexler, *Public Life in Renaissance Florence* (1980), p. 362.

12. Herlihy and Klapisch, *Les Toscans et leur familles*, pp. 370–1 and n. 143; J. Russel, 'How Many of the Population Were Aged?', in M. Sheehan (ed.), *Aging and the Aged in Medieval Europe* (Toronto, 1990), pp. 119–27; Razi, *Life, Marriage and Death in a Medieval Parish*, pp. 1, 151; C. Klapisch, '"A uno pane e uno vino": The Rural Tuscan Family at the Beginning of the 15th Century', in *Women, Family and Ritual in Renaissance Italy* (Chicago, 1985), p. 41; G. Minois, *Histoire de la vieillesse. De l'antiquité à la Renaissance* (Paris, 1987), p. 296.

13. T. Hollingsworth, 'A Demographic Study of British Ducal Familites', *Population Studies* 11 (1957), pp. 5–26; G. Duby, 'Dans la France du nort-ouest au XIIe siècle: les jeunes dans la société aristocratique', *Annales ESC* 19 (1964), pp. 839–43; J. Rosenthal, 'Medieval Longevity and the Secular Peerage 1350–1500', *Population Studies* 27 (1973), pp. 287–93.

14. J. Russel, 'The Effects of Pestilence and Plague 1315–1385', *Comparative Studies in Society and History* 8 (1966), pp. 464–73; D. Herlihy, *Medieval and Renaissance Pistoia. The Social History of an Italian Town* (New Haven, 1987), pp. 90–1; Herlihy and Klapisch, *Les Toscans et leur familles*, p. 200; C. Klapisch-Zuber, 'Demographic Decline and Household Structure. The Example of Prato, Late 14th to Late 15th-Century', in *Women, Family and Ritual in Renaissance Italy*, 27; Russel, 'How Many of the

Population Were Aged?', pp. 12, 126.

15. C. Klapisch, 'Fiscalité et démographie en Toscane (1427–1430)', *Annales* ESC 24 (1969), pp. 1313–37; J. Rosenthal, 'Aristocratic Widows in 15th-Century England', in B. Harris and G. McNamara (eds), *Selected Research from the Fifth Berkshire Conference on History of Women* (Durham, 1984), pp. 36–47; R. Archer, 'Rich Old Ladies. The Problem of Late Medieval Dowagers', in T. Pollard (ed.), *Property and Politics: Essays in Late Medieval English History* (Gloucester, 1984), pp. 15–35.

16. J. Le Goff, *La Civilization médiévale* (Paris, 1966), pp. 26–9.

17. Examples: *Annales S. Iustinae Patavini, M.G.H. Script.*, vol. 19 (Hanover, 1886), p. 179. Matthew Paris, *Chronica majora*, ed. R. Luard, Rolls Series 25 [57] (1877), p. 134; Thomas Aquinas, *Summa Theologiae* 3a, q. 72, art. 8, trans. The Blackfriars (1974), vol. 57, pp. 212–15; M. Lauwers, 'La mort et le corps des saints. La scène de la mort dans les *vitae* du Moyen-Âge', *Le Moyen-Âge*, 94 (1988), pp. 37–8 and n. 110; L. Rapetti (ed) *Li livre de jostice et de plet* (Paris, 1850), p. 98.

18. J. Neufville and A. de Vogüé (eds/trans), *Le règle de Saint Benoit* (Paris, 1942), pp. 642–4.

19. R. Finlay, 'The Venetian Republic as a Gerontocracy: Age and Politics in the Renaissance', *The Journal of Medieval and Renaissance Studies* 8 (1978), pp. 157–8.

20. R. Helmholz, *Marriage Litigation in Medieval England* (Cambridge, 1974), p. 83.

21. G. Lopez (ed.), *Las siete partidas del Rey Don Alfonso el Sabio* (Salamanca, 1555; reprint Madrid, 1974), Ley 2, 74.

22. Roger Bacon, *Opus majus*, ed. J. Bridge (Frankfurt, 1964), vol. 2, p. 206; English trans: Roger Bacon, *Opus majus*, trans. R. Burke (Philadelphia, 1928), vol. 2, p. 619; Roger Bacon, *De retardatione accidentium senectutis cum aliis opusculis medicinalibus*, ed. A. Little and E. Withington (Oxford, 1928), pp. 9, 29, 31, 80.

23. Aristotle, *Rhetorica*, bk 2, ch. 14.

24. Honorius Augustodunensis [Honorius of Autun], *De philosophia mundi libri quatuor*, PL, vol. 172, L. 4, C. 36, col. 99; Vincent de Beauvais, *Speculum naturale*, in *Bibliotheca mundi seu speculum quadruplex* (Douai, 1624), L. 31, C. 87, col. 2360; Arnaldus de Villanova, *De regimine sanitatis*, in *Opera Omnia* (Basel, 1585), col. 372; Albertus Magnus, *De aetate sive de juventute et senectute*, in *Opera Omnia*, ed. A. Borgent (Paris, 1890), vol. 9, tractatus 1, C. 6.

25. M. Carruthers, *The Book of Memory. A Study of Memory in Medieval Culture* (Cambridge, 1993).

26. Vincent de Beauvais, *Speculum naturale*, L. 31, C. 88, col. 2361.

27. It was not only a woman's menstrual blood that was considered impure and harmful. According to both medical and popular conceptions, the foetus in its mother's womb was nourished by her menstrual blood, which was not eliminated from her body during her pregnancy. The blood that served as nourishment for the foetus was thus also considered impure. According to Innocent III, the menstrual blood of a woman which does not flow during her pregnancy is so vile and impure that its touch can cause a tree to wither, grass to shrivel, and the loss of fruit. Dogs which licked it would suffer from rabies. And a child conceived as a result of intercourse with a menstruating woman would be born a leper. Lotharii cardinalis (Innocent III), *De miseria humanae conditionis*, ed. M. Maccarrone (Lugano 1955), L. I, C. 4, 11–12; in the *responsa* of the academic physicians of Salerno it was stated that the infant was incapable of standing, sitting, walking and talking immediately after birth because, unlike the animals, it was nurtured in its mother's womb on menstrual blood from which it was not easily cleansed, while animals were nurtured in the womb on purer food. B. Lawn (ed), *The Prose Salernitan Questions* (Oxford, 1970), Q. 228, 155.

28. *De Secretis mulierum*, in *Les admirables secrets de magie du Grand et du Petit Albert*, cited in D. Jacquart and C. Thomasset, *Sexuality and Medicine in the Middle Ages*, trans. M. Adamson (Oxford, 1988), p. 75; by the end of the 15th century, when *fascinatio* (the process by which certain persons harmed others with the power of sight) was brought into the academic medical domain, women were thought to acquire the power to fascinate in their natural process of ageing.

29. The theory was developed by Diego Alvarez Chanca (*Tractatus de fascinatione*, 1494) and by Antonio de Cartagena (*Libellus de fascinatione*, 1529); according to these writers, the actions of the old women were not controlled by will, but could be much worse if accompanied by bad intentions. The whole discourse in both treatises is based on the potential or actual venomousness of women's bodies, both while menstruating and after the cease of menses. However, old women whose menses ceased, and thus always carried menstrual blood in their bodies, were considered especially prone to fascinate. Their victims were generally children: F. Salmon and M. Cabré, 'Fascinating Women: The Evil Eye in Medical Scholasticism', paper presented at the Barcelona Conference, Cambridge, September 1992 (unpublished).

30. Francesco Petrarca, *De remedies utriusque fortune* (Rotterdam, 1649),, L. I, 18–19; L. II, 94–5, 353, 564–5; Fancesco Petrarca, *Phisick against Fortune*, trans. T. Twyn (1579), ff. 3v, 162r, 267r–268v.

31. Giraldus Cambrensis [Gerald of Wales], *Gemma ecclesiastica*, ed. J. Brewer (Rolls Senes 21, London, 1862), 182; Philippe de Navarre, *Les quatre ages de l'homme*, ed. M. de Fréville (Paris, 1888), p. 90.

32. Guillaume de Deguileville, *Le pélerinage de la vie humaine*, ed. J. Stürzinger (1893), pp. 229, 251–2, 255, 374, 407, 414.

33. C. Walker Bynum, *Holy Feast and Holy Fast. The Religious Significance of Food to Medieval Women* (Berkeley, California, 1987).

34. Aegidius Romanus [Giles of Rome], *De regimine principum* (Rome, 1607), L. 1, pars 4, C. 1–4, 188–203; Aristotle, *Rhetorica*, bk 2, C. 12–14; *Ethica*, bk 4, C. 1, 1121, bk 8, C. 3, 1156a, C. 5, 1157b.

35. Bernardino of Siena, *De calamitatibus et miseries humanae et maxime senectutis*, ed. Fathers of the Collegium S. Bonaventurae (Florence, 1959), vol. 7, sermo 16, 254–6, 258.

36. Vincent of Beauvais, *Speculum naturale*, L. 31, C. 89–90, cols 2361–3.

37. Bromyard John, *Summa praedicantium* (Antwerp, 1614), part II, C. 5, 355.

38. Dante, *Convivio* in *Le opere di Dante*, ed. M. Barbi (Florence, 1921), C. 4, p. 28.

39. Meister Eckhart, *In novitate ambulamus*, in *Die deutschen und lateinischen Werke*, ed. E. Benz et al (Stuttgart, 1956), IV, sermo 15, 145–54, see especially 149–50.

40. Bartholomaeus Anglicus, *Liber de proprietatibus rerum* (Strasbourg, 1505), L. VI, C. 1; Bartolomaeus Anglicus, *On the Properties of Things: John Trevisa's Translation of Bartholomaeus Agnlicus's De proprietatibus rerum*, ed. M. Seymour (Oxford, 1975), p. 290.

41. Bernardino of Siena, *De calamitatibus et miseries humanae et maxime senectutis*, pp. 253, 256–62.

42. Philipe de Navarre, *Les quatre ages de l'homme*, pp. 31, 95–6, 105.

43. Shahar, *Growing Old in the Middle Ages*, pp. 50–1.

44. S. Meech and F. Allen (eds), *The Book of Margery Kempe*, EETS 1940, pp. 179–81.

45. Alvise Cornaro, *Discorsi intorno alla vita sobria*, ed. P. Pancrazzi (Florence, 1946).

46. Philipe de Navarre, *Les quatre ages de l'homme*, p. 105.

47. Vincent de Beauvais, *Speculum naturale*, L. 31, C. 89, col. 2362.

48. Leon Battista Alberti, *I libri della famiglia: The Family in Renaissance Florence*, ed./trans. R. Watkins (Columbia SC, 1969), pp. 35–42, 156–7, 167, 170.

49. A. Pertile, *Storia del diritto italiano della caduca dell'Impero Romano alla codificazione* (Turin, 1892–1902), vol. 3, p. 253 and n. 48.

50. J. Rosenthal, 'Retirement and the Life Cycle in 15th-Century England', in Sheehan, *Aging and the Aged*, pp. 175–6.

51. Rosenthal, 'Retirement and the Life Cycle in 15th-Century England', pp. 180–3; N. Orme, 'The Medieval Almshouse for the Clergy: Clyst Gabriel Hospital near Exeter', *Journal of Ecclesiastical History* 39 (1988), pp. 1–15; N. Orme, 'Suffering the Clergy: Illness and Old Age in Exeter Diocese 1300–1540', in M. Pelling and R. Smith (eds), *Life, Death and the Elderly: Historical Perspectives* (1991), pp. 62–73.

52. D. Barthélemy, 'Kinship', in P. Aries and G. Duby (eds), *A History of Private Life*, vol. 2, *Revelations of the Medieval World*, trans D. Goldhammer (Cambridge, Massachusetts, 1988), pp. 85–116; Bertran de Born, *Définitions de la jeunesse et de la vieillesse*, in J. Anglade (ed./trans.), *Anthologie des troubadours* (Paris, 1927), p. 60.

53. V. Green, *The Madness of Kings* (Stroud, Glocestershire, 1996), p. 74.

54. Shahar, *Growing Old in the Middle Ages*, pp. 132–43.

55. O. Redon, 'Aspects économiques de la discrimination et la "marginalisation" des femmes, XIIIe–XVIIIe siècles', in S. Cavaciocchi (ed.), *La donna nell economia secc. XII–XVIII* (Instituto Internationale di Storia Economica 'F. Datini', Series II, 21, Prato, 1990), pp. 441–60.

56. A. Jewell, 'The Bringing Up of Children in Good Learning and Manners: A Survey of Educational Provisions in the North of England', *Northern History* 18 (1982), p. 11; M. Barteson (ed.), *Cambridge Guild Records* (Cambridge, 1903), p. 9.

57. M. Fagniez (ed.), *Documents relatifs à l'histoire de l'industrie et du commerce en France* (Paris 1898), vol. I, p. 68.

58. Shahar, *Growing Old in the Middle Ages*, pp. 105, 111–12, 123–4, 130, 145.

59. E. Le Roy Ladurie, *Les paysans de Languedoc* (Paris, 1966), pp. 160–8; Klapisch, 'Fiscalité et démographie en Toscane (1427–1430)', pp. 1313–37; Herlihy and Klapisch, *Les Toscans et leur familles*, pp. 370–9, 491–7; Klapisch, '"A uno pane et uno vino"', pp. 160–8.

60. R. Smith, 'The Manorial Court and the Elderly Tenant in Late Medieval England', in Pelling and Smith, *Life, Death and the Elderly: Historical Perspectives*, pp. 36–91; E. Clark, 'The Quest for Security in Medieval England', in Sheehan, *Aging and the Aged in Medieval Europe*, pp. 189–200.

61. Mitterauer and Sieder, *The European Family*, pp. 166–7.

62. R. Harper, 'A Note on Corrodies in the 14th Century', *Albion* 15 (1983), pp. 95–101; B. Harvey, *Living and Dying in England 1110–1540: The Monastic Experience* (Oxford, 1995), pp. 180–90.

4 The 17th Century

1. Maimonides, *Mishneh Torah Hilkhot Issurei Bi'ah*, ch. 9 (5). See M. Singer, '"Honour the Hoary Head": The Aged in the Medieval Jewish Community', in Sheehan, *Aging and the Aged in Medieval Europe*, pp. 42–3.

2. L. Botelho, 'Old Age and Menopause in Rural Women of Early Modern Suffolk', in L. Botelho and P. Thane (eds), *Women and Ageing in Britain since 1500* (London, 2000), pp. 43–65.

3. S.R. Smith, 'Age in Old England', *History Today* 29 (1979), pp. 173–4.

4. N. Guterman (compl.), *A Book of French Quotations with English Translations* (London, 1963), p. 71.

5. T. Cole, *The Journey of Life* (Cambridge, 1992), pp. 1–31, quotation on p. 11.

6. P. Barnum (ed.), *Dives and Pauper* (repr. London, 1992), vol. i, IV, C. 1, p. 304.

7. Lady Montague, *Letters of the Right Honourable L.M.W.M.: Written during her Travels in Europe, Asia and Africa*, vol. 1, iv (London, 1763), p. 26.

8. C.C. Thomas, *A Translation of Galen's Hygiene* (Oxford, 1952), p. 7.

9. Shahar, *Growing Old in the Middle Ages*, pp. 43–4.

10. T. Sheppey, 'A Book of Choice Receipts', c. 1675. Folger Shakespeare Library MS V.a.452.

11. J. Howell, *Proverbs, or, Old Sayed Savves and Adages in English (or the Saxon Toung) Italian, French and Spanish Whereunto the British, for their Great Antiquity, and Weight Are Added. Which Proverbs Are Either Moral, Relating to Good Life; Physical, Relating to Diet, and Health; Topical, Relating to Particular Place; Temporal, Relating to Seasons; or Ironical, Relating to Raillery, and Mirth, etc.* (London, 1659), English proverbs, p. 13; Italian, p. 15. Pagination restarts with every subheading.

12. E. and H. Leigh, *Select and Choyce Observations, Containing All the Romane Emperours. The first eighteen by Edward Leigh, M.A. of Magdalene-Hall in Oxford, the others added by his son Henry Leigh, M.A. also of the same house. Certain choyce French proverbs, alphabetically disposed and Englished added also by the same Edward Leigh* (London, 1657), p. 404.

13. Howell, *Proverbs*, Italian, p. 15; French, p. 12.

14. Quoted in Guterman, *A Book of French Quotations*, p. 67; Leigh, *Select and Choyce Observations*, p. 412; Jean de la Bruyère (1645–1696), as quoted in Guterman, *A Book of French Quotations*, p. 151; ibid., p. 69; Corneille, *Tite et Berenice* (1670), V:1, as quoted in Guterman, *A Book of French Quotations*, p. 85.

15. Howell, *Proverbs*, Portuguese, p. 8; the Marques of Santillana's writing had a long life and was translated into English in 1579 by B. Googe, fol. 23r; Howell, *Proverbs*, French, p. 10; Howell, *Proverbs*, English, p. 1; J.M. Ferraro, *The Marriage Wars in Late Renaissance Venice* (Oxford, 2001), p. 60.

16. Howell, *Proverbs*, Portuguese, pp. 1, 10; Jean Racine, *Athalie* (1691), II:5, as quoted in Guterman, *A Book of French Quotations*, p. 149; W. Baker (ed.), *The Adages of Erasmus* (Toronto, 2001), p. 11; ibid., p. 211; Howell, *Proverbs*, English, p. 6; ibid., Portuguese, p. 14.

17. Howell, *Proverbs*, Italian, p. 15; ibid., English, p. 9; ibid., Italian, p. 3; ibid., Portuguese, p. 9; ibid., Italian, p. 10; ibid.; ibid., French, p. 4.

18. Ferraro, *The Marriage Wars*, pp. 60, 63; Howell, *Proverbs*, English, p. 10; ibid., Italian, p. 3; ibid., English, p. 10.

19. P.L. Duchartre, *The Italian Comedy. The Improvisation, Scenarios, Lives, Attributres, Portraits, and Masks of the Illustrious Characters of the Commedia dell'Arte*, trans. R.T. Weaver (London, 1929), p. 185.

20. Ibid., p. 180; Ferraro, *The Marriage Wars*, pp. 60, 63.

21. Duchartre, *The Italian Comedy*, pp. 202–5.

22. *Chevalier du Soleil* (1680), as quoted in Duchartre, *The Italian Comedy*, p. 202.

23. A. Kugler, *Errant Plagiary: The Life and Writing of Lady Sarah Cowper: 1644–1720* (Stanford, 2002), p. 164; A. Kugler, '"I Feel Myself Decay Apace": Old Age in the Diary of Lady Sarah Cowper (1644–1720)', in

24. A. Burguiere and F. Lebrun, 'The One Hundred and One Families of Europe', in A. Burguiere et al (eds), *The History of the Family, Volume Two: The Impact of Modernity*, trans. S. Hanbury Tenison (Cambridge, MA, 1996), p. 17.

25. Mitterrauer and Sieder, *The European Family*, p. 146.

26. J.S. Grubb, *Provincial Families of the Renaissance: Private and Public Life in the Veneto* (Baltimore, 1996), p. 59.

27. Mitteraur and Sieder, *The European Family*, p. 148.

28. S. Marshall, *The Dutch Gentry, 1500–1650* (New York, 1987), pp. 53–66.

29. A. Favue-Chamoux, 'Marriage, Widowhood, and Divorce', in M. Barbagli and D.I. Kertzer (eds), *Family Life in Early Modern Times, 1500–1789* (New Haven, 2001), pp. 243–4.

30. R. O'Day, *The Family and Family Relationships, 1500–1900: England, France and the United States of America* (Basingstoke, 1994), p. 154.

31. Favue-Chamoux, 'Marriage, Widowhood, and Divorce', pp. 225, 244.

32. Barbagli and Kertzer, *Family Life in Early Modern Times*, 'Introduction', p. xvi.

33. R. Jütte, *Poverty and Deviance in Early Modern Europe* (Cambridge, 1994), pp. 68–9, quotation on p. 88.

34. Ibid., p. 63.

35. Ibid., pp. 63–8, quotation on p. 124.

36. B. Pullan, '"Difettosi, impotenti, inabili": Caring for the Disabled in Early Modern Italian Cities', in his *Poverty and Charity: Europe, Italy, Venice, 1400–1700* (Aldershot, 1994), VI.

37. R. Sarti, *Europe at Home: Family and Material Culture 1500–1800* (New Haven, 2002), p. 31.

38. L. Botelho, '"The Old Woman's Wish": Widows by the Family Fire? Widows' Old Age Provision in Rural England', *The Journal of Family History* 7 (2002), pp. 59–78.

39. Mitterraur and Sieder, *The European Family*, p. 163; Sarti, *Europe at Home*, p. 54.

40. Mitteraur and Sieder, *The European Family*, pp. 159–62.

41. Sarti, *Europe at Home*, p. 54.

42. Ibid., p. 57.

43. Ibid., p. 52.

44. Mitteraur and Sieder, *The European Family*, p. 167.

45. J.E. Smith, 'The Computer Simulation of Kin Sets and Kin Counts', in John Bongaarts, Thomas K. Burch and Kenneth W. Wachter (eds), *Family Demography Methods and their Application* (Oxford, 1987), p. 262.

46. V. Gourdon, 'Are Grandparents Really Absent from the Family Tradition? Forbears in the Region of Vernon (France) around 1800', *The History of the Family* 4 (1999), p. 81.

47. Ibid., p. 90; V. Gourdon, 'Les grands-parents en France du xviiᵉ siècle au début du xxᵉ siècle', *Histoire Économie et Société* 18 (1999), pp. 511–25.

Botelho and Thane, *Women and Ageing in Britain since 1500*, pp. 66–88.

5 The 18th Century

1. Patrice Bourdelais, *L'Âge de la vieillesse: histoire du vieillissement de la population* (Paris, 1993), p. 39; Peter Laslett, 'Introduction: Necessary Knowledge: Age and Aging in the Societies of the Past', in Kertzer and Laslett, *Aging in the Past*, p. 18.

2. David G. Troyansky, *Old Age in the Old Regime: Image and Experience in Eighteenth-Century France* (Ithaca, 1989), pp. 10–11. See also David G. Troyansky, 'The Elderly', in Peter N. Stearns (ed.), *Encyclopedia of European Social History from 1350 to 2000*, vol. 4 (New York, 2001), pp. 219–29.

3. Bourdelais's attempt to arrive at a useful threshold for old age is part of a thorough treatment of the development of the idea of demographic ageing.

4. Paul Johnson, 'Historical Readings of Old Age and Ageing', in Paul Johnson and Pat Thane (eds), *Old Age from Antiquity to Post-Modernity* (London, 1998), pp. 1–18.

5. Susannah R. Ottaway, 'Introduction: Authority, Autonomy, and Responsibility among the Aged in the Pre-Industrial Past', in Ottaway, Botelho and Kittredge, *Power and Poverty*, pp. 1–12.

6. Susannah R. Ottaway, *The Decline of Life: Old Age in Eighteenth-Century England* (Cambridge, 2004), p. 219.

7. Lutz K. Berkner, 'The Stem Family and the Developmental Cycle of the Peasant Household', *American Historical Review* 77, pp. 398–418; David Gaunt, 'The Property and Kin Relationships of Retired Farmers in Northern and Central Europe', in Richard Wall, with Jean Robin and Peter Laslett (eds), *Family Forms in Historic Europe* (Cambridge, 1983), pp. 249–79; Rudolf Andorka, 'Household Systems and the Lives of the Old in Eighteenth- and Nineteenth-Century Hungary', in Kertzer and Laslett, *Aging in the Past*, pp. 129–55.

8. Yves Castan, *Honnêteté et relations sociales en Languedoc, 1715–1780* (Paris, 1974), p. 231.

9. Troyansky, *Old Age in the Old Regime*, ch. 6; Alain Collomp, *La maison du père: famille et village en Haute-Provence aux XVIIe et XVIIIe siècles* (Paris, 1983).

10. Louis-Sébastien Mercier, *Le vieillard et ses trois filles* (Paris, 1792), cited in Troyansky, *Old Age in the Old Regime*, p. 61.

11. Troyansky, *Old Age in the Old Regime*, p. 136.

12. Vincent Gourdon, *Histoire des grands-parents* (Paris, 2001). Gourdon distinguishes between *grands-parents* and the older form of *ayeux*.

13. Ottaway, *The Decline of Life*, ch. 3.

14. Amy M. Froide, 'Old Maids: The Lifecycle of Single Women in Early Modern England', in Botelho and Thane, *Women and Ageing in Britain since 1500*, p. 90.

15. Lois W. Banner, *In Full Flower: Aging Women, Power and Sexuality* (New York, 1992).

16. Sherri Klassen, 'Old and Cared For: Place of Residence for Elderly Women in Eighteenth-Century Toulouse', *Journal of Family History* 24 (1999), pp. 35–52; 'Social Lives of Elderly Women in Eighteenth-Century Toulouse,' in Ottaway, Botelho and Kittredge, *Power and Poverty*, pp. 49–66.

17. Angela Groppi, 'Old People and the Flow of Resources between Generations in Papal Rome, Sixteenth to Nineteenth Centuries', in Ottaway, Botelho and Kittredge, *Power and Poverty*, p. 102.

18. On old-age pensions and the state, see Vida Azimi, 'Les pensions de retraite sous l'Ancien Régime', in *Mémoires de la société pour l'histoire du droit et des institutions des anciens pays bourguignons, comtois et romands*, 43e fascicule (1986), pp. 77–103; Bruno Dumons and Gilles Pollet, *L'État et les retraites: genèse d'une politique* (Paris, 1994); Guy Thuillier, *Les retraites des fonctionnaires: débats et doctrines (1790–1914)* (2 vols, Paris, 1996); David G. Troyansky, 'Aging and Memory in a Bureaucratizing World: A French Historical Experience', in Ottaway, Botelho and Kittredge, *Power and Poverty*, pp. 15–30; Bernd Wunder, 'Die Einführung des staatlichen Pensionssystems in Frankreich (1760–1850)', *Francia* 11 (1983), pp. 417–74.

19. David Hackett Fischer, *Growing Old in America* (New York, 1978); Achenbaum, *Old Age in the New Land*.

20. Lynn Hunt, *The Family Romance of the French Revolution* (Berkeley, 1993).

21. Mona Ozouf, *La fête révolutionnaire* (Paris, 1976).

22. Troyansky, *Old Age in the Old Regime*, pp. 209–10.

23. Ibid., p. 212.

24. Ibid., p. 213.

25. See Dumons and Pollet, *L'État et les retraites*; Josef Ehmer, *Sozialgeschichte des Alters* (Frankfurt, 1990); David G. Troyansky, 'Balancing Social and Cultural Approaches to the History of Old Age and Ageing in Europe: A Review and an Example from Post-Revolutionary France', in Johnson and Thane, *Old Age from Antiquity to Post-Modernity*, pp. 96–109.

26. Troyansky, *Old Age in the Old Regime*, pp. 113, 24–6.

27. Ibid., p. 114.

28. However, Ottaway, *The Decline of Life*, sees increasing recourse to the workhouse in the period.

29. Georges Louis Leclerc, comte de Buffon, 'De la vieillesse et de la mort', in *Histoire naturelle de l'homme*, in *Oeuvres complètes*, vol. 4 (Paris, 1774), pp. 351–2, cited in Troyansky, *Old Age in the Old Regime*, p. 116.

30. Troyansky, *Old Age in the Old Regime*, pp. 86–8.

31. Ibid., pp. 99–100.

32. Troyansky, 'Balancing Social and Cultural Approaches', p. 100.

33. Joan Hinde Stewart, 'Le *De Senectute* de Madame de Lambert', in *Sciences, musiques, lumières: mélanges offerts à Anne-Marie Chouillet*, publiés par Ulla Kölving et Irène Passeron (Ferney-Voltaire, 2002), pp. 331–8.

34. Troyansky, *Old Age in the Old Regime*, pp. 103–7.

35. Peter Borscheid, *Geschichte des Alters* (Münster, 1987).

36. Kittredge, '"The Ag'd Dame to Venery Inclin'd"', pp. 247–63.

37. Thane, *Old Age*, pp. 65–8.

38. Joan Hinde Stewart, 'Reading Lives "à la manière de Crébillon"', *Eighteenth-Century Fiction* 13 (2001), pp. 415–35.

39. Joan Hinde Stewart, 'Fifteen Minutes till Fifty', *Studies on Voltaire and the Eighteenth Century* (2002:06), pp. 7–16. For Graffigny's death, see Stewart, '"Still Life": La Vieille Dame et la mort,' *Studies on Voltaire and the Eighteenth Century* (2004:12).

40. Kugler, '"I Feel Myself Decay Apace": Old Age in the Diary of Lady Sarah Cowper (1644–1720)', pp. 66–88.

41. Anne Kugler, 'Women and Aging in Transatlantic Perspective', in Ottaway, Botelho and Kittredge, *Power and Poverty*, pp. 67–85.

6 The 19th Century

1. P.M. Roget, 'Age', in John Forbes et al (eds), *The Cyclopaedia of Practical Medicine* (London, 1833), pp. 34–46.

2. Michael Anderson, *Approaches to the History of the Western Family, 1500–1914* (Cambridge, 1995), p. 64.

3. Letter to John Vaughan, 1815; quoted in Anthony and Sally Sampson, *The Oxford Book of Ages* (Oxford, 1985), p. 139.

4. Ibid., pp. 62–3.

5. For a good example of how our knowledge on the history of old age evolved over time, see Carole Haber, 'Historians' Approach to Aging in America', in T.R. Cole, R. Kastenbaum and R. Ray, *Handbook of the Humanities and Aging* (New York, 2nd edn, 2000), pp. 25–40.

6. Letter to V.V. Stasov, 1906; quoted in Sampson, *The Oxford Book of Ages*, p. 148.

7. Julian Treuherz, *Victorian Painting* (London, 1993), p. 180.

8. Achenbaum, *Old Age in the New Land*, p. 60.

9. Troyansky, *Old Age in the Old Regime*, p. 9.

10. Richard M. Smith, 'The Structured Dependence of the Elderly as a Recent Development: Some Sceptical Historical Thoughts', *Ageing and Society* 4 (1984), p. 414.

11. *The Poor Law Report of 1834* (repr. London, 1970), p. 115.

12. Anderson, *Approaches to the History of the Western Family*.

13. Michael R. Haines and Allen C. Goodman, 'A Home of One's Own: Aging and Home Ownership in the United States in the Late Nineteenth and Early Twentieth Century', in Kertzer and Laslett, *Aging in the Past*, pp. 203–26.

14. Ibid., pp. 220–1.

15. Anderson, *Approaches to the History of the Western Family*, p. 16.

16. Rudolf Andorka, 'Household Systems and the Lives of the Old in Eighteenth- and Nineteenth-Century Hungary', in Kertzer and Laslett, *Aging in the Past*, pp. 129–55.

17. Quoted in Achenbaum, *Old Age in the New Land*, p. 48.

18. Ibid. p. 68.

19. P. Johnson, 'The Employment and Retirement of Older Men in England and Wales, 1881–1981', *Economic History Review* 47 (1994), p. 118.

20. David R. Green, *From Artisans to Paupers: Economic Change and Poverty in London, 1790–1870* (Aldershot, 1995), p. 25.

21. Thane, *Old Age*.

22. James C. Riley, *Sick, Not Dead: The Health of British Workingmen during the Mortality Decline* (Baltimore and London, 1997); C. Edwards et al, 'Sickness, Insurance and Health: Assessing Trends in Morbidity through Friendly Society Records', *Annales de Démographie Historique* 1 (2003), pp. 131–67.

23. Achenbaum, *Old Age in the New Land*, pp. 82–3.

24. Thomas Scharf, *Ageing and Ageing Policy in Germany* (Oxford, 1998), p. 25.

25. Ibid., pp. 26–7.

26. Marco H.D. van Leeuwen, 'Surviving with a Little Help: The Importance of Charity to the Poor of Amsterdam 1800–50, in a Comparative Perspective', *Social History* 18 (1993), pp. 319–38.

27. The second-largest provider was the municipality. However, Amsterdam authorities only considered applicants who had been rejected by religious charities.

28. Achenbaum, *Old Age in the New Land*, p. 82.

29. Paul Slack, *The English Poor Law, 1531–1782* (Cambridge, 1995), pp. 42–3. Some 650 hospitals were founded in England during the 19th century. Robert Pinker, *English Hospital Statistics 1861–1938* (London, 1966), p. 57.

30. Claudia Edwards, 'Age-Based Rationing of Medical Care in Nineteenth-Century England', *Continuity and Change* 14 (1999), pp. 227–65.

31. Slack, *English Poor Law*, p. 22; Claudia Edwards, 'Inequality in Nineteenth-Century Welfare Provision: A Study of Access to and Quality of Institutional Medical Care for the Elderly in England' (unpubl. PhD dissertation, London, 2002), p. 146.

32. David Thomson, 'The Decline of Social Welfare: Falling State Support for the Elderly since Early Victorian Times', *Ageing and Society* 4 (1984), pp. 451–82.

33. David Thomson, 'Workhouse to Nursing Home: Residential Care of Elderly People in England since 1840', *Ageing and Society* 3 (1983), p. 49.

34. Ibid., p. 51.

35. Achenbaum, *Old Age in the New Land*, p. 80.

36. Reinhard Spree, 'Krankenhausentwicklung und Sozialpolitik in Deutschland während des 19. Jahrhunderts', *Historische Zeitschrift* 260 (1995), pp. 76–7.

37. Peter N. Stearns, *Old Age in European Society: The Case of France* (London, 1977), p. 83.

38. Ibid., p. 102.

39. C. Booth, *The Aged Poor in England and Wales* (London, 1894), p. 339.

40. Harry T. Phillips and Susan A. Gaylord (eds), *Aging and Public Health* (New York, 1985).

41. Hans-Joachim Voth, 'Living Standards and the Urban

Environment', in Roderick Floud and Paul Johnson, *The Cambridge Economic History of Modern Britain Volume I: Industrialisation, 1700–1860* (Cambridge, 2004), pp. 268–94.

42. Emily Grundy, 'The Health and Health Care of Older Adults in England and Wales, 1841–1994', in J. Charlton and M. Murphy (eds), *The Health of Adult Britain* (London, 1997), vol. 2, pp. 182–203.

43. Riley, *Sick, Not Dead*, pp. 153–87.

44. Henry Power and Leonard W. Sedgwick, 'Age', *The New Sydenham Society's Lexicon of Medicine and the Allied Sciences* (London, 1879).

45. Edwards, 'Inequality in Nineteenth-Century Welfare Provision', pp. 286–7.

46. J. Grimley Evans, 'Geriatric Medicine: A Brief History', *British Medical Journal* 315 (1997), pp. 1075–7.

47. Stearns, *Old Age*; Christoph Conrad, 'Old Age and the Health Care System in the Nineteenth and Twentieth Centuries', in Johnson and Thane, *Old Age from Antiquity to Post-Modernity*, pp. 132–45.

48. Stearns, *Old Age*, pp. 96–7.

49. Ibid., p. 83.

50. Ibid., p. 89.

51. Ibid., p. 81.

52. Hans-Joachim von Kondratowitz, 'The Medicalization of Old Age: Continuity and Change in Germany from the Late Eighteenth to the Early Twentieth Century', in Pelling and Smith, *Life, Death and the Elderly: Historical Perspective*, pp. 134–64.

53. Carole Haber, *Beyond Sixty-Five: The Dilemma of Old Age in America's Past* (Cambridge, 1983), p. 80.

54. Ibid., pp. 47–81.

55. Daniel Maclachlan, *A Practical Treatise on the Diseases and Infirmities of Advanced Life* (London, 1863), p. iv.

56. Anthony Carlisle, *An Essay on the Disorders of Old Age and on the Means for Prolonging Human Life* (London, 1817); Sir Henry Halford, *Essays and Orations, Read and Delivered at the Royal College of Physicians; To Which Is Added an Account of the Opening of the Tomb of King Charles I* (London, 1831), pp. 1–15; Henry Holland, *Medical Notes and Reflections* (London, 1839), pp. 269–88; George E. Day, *A Practical Treatise on the Domestic Management and Most Important Diseases of Advanced Life* (Philadelphia, 1849); Barnard van Oven, *On the Decline of Life in Health and Disease, Being an Attempt to Investigate the Causes of Longevity; and the Best Means of Attaining a Healthful Old Age* (London, 1853); Maclachlan, *Practical Treatise*.

57. Maclachlan, *Practical Treatise*.

58. Van Oven, *On the Decline of Life*, p. 29.

59. Ibid., pp. vii–ix.

60. David Mitch, 'Education; and Skill of the British Labour Force', in Floud and Johnson, *The Cambridge Economic History of Modern Britain: Volume I*, p. 351.

61. Quoted in Achenbaum, *Old Age in the New Land*, p. 16.

62. Halford, *Essays and Orations*, p. 15.

63. Quoted in Cole, *The Journey of Life*, p. 135.

64. Sir James Stonhouse, *Friendly Advice to a Patient: Calculated More Particularly for the Use of the Sick Belonging to the Infirmaries, As Well the Out-Patients, as Those within the House; Though the Greatest Part Is Suitable and of Equal Service to Every Sick Person* (London, 22nd edn, 1824), p. 4.

65. F.K. Prochaska, *Women and Philanthropy in Nineteenth-Century England* (Oxford, 1980), p. 158.

66. Stonhouse, *Friendly Advice to a Patient*.

67. Bristol Record Office: Bristol Infirmary Weekly Committee Book, entry of 16/5/1849.

68. Ibid., 6/9/1848.

69. Bristol Record Office: Bristol Royal Infirmary Committee Book, entry of 26/3/1872.

70. Ibid., 22/5/1860.

71. Ibid., 9/7/1861.

72. This section is based on Cole, *Journey of Life*, ch. 6, pp. 110–38; see also Achenbaum, *Old Age in the New Land*, pp. 33–6.

73. Cole, *Journey of Life*, p. 129, n. 28.

74. Ibid., pp. 133–4.

75. Brian Hollingworth (ed.), *Songs of the People: Lancashire Dialect Poetry of the Industrial Revolution* (Manchester, 1982), pp. 117–18, 148.

76. Quoted in Scharf, *Ageing and Ageing Policy in Germany*, p. 23.

7 The 20th Century

1. Thane, *Old Age*, pp. 475–80.

2. P. Thane, 'The Debate on the Declining Birth-rate in Britain: The "Menace" of an Ageing Population, 1920s–1950s', *Continuity and Change* 5:2 (1990), pp. 283–305; A. Sauvy, 'Social and Economic Consequences of Ageing of Western Populations', *Population Studies*, 2:1 (June 1948), pp. 115–24; M.S. Quine, *Population Politics in Twentieth-Century Europe* (1996).

3. World Bank, *Averting the Old Age Crisis: Policies to Protect the Old and Promote Growth* (Oxford, 1994).

4. Thane, *Old Age*, pp. 476–7.

5. P.R. Kaim-Caudle, *Comparative Social Policy and Social Security. A Ten-Country Study* (1973).

6. S.A. Bass (ed.), *Older and Active. How Americans over 55 Are Contributing to Society* (1995); A. Pifer and L. Bronte, *Our Ageing Society. Paradox and Promise* (1986).

7. M. Rahikainen, 'Ageing Men and Women in the Labour Market – Continuity and Change', *Scandinavian Journal of History* (2001), pp. 297–314.

8. Achenbaum, *Old Age in the New Land*, pp. 127–42; Haber and Gratton, *Old Age and the Search for Security*.

9. G. Orwell, *The Road to Wigan Pier* (Harmondsworth, 1962 edn), pp. 8–9.

10. S. Lovell, 'Soviet Socialism and the Construction of Old Age', *Jahrbücher für Geschichte Osteuroopas*, 51 (2003), pp. 564–85.

11. C. Phillipson, 'The Experience of Retirement: A

Sociological Study' (PhD dissertation, University of
Durham, 1978), pp. 135, 272–3.

12. M. Kohli et al, *Time for Retirement: Comparative Studies
of Early Exit from the Labour Force* (Cambridge, 1991);
J. Falkingham and P. Johnson, *Ageing and Economic
Welfare* (1992), pp. 50–1, 76–8; Pifer and Bronte, *Our
Ageing Society*, pp. 341–65.

13. T. Kirkwood, *The End of Age* (London, 2001); Bass,
Older and Active, pp. 10–70, 263–94; Pifer and Bronte,
Our Ageing Society, pp. 341–90.

14. Thane, *Old Age*, p. 476; World Bank, *Averting the Old
Age Crisis*.

15. Thane, *Old Age*, pp. 475–93; Tom Kirkwood, *The End
of Age. Why Everything about Ageing Is Changing*
(London, 2001).

16. E.g., UK Government, *Pensions: Challenges and Choices.
The First Report of the Pensions Commission* (2 vols,
London, 2004).

17. P. Thane, 'Geriatrics', in W.F. Bynum and R. Porter (eds),
Companion Encyclopaedia of the History of Medicine
(1993), vol. 2, pp. 1092–118.

18. Lovell, 'Soviet Socialism and the Construction of
Old Age'.

19. Thane, 'Geriatrics'; Kirkwood, *The End of Age*.

20. Bass, *Older and Active*, pp. 236–62; Thane, *Old Age*,
pp. 407–35.

21. Kirkwood, *The End of Age*; Bass, *Older and Active*,
pp. 10–34.

22. N. and J. MacKenzie (eds), *The Diaries of Beatrice Webb*,
vol. 4 (1986).

23. Simone De Beauvoir, *Old Age*, p. 15.

24. Ibid., pp. 268–9.

25. Ibid., p. 290.

26. Ibid., pp. 605–6.

27. R.E. Yahnke, 'Intergeneration and Regeneration:
The Meaning of Old Age in Films and Videos', in
R. Cole, R. Kastenbaum and R.E. Ray, *Handbook of the
Humanities and Aging* (2nd edn, 2000), pp. 293–323.

28. Mass Observation Archive (University of Sussex),
Growing Older, files B and C.

29. B. Kamler and S. Feldman. 'Mirror, Mirror on the Wall:
Reflections on Ageing', *Australian Cultural History* 14
(1995), pp. 1–22.

30. I. Loewenberg, *The View from Seventy. Women's
Recollections and Reflections* (Iowa City, 2004).

31. P. Thompson, C. Itzin and M. Abendstern, *I Don't
Feel Old. Understanding the Experience of Later Life*
(Oxford, 1991).

Further Reading

1 Introduction: The Age of Old Age

Achenbaum, W.A. *Old Age in the New Land. The American Experience since 1790* (1979)

Bois, J.-P. *Les Vieux, de Montaigne aux premières retraites* (Paris, 1989)

De Beauvoir, S. *La Vieillesse* (Paris, 1970)/*Old Age* (1977)

Haber, C. and B. Gratton. *Old Age and the Search for Security. An American Social History* (Bloomington, 1994)

Jütte, R. *Poverty and Deviance in Early Modern Europe* (Cambridge, 1994)

Ottaway, S. *The Decline of Life. Old Age in Eighteenth-Century England* (Cambridge, 2004)

Ottaway, S., L. Botelho and K. Kittredge (eds). *Power and Poverty. Old Age in the Pre-Industrial Past* (Greenwood, Connecticut, 2002)

Shahar, S. *Growing Old in the Middle Ages* (London, 1997)

Thane, P. *Old Age in English History. Past Experiences, Present Issues* (Oxford, 2000)

Wrigley, E., R. Davies and J. Oeppen. *English Population History from Family Reconstitution 1580–1837* (Cambridge, 1997)

2 The Ancient Greek and Roman Worlds

Bakhouche, B. (ed). *L'Ancienneté chez les Anciens* (Montpellier, 2003)

Brandt, H. *Wird auch silbern mein Haar* (Munich, 2002)

Cokayne, K. *Experiencing Old Age in Ancient Rome* (London, 2003)

David, E. *Old Age in Sparta* (Amsterdam, 1991)

Eyben, E. 'Roman Notes on the Course of Life', *Ancient Society* 4 (1973), pp. 213–38

Falkner, T.M. *The Poetics of Old Age in Greek Epic, Lyric, and Tragedy* (Norman and London, 1995)

Falkner, T.M. and J. de Luce (eds). *Old Age in Greek and Latin Literature* (Albany, New York, 1989)

Garland, R. *The Greek Way of Life from Conception to Old Age* (London, 1991)

Gutsfeld, A. and W. Schmitz (eds). *Am schlimmen Rand des Lebens?* (Köln, 2003)

Mattioli, U. (ed.). *Senectus: La vecchiaia nel mondo classico* (Bologna, 1995)

Parkin, T.G. *Old Age in the Roman World: A Cultural and Social History* (Baltimore, 2003)

Powell, J.G.F. (ed.). *Cicero: Cato Maior de Senectute* (Cambridge, 1988)

Richardson, B.E. *Old Age among the Ancient Greeks* (Baltimore, 1933)

Stahmer, H.M. 'The Aged in Two Ancient Oral Cultures: The Ancient Hebrews and Homeric Greece', in S.F. Spicker, K.M. Woodward and D.D. van Tassel (eds), *Aging and the Elderly: Humanistic Perspectives in Gerontology* (Atlantic Highlands, New Jersey, 1978), pp. 23–36

Suder, W. (ed.). *Geras. Old Age in Greco-Roman Antiquity: A Classified Bibliography* (Wroclaw, 1991)

3 The Middle Ages and Renaissance

Carruthers, M. *The Book of Memory. A Study of Memory in Medieval Culture* (Cambridge, 1993)

Harvey, B. *Living and Dying in England 1110–1540: The Monastic Experience* (Oxford, 1995)

Herlihy, D. and C. Klapisch. *Les Toscans et leur familles: étude du Catasto florentin de 1427* (Paris, 1980)

Jacquart, D. and C. Thomasset. *Sexuality and Medicine in the Middle Ages*, trans. M. Adamson (Oxford, 1988)

Laslett, P. and K. Osterveen (eds). *Family Life and Illicit Love in Earlier Generations* (Cambridge 1977)

Le Roy Ladurie, E. *Les paysans de Languedoc* (Paris, 1966)

Minois, G. *Histoire de la vieillesse. De l'antiquité à la Renaissance* (Paris, 1987)

Mitterauer, M. and R. Sieder. *The European Family. Patriarchy to Partnership from the Middle Ages to the Present*, trans. K. Osterveen and M. Hörziager (Oxford, 1982)

Pelling, M. and R. Smith (eds). *Life, Death and the Elderly: Historical Perspectives* (1991)

Pullan, B. *Rich and Poor in Renaissance Venice* (Oxford, 1971)

Razi, Z. *Life, Marriage and Death in a Medieval Parish* (Cambridge, 1980)

Shahar, S. *Growing Old in the Middle Ages* (London, 1997)

Sheehan, M. (ed.). *Aging and the Aged in Medieval Europe* (Toronto, 1990)

Smith, R. (ed.). *Land, Kinship and Life Cycle* (Cambridge, 1984)

Walker Bynum, C. *Holy Feast and Holy Fast. The Religious Significance of Food to Medieval Women* (Berkeley, California, 1987)

4 The 17th Century

Barbagli, M. and D.I. Kertzer, *Family Life in Early Modern Times, 1500–1789* (New Haven and London, 2001)

Botelho, L. and P. Thane (eds). *Women and Ageing in British Society since 1500* (Harlow, 2001)

Gottlieb, B. *The Family in the Western World from the Black Death to the Industrial Age* (New York and Oxford, 1993)

Groppi, A. 'Roman Alms and Poor Relief in the Seventeenth Century', in P.J. van Kessel and E.M.R. Schulte (eds), *Rome-Amsterdam, Two Growing Cities in Seventeenth-Century Europe* (Amsterdam, 1997)

Johnson, P. and P. Thane (eds). *Old Age from Antiquity to Post-Modernity* (London, 1998)

Klapisch-Zuber, C., M. Segalen and F. Zonabend (eds). *History of the Family, Volume Two: The Impact of Modernity*, trans. Sarah Hanbury Tenison (Cambridge, Massachusetts, 1996)

Kugler, A. *Errant Plagiary: The Life and Writing of Lady Sarah Cowper: 1664–1720* (Stanford, 2002)

Marshall, S. *The Dutch Gentry, 1500–1650* (New York; Westport, Conn., 1987)

Mitterauer, M. and R. Sieder, *The European Family* (Oxford, 1982)

Murstein, B.I., *Love, Sex and Marriage through the Ages* (New York, 1974)

O'Day, R. *The Family and Family Relationships, 1500–1600: England, France and the United States of America* (Basingstoke, 1994)

Ottaway, S., L.A. Botelho and K. Kittredge (eds). *Power and Poverty: Old Age in the Pre-Industrial Past* (Westport, Connecticutt, 2002)

Sarti, R., *Europe at Home: Family and Material Culture 1500–1800* (New Haven, 2002)

Thane, P., *Old Age in English History: Past Experiences, Present Issues* (Oxford, 2000)

5 The 18th Century

Achenbaum, W.A. *Old Age in the New Land: The American Experience since 1790* (Baltimore, 1978)

Banner, L.W. *In Full Flower: Aging Women, Power and Sexuality* (New York, 1992)

Borscheid, P. *Geschichte des Alters* (Münster,1987)

Botelho, L. and P. Thane (eds). *Women and Ageing in British Society since 1500* (2001)

Bourdelais, P. *L'Âge de la vieillesse: histoire du vieillissement de la population* (Paris, 1993)

Castan, Y. *Honnêteté et relations sociales en Languedoc, 1715–1780* (Paris, 1974)

Collomp, A. *La Maison du père : Famille et village en Haute-Provence aux XVIIe et XVIIIe siècles* (Paris, 1983)

Dumons B. and G. Pollet. *L'État et les retraites: Genèse du'une politique* (Paris, 1994)

Ehmer, J. *Sozialgeschichte des Alters* (Frankfurt, 1990)

Fischer, D.H. *Growing Old in America* (1978)

Gourdon, V. *Histoire des grands-parents* (Paris, 2001)

Kertzner, D. and P. Laslett (eds), *Aging in the Past: Demography, Society and Old Age* (Berkeley, 1995)

Ottaway, S. *The Decline of Life: Old Age in Eighteenth-Century England* (Cambridge, 2004)

Ottaway, S., L. Botelho and K. Kittredge (eds). *Power and Poverty: Old Age in the Pre-Industrial Past* (Westport, Conn., 2002)

Thane, P. *Old Age in English History: Past Experiences, Present Issues* (Oxford, 2000)

Troyansky, D. *Old Age in the Old Regime: Image and Experience in Eighteenth-Century France* (Ithaca, 1989)

6 The 19th Century

Achenbaum, W.A. *Old Age in the New Land: The American Experience since 1790* (London, 1979)

Cole, T.R. *The Journey of Life: A Cultural History of Aging in America* (Cambridge, 1992)

Edwards, C. 'Age-Based Rationing of Medical Care in Nineteenth-Century England', *Continuity and Change* 14 (1999), pp. 227–65

Evans, J.G. 'Geriatric Medicine: A Brief History', *British Medical Journal* 315 (1997), pp. 1075–7

Haber, C. *Beyond Sixty-Five: The Dilemma of Old Age in America's Past* (Cambridge, 1983)

Hepworth, M. 'Framing Old Age in Victorian Painting, 1850–1900: A Sociological Perspective', in J. Hughson and D. Inglis (eds), *The Sociology of Art* (London, 2004)

Johnson, P. and P. Thane (eds). *Old Age from Antiquity to Post-Modernity* (London, 1998)

Kertzer, D.I. and P. Laslett (eds). *Aging in the Past: Demography, Society and Old Age* (London, 1995)

Pelling, M. and R.M. Smith (eds). *Life, Death and the Elderly: Historical Perspective* (London, 1991)

Stearns, P.N. *Old Age in European Society: The Case of France* (London, 1977)

Thomson, D. 'The Decline of Social Welfare: Falling State Support for the Elderly since Early Victorian Times', *Ageing and Society* 4 (1984), pp. 451–82

7 The 20th Century

Achenbaum, W.A. *Old Age in the New Land. The American Experience since 1790* (1978)

Bass, S.A. (ed.). *Older and Active. How Americans over 55 Are Contributing to Society* (1995)

Bynum, W.F. and R. Porter (eds). *Companion Encyclopaedia of the History of Medicine* (2 vols, 1993)

Cole, T., R. Kastenbaum and R.E. Ray. *Handbook of the Humanities and Aging* (2nd edn, 2000)

Falkingham, J. and P. Johnson. *Ageing and Economic Welfare* (1992)

Haber, C. and B. Gratton. *Old Age and the Search for Security. An American Social History* (Bloomington, 1994)

Johnson, P. and P. Thane (eds). *Old Age from Antiquity to Post-Modernity* (1998)

Kirkwood, T. *The End of Age* (2001)

Kohli, M., et al. *Time for Retirement: Comparative Studies of Early Exit from the Labour Force* (Cambridge, 1991)

Loewenberg, I. *The View from Seventy. Women's Recollections and Reflections* (Iowa City, 2004)

Pifer, A. and L. Bronte. *Our Ageing Society. Paradox and Promise* (1986)

Quine, M.S. *Population Politics in Twentieth-Century Europe* (1996)

Thane, P. *Old Age in English History. Past Experiences, Present Issues* (Oxford, 2000)

Thompson, P., C. Itzin and M. Abendstern. *I Don't Feel Old. Understanding the Experience of Later Life* (Oxford, 1991)

World Bank. *Averting the Old Age Crisis: Policies to Protect the Old and Promote Growth* (Oxford, 1994)

Sources of Illustrations

p. 2   Peter Arno/©1931 The New Yorker, Condé Nast Publications Inc. Reprinted by permission. All Rights Reserved

p. 8   The British Library, London

p. 10   Musée d'Orsay, Paris. *Photo:* Scala

p. 12   Private Collection

p. 13   *Photo:* Popperfoto

p. 14   Private Collection

p. 15   Prado, Madrid. *Photo:* Scala

p. 17   From J. Caulfield, *Portraits*, London, 1794

pp. 18–19 *Photo:* Scala

p. 20   Bibliothèque Nationale, Paris

p. 22   Galleria Palatina, Florence. *Photo:* Scala

p. 23   Prado, Madrid. *Photo:* Scala

p. 24   Albertina, Vienna

p. 26   Galleria d'Arte Moderna, Roma. *Photo:* Scala

p. 27   Reprinted by permission of PDF on behalf of Posy Simmonds ©; as printed in the original volume

p. 30   National Museum, Athens

p. 32   Museo Nazionale, Naples

p. 33   Palazzo dei Conservatori, Rome. *Photo:* Alinari

p. 34   The British Museum, London

p. 35   Museo Nazionale, Naples. *Photo:* Bridgeman Art Library

pp. 36–7 Martin von Wagner Museum, Würzburg

pp. 38–9 Antikenmuseum, Berlin. *Photo:* Erich Lessing, AKG, London

p. 40   National Archeological Museum, Athens. *Photo:* Roloff Beny

p. 41   Ny Carlsberg Glyptothek, Copenhagen

p. 42   Museo Nazionale, Naples

p. 43   J. Paul Getty Museum, California

p. 44   Kunsthistorisches Museum, Vienna

p. 46   Martin von Wagner Museum, Wurzburg

p. 47   Metropolitan Museum of Art, New York NY. *Photo:* Erich Lessing, AKG, London

p. 48   The British Museum, London

p. 49   Vatican Museums, Rome

p. 50   The British Museum, London

p. 51   The British Museum, London

p. 52   J. Paul Getty Museum, California

p. 53   Museo Capitolino, Rome

p. 54   Metropolitan Museum of Art, New York, NY

p. 55   Allard Preisson Museum, Amsterdam

p. 56   Louvre, Paris. *Photo:* Maurice Chuzeville, RMN

p. 57   National Museum, Athens

p. 58   Louvre, Paris. *Photo:* RMN

p. 59   Villa Albani, Rome

p. 61   Louvre, Paris. *Photo:* M. Chuzeville, RMN

p. 62   Museo di Villa Giulia, Rome

p. 63   Staatliche Museen, Berlin

p. 64   Louvre, Paris. *Photo:* RMN

pp. 66–7 The British Museum, London

p. 68   The British Museum, London

p. 69   Metropolitan Museum of Art, New York, NY

p. 70   Bibliothèque Nationale, Paris

p. 195   From J. Caulfield, *Portraits*, London 1794

pp. 194–5 J. Paul Getty Museum, California

p. 196   Staatliche Museen, Berlin. *Photo:* AKG, London

pp. 198–9 Popular print. Bibliothèque Nationale, Paris

p. 199   Popular print. Bibliothèque Nationale, Paris

p. 200   Musée des Beaux Arts, Marseilles. *Photo:* Bridgeman Art Gallery

p. 201   Germanischesnationalmuseum, Nuremberg. *Photo:* Scala

p. 202   Musée d'Art et d'Histoire, Geneva. *Photo:* Bridgeman Art Library

p. 203   (left) Louvre, Paris. *Photo:* Bridgeman Art Library
           (right) The Iveagh Bequest, Kenwood

p. 204   Historical Museum, Amsterdam

p. 205   Bibliothèque Nationale, Paris

p. 206   From J. Caulfield, *Portraits*, London, 1794

p. 207   Gemaldegalerie, Dresden. *Photo:* Bridgeman Art Library

p. 208   By courtesy of Brooklin Historical Society, Brooklin, Mass., USA

p. 210   Photo by Berthes of Warrington, Gersheim Collection, Houston, Texas

p. 212   From Henry Mayhew, *London Labour*, 1861

p. 213   (top) Museum of Fine Arts, Boston, Tompkin Collection
           (bottom) *Photo:* Mary Evans Picture Library

p. 214   Museum Mesdag, The Hague

p. 215   Rijksmuseum Kröller-Müller, Otterlo

p. 216   Mary Evans Picture Library

p. 218   Collection of Georg Schäfer, Schweinfort. *Photo:* AKG, London

p. 219   (left) The Hirschsprung Collection, Copenhagen
           (right) Stiftung für Kunst and Kulturgeschichte, Zurich

p. 220   G. Doré, *London, a Pilgrimage*, 1872

pp. 222–3 Museo d'Arte Moderna di Cà Pesaro, Venice. *Photo:* Bridgeman Art Library

p. 224   (top) Märkisches Museum, Berlin. *Photo:* AKG, London
           (bottom) Harrogate Art Gallery, Yorkshire

pp. 226–7 Musée des Beaux-Arts André Malraux, Le Havre. *Photo:* Bridgeman Art Library

p. 228   Mary Evans Picture Library

p. 231   Staatsgalerie, Stuttgart. Max Liebermann © DACS 2005. *Photo:* AKG, London

p. 232   G. Doré, *London, a Pilgrimage*, 1872

p. 234   Louvre, Paris. *Photo:* Scala

p. 235   J. Paul Getty Museum, California

p. 236   The British Library, London

p. 238   (both) *Photo:* Mary Evans Picture Library

p. 240   Courtesy of the Royal Photographic Society, Bath

p. 241   Collection Sam Wagstaff, New York

p. 242   Wellcome Historical Medical Library, London

p. 245   Kobel Collection, courtesy of Thackrey & Robertson, San Francisco

pp. 246–7 National Museum, Liverpool. *Photo:* Bridgeman Art Library

p. 248   Galeria d'Arte Moderna, Florence. *Photo:* Scala

p. 249   Statensmuseum for Kunst, Copenhagen. Detail.

p. 251   J. Paul Getty Museum, California

p. 252   National Museum and Galleries on Merseyside. *Photo:* Bridgeman Art Library

p. 254   National Gallery of Art, Washington DC

p. 256   (both) National Gallery of Art, Washington DC. *Photo:* Bob Grove

p. 257   (both) National Gallery of Art, Washington DC. *Photo:* Bob Grove

p. 260   (both) Library of Congress, Washington DC

p. 262   Library of Congress, Washington DC

p. 265   (left) Musée d'Histoire Contemporaine, Paris
           (right) *Photo:* AKG, London

p. 266   *Photo:* AKG London

p. 267   Bibliothèque Nationale, Paris

p. 268   Atheneum, Helsinki, Rissanen © DACS 2005

p. 270   Nationalgalerie, Berlin. Otto Nagel © DACS 2005

p. 272   Hulton Getty Images

p. 273   *L'Assiette au Beurre*, Paris, 1903

p. 274   Novosti Press Agency

p. 275   *Photo:* Giraudon/Bridgeman Art Library

p. 276   Published in Steinberg THE PASSPORT, Hamish Hamilton, London 1974.
           Ink and graphite on paper, 14¹¹⁄₄₂ x 23¹¹⁄₄₄ inches.
           © The Saul Steinberg Foundation/Artists Rights Society (ARS), NY, and DACS, London

p. 278   Hulton Getty Images

p. 280   *Photo:* Novosti Press Agency

p. 281   *Photo:* Novosti Press Agency

p. 282   Department of Health, UK

p. 283   Science Photo Library, London

p. 284   By courtesy of *The Oldie* magazine

p. 286   Goodman Derrick Solicitors. Copyright of the artist

p. 287   Copyright of the artist. National Portrait Gallery, London

p. 288   Time-Life Pictures – Getty Images

p. 289   (both) *Photo:* Camera Press

p. 290   *Photo:* Hulton Getty Images

p. 291   Passfield Papers. LSE Archives

p. 292   Cecil Beaton Archives. Sotheby's London

p. 294   (both) *Photo:* Ronald Grant Archives

p. 296   Robert Miller Gallery, New York. Copyright of the artist

p. 298   *Photo:* John Birdsall Photos

LIFE AND

STAGES OF MAN'S LIFE FRO...

Fear...
and ke...
Comma...

Resist the Devil, an...

20

30

40

10

5

Until the first Five years be spent, the Child is lamblike innocent

At Ten, he goat like skips and joys in games & sports and foolish toys.

At Twenty, love doth swell his veins and eagle like untamed remains.

With bull like strength to smite his foes, At Thirty to the field he goes.

At Forty nought his courage quails but lion like, by force prevails.

Strengt... Fifty, b... fox like... man...